for GBBH

Logic 531
D 3C

Trying to Make Sense

Trying to Make Sense

PETER WINCH

Basil Blackwell

Copyright © Peter Winch 1987

First published 1987

Basil Blackwell Ltd
108 Cowley Road, Oxford, OX4 1JF, UK

Basil Blackwell Inc,
432 Park Avenue South, Suite 1503
New York, NY 10016, USA

British Library Cataloguing in Publication Data

Winch, Peter
   Trying to make sense.
   1. Wittgenstein, Ludwig
   I. Title
   192   B3376.W564

   ISBN 0–631–15336–5
Library of Congress Cataloging-in-Publication Data

Winch, Peter.
   Trying to make sense.
   Includes index.
   1. Philosophy.   2. Wittgenstein, Ludwig, 1889–1951.
I. Title.
B29.W52 1987   149'.94   86-30956
ISBN 0–631–15336–5
     Typeset in 11 on 12 pt Ehrdardt
       by Columns of Reading
     Printed in Great Britain by
    Billing & Sons Limited, Worcester

Contents

Acknowledgements

'Text and Context' was published in *Philosophical Investigations*, January 1982. *'Im Anfang war die Tat'* is a revision and expansion of a paper read to the Wittgenstein Colloquium held in London, Ontario in 1976 and has been printed in *Perspectives on the Philosophy of Wittgenstein*, edited by Irving Block (Blackwell 1981). 'Facts and Superfacts' was a critical notice published in *The Philosophical Quarterly*, October 1983. 'Ceasing to Exist' was the Annual Philosophical Lecture 1982 delivered to the British Academy under the Henriette Hertz Trust and was published in *Proceedings of the British Academy* (Oxford University Press). 'Meaning and Religious Language' is a revised and extended version of a paper read to a conference on the philosophy of religion sponsored by the Royal Institute of Philosophy and held at the University of Lancaster in 1975; it has been published in *Reason and Religion*, edited by Stuart C. Brown (Cornell University Press 1977). 'Darwin, *Genesis* and Contradiction' was a talk first broadcast on BBC Radio 3 in 1976 in the context of the Open University's course: 'Thought and Reality: Central Themes in Wittgenstein's Philosophy'. *'Eine Einstellung zur Seele'* was the Presidential Address to the Aristotelian Society in the Session 1980–1 and is published in *Proceedings of the Aristotelian Society* 1980–1981. 'Who is my Neighbour?' was an Inaugural Lecture delivered at the University of Illinois at Urbana/Champaign in 1986. 'Ethical Relativism' is a revised version of a paper delivered to a conference on *Lebensformen und soziale Verständigung* organized by the *Institut für die Wissenschaften vom Menschen* in Vienna in 1982. 'Particularity and Morals' was a lecture delivered at the University of Vienna in 1983 in a series of lectures organized by the *Institut für die Wissenchaften vom Menschen*. 'Language, Belief and Relativism' was published in *Contemporary British Philosophy, Fourth Series*, edited by H. D. Lewis (Allen and Unwin 1976).

Some of the above essays have been revised to make them more suitable to the context of the present volume.

I should like to thank Elizabeth Dimm, Elizabeth Betts and Kendal Anderson for their help in getting these essays ready for publication in their present form.

1

Introduction

This volume consists of papers written since the publication of a previous collection.[1] It contains five essays previously unpublished. 'Language, Thought and World in Wittgenstein's *Tractatus*', 'Wittgenstein: Picture and Representation', 'Particularity and Morals', 'Ethical Relativism' and 'Who is my Neighbour?'. Some of the others are not very accessible.

The topics discussed are ostensibly very diverse: the relations between language, thought, world and action; the nature of representation; questions in the philosophy of religion, the notion of existence; our knowledge of ourselves and of each other; our responses to literature and art; certain ethical issues; various forms of relativism. Anything I have had to say about any of these topics is grounded in such understanding as I have of Wittgenstein's philosophy. Some of the essays are explicitly exegetical in form of Wittgenstein's thinking. But there is certainly no attempt here at any systematic exposition; my attitude to Wittgenstein's work has always been one of gratitude for the help it has given me in seeing what are the important questions, and what kinds of questions they are, rather than that of an aspiring exegete. For this reason I have not grouped all the 'exegetical' pieces together. I have aimed at an arrangement which will help to display some of the important connections between the various issues discussed. But quite different arrangements would have been valid; and the pieces which different readers will see as belonging together will undoubtedly vary according to the particular directions of readers' own interests and approaches to philosophy.

1 Peter Winch, *Ethics and Action*.

I said that the topics discussed are 'ostensibly' very diverse. But I do as a matter of fact believe that they are all very intimately interconnected. At any rate I have certainly never had the feeling in writing them of turning from one topic to an entirely different one. Rather, it has been as though the same concerns and difficulties have made it necessary for me to make tentative explorations in various directions. I do not think there would be much positive value in my trying to say explicitly what these common concerns and difficulties are. If the essays have any value taken together, it will lie in their capacity to excite these concerns and sharpen the sense of these difficulties in their reader. If they do not do this no introduction I could write would do it for them.

2

Language, Thought and World in Wittgenstein's *Tractatus*

Wittgenstein suggests in his preface to *Philosophical Investigations* that his new thoughts can 'be seen in the right light only by contrast with and against the background of my old way of thinking', his old way of thinking in the *Tractatus*, that is. And it is clear enough that certain of the arguments in *Investigations* are directed immediately against things said in the earlier work. In three places the *Tractatus* is mentioned by name: these references concern the relation between language and logic, the idea that logic is something 'sublime': an absolutely hard and determinate structure underlying the shifting and fuzzy variety characteristic of our ordinary ways of speaking and making it possible for us to speak of 'the general form of proposition'.

Wittgenstein's treatment of these issues in *Philosophical Investigations* and other later writings is closely intertwined with criticisms of other ideas about language and the world which he sees as characteristic philosophical confusions. For instance, that the grammar of our language needs to be justified by showing that it adequately reflects the nature of things; that our speech acquires its sense through hidden mental processes of thinking, meaning, understanding and the like. And there seems little doubt that he saw the temptations to these two sorts of error as closely associated: perhaps even as having a common source. That being so, it is natural that we should ask ourselves whether these ideas too are to be found in the *Tractatus*. Many claim that they are. My purpose here is to contest that claim.[1]

1 A very clear articulation of such a reading of the *Tractatus* is given by Norman Malcolm in his *Memory and Mind*, pp. 132–9. This interpretation was elaborated by Professor Malcolm in seminars at King's College, London and I have benefited greatly from discussion with him there and elsewhere. Since my own discussion was written he has published an account of his present position in his *Nothing is Hidden*.

It is certainly not difficult to find in the *Tractatus* remarks which look as though they can be so read as to support the claim. And there are general structural features of the work which may seem to point in the same direction: I mean the fact that it starts with a discussion of the *world* and goes on to introduce the notion of a *thought* as a prelude to the discussion of the *proposition*. That certainly can be made to look as though a philosophy of language is being based on a metaphysics, mediated by a philosophy of mind.

On the other hand it can hardly be said that the *Tractatus* argues for a view of these matters that *Philosophical Investigations* rejects. There is very little at all in the text of the *Tractatus* corresponding to the lengthy and involved discussions of the mental in *Philosophical Investigations*, and very little on the proper construal of concepts like meaning, understanding and thinking that occupy so much of that book. There is rather more in the *Notebooks 1914–1916*. But this is a source that ought to be used with caution. Where the *Notebooks* contain material that is not included in the *Tractatus* it cannot be assumed that this material can safely be used to fill out what is said in the *Tractatus*. It would surely be extremely odd for Wittgenstein deliberately to have excluded from his final text material vital to its correct interpretation. And the *Notebooks* are not an album of possible formulations of *Tractatus* views from which he selected the best for publication. They record a wrestling with the problems and temptations that Wittgenstein thought he had finally dealt with at the time of the completion of his first book. In the course of this wrestling he naturally tried to state as forcefully as possible the difficulties and temptations around which he found it hard to see his way. The mentalistic conception of the sense of propositions was indeed one of the strongest of such temptations. But in my view, so far from being an unstated assumption behind the *Tractatus*, it is one of its main targets for *criticism*. And if that is so, it is hardly surprising that it is a conception which often receives forceful expression in the *Notebooks*; and this by itself lends little support to the view that it is the theory of the *Tractatus*.

Let me now give an extremely condensed (and therefore rough) outline of the main features of what the *Tractatus* says about language, thought and the world. I will then offer an equally condensed sketch of the 'metaphysical' reading of this account which I will subsequently criticize.

The world consists of elementary facts or states of affairs

(*Sachverhalte*)[2] which are articulated concatenations of objects (*Gegenstände*). It is essential to any object that it can combine with other objects to form *Sachverhalte* only in certain determinate ways; and an object appears in the world only in the context of such *Sachverhalte*. We make pictures of facts, pictures composed of elements which correspond to the objects constituting the *Sachverhalte* which go to form the pictured facts. These pictorial elements are mutually interrelated just as are the objects in the pictured state of affairs; and they form a true picture when the objects corresponding to the pictorial elements are mutually interrelated as depicted, that is, when the pictured state of affairs exists or obtains. A thought is a logical picture of the facts (and every picture, whatever other features it may have, is also a logical picture). A proposition is the expression of a thought in a way that is perceptible to the senses; it is a complex sign, composed of simple signs in a projective relation to the world. Such simple signs are names, the meanings of which are the objects in pictured states of affairs, which the names represent in propositions. A name has a meaning independently of the obtaining of any *particular* state of affairs; but it stands for an object to the nature of which certain quite determinate possibilities of combination with other objects are essential; and correspondingly it too will be characterized by quite determinate possibilities of combination with other names into propositions. However, since its meaning is independent of the obtaining of any particular state of affairs, a proposition in which it occurs may be either true or false according as the objects corresponding to its constituent names are or are not related as are the names themselves in that proposition.

So far I have tried to present a summary of the *Tractatus* account of these matters which is neutral as between conflicting interpretations. I now turn to questions of interpretation.

Here is a natural, and very widespread reading of the account I have just outlined. The discussion of notions like the *world, states of affairs, facts, objects* provides an attempted explanation of why it is that some strings of words form combinations which have a sense, express propositions, while others do not. Namely, it depends on the internal properties and relations of the objects for which the words stand. If those objects are such as to be capable of combining in a

---

2   The noun '*Sachverhalt*' corresponds to the verb '*sich verhalten*', which occurs in one of the *Tractatus* formulations of 'the general form of proposition': *es verhält sich so und so* ('this is how things are'). A *Sachverhalt* is a way things are.

certain way, then their names will combine in that way too and yield a proposition; otherwise not. It is by virtue of the fact that the names *mean*, are *the representatives of*, those objects that the objects exercise, as it were, this logical power over the combination of names.

But how does meaning, this all-important correlation which bestows the same internal properties on names as are already possessed by the correlated objects, come about? The *Tractatus* seems not to discuss this question; or at least what it *does* say does not seem to help the present interpretation. (I am thinking of 3.263 which I will discuss later.) However, having travelled so far already along this path, it is natural to take the further step of supposing that the relation between name and object is established by some mental act which, as it were, *fastens* the name to a particular object in a particular way. It is strange, to be sure, that the *Tractatus* does not unequivocally *say* this all-important thing, but perhaps it is meant to be understood in the last sentence of 3.11 (about the sense of a proposition, rather than about the meaning of a name): 'The method of projection is to think of the sense of the proposition'. And then there is Wittgenstein's postscript to his letter to Russell of 19 August 1919,

> Does a Gedanke consist of words? No! But of psychical constituents that have the same sort of relation to reality as words. What those constituents are I don't know.[3]

But anyway, across this supposed psychical link between name and object flow all the logical properties of the world into the perceptible signs that constitute our language. The real link between language, the proposition and the world is to be found in the psychic act within which name and object become fused.

This is certainly a view which has attracted a lot of philosophers, including Russell. In fact something like this is involved in the discussion of causation by Russell in 'The Limits of Empiricism' which Wittgenstein attacks in 'Cause and Effect: Intuitive Awareness'.[4] And it would be sufficiently recognizable as a target for the discussions of the idea that meaning is an occult mental process that occupy so much of *Philosophical Investigations*. All the same there are serious obstacles to accepting it as a tenable interpretation of the *Tractatus*; and to these I now turn.

3 *Notebooks 1914–1916*, p. 130.
4 The Wittgenstein material comes from a notebook written in 1937.

Wittgenstein himself gives an account of his aim in the *Tractatus* which flies in the face of the above interpretation. He writes in his preface:

> The book deals with the problems of philosophy, and shows, I believe, that the reason why these problems are posed is that the logic of our language is misunderstood. The whole sense of the book might be summed up in the following words: what can be said at all can be said clearly, and what we cannot talk about we must pass over in silence.
>
> Thus the aim of the book is to set a limit to thought, or rather – not to thought, but to the expression of thoughts: for in order to be able to set a limit to thought, we should have to find both sides of the limit thinkable (i.e. we should have to be able to think what cannot be thought).
>
> It will therefore only be in language that the limit can be set, and what lies on the other side of the limit will simply be nonsense.

Now if the *Tractatus* does indeed try to account for the distinction between sense and nonsense in terms of something which is supposed to be understandable independently of that distinction – the nature and interrelations of objects – then it certainly does seem to be trying to think both sides of the limit to thought in just the way the preface to the book rules out. When the preface says that the boundary limiting the expression of thought must be drawn 'in language', it is not of course making the quite trivial point that we must use language in stating where the boundary lies; instead it says that the boundary itself must be thought of as in some sense a linguistic boundary. That is, we cannot decide that one form of words expresses a proposition and another does not by comparing these expressions with something non-linguistic (as we do when it is a question of determining a proposition's *truth*). We can make the distinction only by referring to certain features of the linguistic expressions themselves.

It is equally inadmissible to try to account for the meanings of names by reference to their relation to something non-linguistic. What distinguishes an expression which has a meaning (and is, therefore, a name) from one which does not can only be something to do with its role *in* language. And proposition 3.203 will have to be interpreted as saying something about that role. This rules out as unnecessary (and *therefore* according to 5.47321 meaningless) any talk about a psychic act which links the name with something outside language. (Incidentally, this is not to say that 'objects are purely linguistic entities' – whatever precisely that would mean; it is to say that the role of the word 'object' according to the *Tractatus* lies in its logico-syntactic relation with the word 'name'.)

Terms like *world, fact, object* are terms of our language which, on the *Tractatus* view, have a peculiarly fundamental role in the description of language. I say 'on the *Tractatus* view', because in *Philosophical Investigations* Wittgenstein argues that assigning to them this role is a confusion which results from the tendency 'to sublime the logic of our language' which he has by then come to think of as the main error of his earlier work. What the opening sentences of the *Tractatus* do is to establish certain fundamental features of the 'logical syntax' of these terms by exhibiting their use in relation to each other in sentences. This process is subsequently extended to include such terms as *picture, proposition, thought, name*.

Proposition 3.203, 'A name means an object. The object is its meaning', is an example of this procedure. It does not state that a certain relation holds between two terms. The only 'relation' that could be in question here is an *internal* relation and, as such, it could not be stated in a proposition, but will be exhibited in the propositions which describe states of affairs involving such terms. (See *Tractatus* 4.122.) The words "name", "object", "meaning", express formal concepts; and no proposition can state that something is an object falling under a formal concept: that it is such an object is exhibited in the sign for that object. (See 4.126.) Proposition 3.203 can be read as a gesture towards the syntactical role of names in our language and towards the way in which the use of the word 'meaning' is intertwined in that role. It is certainly not intended as, and is not, the last word in the *Tractatus* on the role which names play in language.

What *is* said about this should be startling to anyone who takes 3.203 to be saying that the meaning of any particular name consists in its standing in relation to something extralinguistic, an object. Consider for example 3.326–3.33:

> In order to recognize a symbol by its sign we must observe how it is used with a sense.
>
> A sign does not determine a logical form unless it is taken together with its logico-syntactic employment.
>
> If a sign is *useless*, it is meaningless. That is the point of Occam's maxim.

(If everything behaves as if a sign had meaning, then it does have meaning.)

In logical syntax the meaning of a sign should never play a role. It must be possible to establish logical syntax without mentioning the *meaning* of a sign: only the description of expressions may be presupposed.

Is it not rather extraordinary that Wittgenstein should say this? *If*, that is, he thinks that the essential thing about a name, what makes it a name, is its correlation with something extralinguistic, is it not strange that we should be prohibited from mentioning this essential something which determined the sign's use? Of course, I am not suggesting that, according to Wittgenstein, the name *does not* stand for an object. What is being attacked is a misleading conception of what it is for this to be so. A name has a meaning if it behaves in language just as though it had one; in fact its having the meaning it does just consists in its 'significant use' (*sinnvollen Gebrauch*).

Proposition 3.334 reads: 'The rules of logical syntax must go without saying, once we know how each individual sign signifies.' It is important that Wittgenstein writes *wie* ('how') rather than *was* ('what'). The what will already have been settled once the how is established. One is reminded of Wittgenstein's point in *Philosophical Remarks* where, discussing the expression of expectancy, he says 'Tell me *how* you are searching, and I will tell you *what* you are searching for'.[5] Of course this already represents an advance beyond the *Tractatus* preoccupation with mere syntax in its reference to the behavioural manifestations of expecting; but it is a development the seeds of which are already present in the *Tractatus*, rather than an out-and-out rejection of that book's conception of the connection between language and the world.

The view of the connection between meaning and syntax in the *Tractatus* that I have been putting forward is obviously close to that of some other writers: for instance that of Professor Hidé Ishiguro in her paper 'Use and Reference of Names'.[6] My main worry with her way of expressing the point has to do with her talk about *Tractatus* names as 'dummy names'. This carries the unfortunate (though I believe unintended) suggestion that such 'names' are to be contrasted with *real* names and are not to be thought of as really referring to anything. That was anyway certainly not Wittgenstein's

5 *Philosophical Remarks*, p. 67.
6 Peter Winch (ed.), *Studies in the Philosophy of Wittgenstein*.

intention. The discussion of what it is for a name to function in a certain way in a symbolism *is* a discussion of what it is for it to have a reference. Proposition 3.203 is in no way rescinded, or even qualified, by 3.328 or even 3.33. These later remarks *amplify* the earlier one and warn against misunderstanding: the misunderstanding of supposing that a name's meaning is something other than and prior to its logico-syntactic role. And though the names of the *Tractatus* cannot of course be identified with names in ordinary speech, which lack the necessary simplicity, nevertheless, what is said about the connection between meaning and syntax must be taken to apply to the latter too. This is clear, for instance, from the parenthesis at the end of 3.323: '(In the proposition, 'Green is green' – where the first word is the proper name of a person and the last an adjective – these words do not merely have different meanings: they are *different symbols*.)'

It is no objection to what I am saying to point out that one undoubtedly can teach someone the meaning of a sign, or introduce a sign into the language, by means of a stipulation combined with ostensive definition. It has to be remembered that the ostensive gesture and its connection with the words which are uttered have to be understood first if the ceremony is to have the desired consequences. *These procedures, then, form part of the symbolism* – and a part that is presupposed by the meaning of the sign thus introduced: which can, therefore, not be regarded as a *primitive* sign, a 'name' in the *Tractatus* sense of the word, if that is interpreted as being a sign which gets its significance simply from being correlated with something extralinguistic. The point is that this 'correlation', understood in this way, turns out to presuppose further signs which are, therefore, *more primitive* than the sign thus introduced.

So the correlation between name and object, of which the *Tractatus* speaks, has to be understood differently. And this is to be expected, given the prominent and often quoted: 'Only propositions have sense; only in the nexus of a proposition does a name have meaning.' (3.3)

This remark follows another very important and *prima facie* puzzling one: 'The meanings of primitive signs can be explained by means of elucidations. Elucidations are propositions that contain the primitive signs. So they can only be understood if the meanings of the signs are already known.' (3.263) The last sentence might be taken by itself to mean that the meanings of primitive signs must be known independently of their use in propositions (since they must 'already' be known if the propositions in which they occur are to be understood); and this might be taken to support the view that according to the *Tractatus* names get their meaning from an immediate confrontation with and, as it were, welding to objects such as to equip them for subsequent use in propositions. But this seems to run counter to the first two sentences of 3.263, which speak of 'explaining the meaning' of primitive signs by presenting them in propositions; to say nothing of 2.0122: 'It is impossible for words to appear in two different roles: by themselves, and in propositions.'

It seems to me there are two possible ways of interpreting these remarks satisfactorily. One consists in taking the 'explanation' here spoken of to be the kind of explanation of meaning aimed at in philosophy: not, that is, an explanation which teaches the term to someone who is ignorant of it, nor yet one that introduces a new term into the language; but one, rather, that clarifies one's understanding of the meaning of an already familiar term. This is an interpretation that fits the text with ease.

But it is possible too to make sense of it while allowing that what is being spoken of is an explanation by virtue of which an expression acquires a meaning it did not have before. On this reading 3.263 seems at first blush to imply a vicious circle: the elucidations have to be understood if we are to grasp the meanings of the names they contain; and the meanings of those names have to be grasped if we are to understand the sense of the elucidations. But the circle is not vicious. The point is that one cannot learn the meanings of names separately from each other; to learn their meanings *is* to learn how they combine in sentences. In order to learn that, one has to be presented with sentences and learn to distinguish them from senseless strings of words. To have come to grasp the sense of a sentence is to have come to grasp the meanings of the names of which it is composed. More than that: because grasping those meanings involves appreciating the countless further combinations into which the names may enter, it is something that comes only with mastery of a whole calculus, a calculus which it is one of the main concerns of the *Tractatus* to describe. What the acquisition of such a mastery looks like in detail is not discussed; realization of the need for such a discussion was to come much later and to be responsible for much of *Philosophical Investigations* and *On Certainty*.

This interpretation, in making syntax autonomous, might also seem to make it arbitrary in a sense which is foreign to the *Tractatus*.

In this connection 3.342–3.3421 are important:

> Although there is something arbitrary in our notations, *this* much is not arbitrary – that *when* we have determined one thing arbitrarily, something else is necessarily the case. (This derives from the *essence* of notation.)
>
> A particular mode of signifying may be unimportant but it is always important that it is a *possible* mode of signifying. And that is generally so in philosophy: again and again the individual case turns out to be unimportant, but the possibility of each individual case discloses something about the essence of the world.

What is not arbitrary in our notation is said here to depend on the essence of the *notation* (that is, on something linguistic). It is not said to be determined by the nature of any 'extralinguistic objects'. What is being said is that if we arbitrarily determine that a certain perceptible sign is to play a certain role, we do so *within the framework of language*; that is, the presupposition is that this sign is to combine with others so as to stand in a projective relation to the world. That being so, our arbitrary determination has as its non-arbitrary consequence that only certain combinations with other signs are permissible for it. This is a consequence of the nature of symbolism, nothing else. Of course, to speak of 'symbolism' is *eo ipso* to speak of a projective relation to the world; and that is why Wittgenstein is able to add as a corollary that the possibility of a certain method of symbolizing 'reveals something about the nature of the world'.

So much for the idea that the *Tractatus* offers a metaphysical underpinning for a theory of language. I turn now to the closely connected idea that it contains, or assumes, a philosophy of mind to account for the relation between language and the world. Stated very briefly the case for such an interpretation could be put like this.

The *Tractatus* speaks of *both* 'thoughts' and 'propositions' and makes a distinction between them. Thus 3 reads: 'A logical picture of facts is a thought.' and 3.1: 'In a proposition a thought finds expression that can be perceived by the senses.' A correct inference to draw so far is that the word 'thought' expresses a more general concept than does 'proposition', in that there may be thoughts which are *not* 'expressed perceptibly through the senses' and for which, therefore, no corresponding proposition is uttered.

But it would be a further (and in my view incorrect) move to conclude that for every state of affairs correctly designated a proposition there is another – that is to say, a *different* – state of affairs, designated a thought. This would be the view that what makes a given string of signs into a proposition is that something else stands behind it, another state of affairs, a thought, which confers sense on (and *is* the sense of) that string of signs, which thereby takes on the status of a proposition. Such a view may seem to be supported by Wittgenstein's remark in his letter to Russell of 19 August 1919.[7] This remark certainly does add to what I have acknowledged as being involved in the *Tractatus* distinction between 'thought' and 'proposition' (that there may be thoughts which are not expressed in propositions). It suggests the kind of account that should be given of those thoughts which are not perceptibly expressed: an account which simply substitutes certain unknown psychical constituents for words in the account of propositions. But it still stops well short of the further claim that such a psychical state of affairs is needed in order to transmute a string of perceptible signs into a proposition. That is the key claim of the interpretation of the *Tractatus* I now want to consider.

There is one sentence in the *Tractatus* which is sometimes taken to make this claim explicitly, namely the last sentence of 3.11, which I now quote in full: 'We use the perceptible sign of a proposition (spoken or written, etc.) as a projection of a possible situation. The method of projection is to think of the sense of the proposition.' That is the Pears and McGuiness translation. The German text of the last sentence is: '*Die Projektionsmethode ist das Denken des Satz-Sinnes.*' The Pears and McGuiness version (unlike Ogden's) obscures the ambiguity of the original which (taken on its own at least) can be regarded in either of the following ways: (a) as explaining what the method of projection is, namely thinking the sense[8] of the proposition; or (b) as explaining what thinking the sense of the proposition is, namely the method of projection.

Which reading we adopt is obviously of vital importance. (a) opens

7   *Notebooks 1914–1916*, p. 130; quoted above p. 6.
8   I prefer 'think the sense' to 'think of the sense' (which is used by both Ogden and Pears and McGuiness). This latter sounds too much like *contemplating* the sense, making it the *object* of one's thinking; but the context clearly requires the sense to be the content of one's thinking. In 'thinking the sense' the expression 'the sense', *characterizes* the thinking activity; in 'thinking of the sense' it seems to refer to a quasi-independent object of the activity.

the door wide to the mentalistic interpretation of sense; whereas (b) looks precisely as though it were calculated to guard against that interpretation. It will come as no surprise that I favour reading (b).

However, I do not believe that this is a matter of 'You pays your money and you takes your choice'. I said that the German original of 3.11 is ambiguous 'taken on its own at least'. But taken in its context, I must say that it does not seem to me in the least ambiguous. The main proposition (3) to which it is subsidiary reads: 'A logical picture of facts is a thought.' Its subject phrase, 'A logical picture of facts', expresses continuity with what has gone before, namely an extended discussion of what a picture (*Bild*) is and how a picture depicts a state of affairs. We have just been told (2.182) that 'Every picture is *at the same time* a logical one'. Proposition 3 formally introduces the new term 'thought' (*Gedanke*) into the discussion in a way that is obviously intended to connect it with what has gone before. Everything possible is done to emphasize that it is a *logical* term; there is no mention of psychology. And in what follows, equally, what is singled out as essential to a thought is the logico-linguistic notion of 'projection'. Proposition 3.1 characterizes a proposition as a sensuously perceptible expression of a thought (that is, of a logical picture). The first part of 3.11 takes this up by using the term 'projection' to express the relation between the sensuously perceptible sign and the possible state of affairs. In its problematic last sentence this term ('projection') is *then* used to explain how we are to understand what 'thinking the sense of the proposition' is. In fact this sentence is really an amplification of the explanation of 'thought' in 3, making use of the intervening explanation of the term 'propositional sign' in terms of 'projection'.

There is another place in the *Tractatus* in which something important is said that is incompatible with the mentalistic interpretation of thought. I am thinking of the discussion of 'certain propositional forms of psychology, like "A thinks, that p is the case", or "A thinks p", etc.' which runs from 5.541 to 5.5423. Wittgenstein there objects to Russell's theory that in the situation described by such propositions the subject, A, stands in a certain relation to the proposition p. The relation in question is surely that which the interpretation of 3.11 that I am rejecting understands by 'thinking the sense of the proposition'. On this interpretation it is this thinking that actually gives the proposition its sense. But Wittgenstein's objection to Russell in 5.5422 is: 'The correct explanation of the form of the proposition "A makes the judgment p" must show that it is impossible for a judgment to be a piece of nonsense. (Russell's theory does not satisfy this requirement.)' So it is quite clear that Wittgenstein did not think that an act of thought could *confer* sense on an expression which otherwise would not possess it. On the contrary, he thought that any account of thought must be *based* on an account of what it is for an expression to have sense.

Let me try to state at this point what I take to be the *Tractatus* account of the relation between proposition and thought. I may *think* that p and I may *say* that p. Saying that p is *one* form that thinking that p may take. So: if I assert the proposition p I also have the thought that p, not in the sense that besides asserting the proposition p I am also doing something else, thinking that p, but in the sense that asserting the proposition p *is* (one form of) thinking that p. But I may also think that p without asserting the proposition that p, that is, without expressing my thought in a way that is perceptible to the senses. In such a case my thought is made up of certain psychic components (nature unknown) which have exactly the same relation to each other, and also exactly the same projective relation to the world, as do the words in which the proposition p is expressed. This psychic state of affairs, which (in *these* circumstances) is the form which my thought takes, is no more and no less qualified to bear sense than the linguistic state of affairs that constitutes the proposition (in those cases where I express my thought in the form of a proposition). All that is needed in either case is the requisite projective relation to the world. Wittgenstein could afford to be as unconcerned about the nature of the 'psychic constituents' as he appeared to be in his letter to Russell because these were quite irrelevant to what made a thought a thought and (*a fortiori*) to what made a proposition a proposition. On the other interpretation, however, such insouciance would surely be remarkable. How could Wittgenstein fail to be interested in the nature of the ultimate bearer of sense? Isn't that what the whole book is supposed to be about?

In *Philosophical Investigations* Wittgenstein criticizes the *Tractatus* not for the doctrine that the real thought which constitutes the sense of the perceptible propositional sign is something psychical (for this is *not* a doctrine of *Tractatus*), but rather for regarding the 'real thought' as something that is in any sense *concealed* and which can be exhibited by 'analysis'. Part of *Tractatus* 4.002 reads: 'Language disguises thought. So much so, that from the outward form of the clothing it is impossible to infer the form of the thought beneath it, because the outward form of the clothing is not designed to reveal the form of the body, but for entirely different purposes.'

The contrast *external/internal* is of course often used in philosophy in discussions of the relation between the physical and the mental. But there is no suggestion that this is the contrast intended here. The image of the clothes and the shape of the body beneath clearly has to be understood in terms of the *logical* conception of an *analysis* of propositions which displays them as truth-functions of elementary propositions: a conception which it is precisely the aim of the propositions following and subordinate to 4 to expound.

Indeed, the physical/mental interpretation of the contrast is pretty explicitly rejected in these sections. 4.112 presents philosophy as a process of logical clarification (later amplified as truth-functional analysis). 'Without philosophy thoughts are, as it were, cloudy and indistinct: its task is to make them clear and to give them sharp boundaries.' And then, in a proposition so numbered (4.1121) as to emphasize its role as expounding that, he denies that this clarification has anything to do with psychology:

> Psychology is no more closely related to philosophy, than any other natural science.
>
> Theory of knowledge is the philosophy of psychology.
>
> Does not my study of sign-language correspond to the study of thought-processes which philosophers used to consider so essential to the philosophy of logic? Only in most cases they got entangled in unessential psychological investigations, and with my method too there is an analogous risk.

It could hardly be more clearly stated that mental processes (thought processes even) have nothing more closely to do with the concerns of philosophy (with the study of sense, that is) than does sign language itself. What has to be studied is the general rule of transition from one structure to another (compare 4.0141) rather than anything about those structures considered in themselves.

I am not suggesting that everything in what the *Tractatus* says about these things is perfectly in order. The idea that unexpressed thoughts must be structures analogous to propositions, simply composed of different 'constituents', does come under damaging fire in *Philosophical Investigations*. The *Investigations* attack is directed at the same time at the idea that such a psychic structure is the *real* bearer of sense. But I think, and have argued, that the *Tractatus* had already given up *that* idea and had seen that such a psychic structure would be in no better or worse position for bearing sense than a perceptibly expressed thought (namely a proposition). But I think Wittgenstein had not, in the *Tractatus*, properly appreciated that to think of the relation between proposition and thought in that way really still left the notion of sense in darkness.

In *Investigations* Wittgenstein faces this issue in his criticisms of the idea that the sense of a sign is to be given in an *interpretation*. I think that even in the *Tractatus* he had realized that to unravel this puzzle the notion of the *application* of signs is fundamental. But what this notion comes to is not even much discussed in the *Tractatus*. We are not given much more than the notion of a 'method of projection'. Such explanation as there is of this term is mainly through geometrical analogies; this inhibits proper realization of the *variety* of applications with which we have to deal.[9] It is precisely the attainment of this realization that really marks off *Philosophical Investigations* and makes it such a radically new departure. The discussion of the notion of application did not really advance until the introduction and development of 'language games'; but I am not going into that now. My aim has been rather to show that these later developments were not directed against a view maintained in the *Tractatus*, but were attempts to deal more successfully with confusions which had already been identified as such there.

9 See below, ch. 6.

3

Text and Context

I

I was originally asked to talk on this subject at a conference of
university teachers of English Literature in Southampton. The
general topic of the conference was the idea of the context of a
literary work and its relation to the work's meaning.

Literary critics have, of course, devoted much attention to this
topic and have constructed elaborate theories in attempts to explain
this relation – theories of widely different types, sociological,
economic, political, psychological and 'structural', for example. I
have no more than a very superficial acquaintance with such theories
and am not going to attempt to expound or criticize any of them. In
fact I shall more or less completely ignore all of them.

Instead I am going to look directly at some questions concerning
our understanding of and sensibility towards works of art which
seem to me of philosophical interest; and I shall discuss these
questions in what I understand to be a philosophical fashion. Before
starting, however, I should like to mention the terms in which the
organizer of the conference I have mentioned wrote to me and the
problem that he started running through my head.

He spoke of the way in which the so-called 'New Critics' of the
1940s and 1950s had insisted on the textual 'autonomy' of literary
works and how, subsequently, critics had become dissatisfied with
the way in which such an approach seemed to ignore the work's
complex and varied backgrounds. He spoke about how various
contextual 'theories' of the sort I have mentioned were developed in
response to this dissatisfaction. But, he went on, increasingly some
critics had come to feel that these theories were in danger of going

too far and 'explaining away' the original works under examination in a 'reductionist' way – so that the intrinsic meaning of the work was lost sight of.

This then is the context of my own discussion. I shall start it by quoting a savage description of a bad critic at work and shall go on to try to isolate precisely what is wrong with the way he goes about things. I shall then continue my discussion independently of this example.

The example is from George Eliot's *Middlemarch* (chapter 20). The dried up middle-aged scholar, Mr Casaubon, has taken his enthusiastic and idealistic young bride, Dorothea, to Rome on their honeymoon and they are visiting the artistic wonders of that city, she for the first time.

> ... her husband's way of commenting on the strangely impressive objects around them had begun to affect her with a sort of mental shiver: he had perhaps the best intention of acquitting himself worthily, but only of acquitting himself. What was fresh to her mind was worn out to his; and such capacity of thought and feeling as had ever been stimulated in him by the general life of mankind had long shrunk to a sort of dried preparation, a lifeless embalment of knowledge.
>
> When he said "Does this interest you, Dorothea? Shall we stay a little longer? I am ready to stay if you wish it", it seemed to her as if going or staying were alike dreary. Or, "Should you like to go to the Farnesina, Dorothea? It contains celebrated frescoes designed or painted by Raphael, which most persons think worth while to visit."
>
> "But do you care about them?" was always Dorothea's question.
>
> "They are, I believe, highly esteemed. Some of them represent the fable of Cupid and Psyche, which is probably the romantic invention of a literary period, and cannot I think be reckoned as a genuine mythical product. But if you like these wall-paintings, we can easily drive thither; and you will then, I think, have seen the chief work of Raphael, any of which it were a pity to omit in a visit to Rome. He is the painter who has been held to combine the most complete grace of form with sublimity of expression. Such at least I have gathered to be the opinion of conoscenti."

Casaubon is a rather extreme example of how a certain way of considering the context of a work of art may have the result of obliterating the work instead of bringing it into clearer focus. He reminds me of a nice remark of Wittgenstein's from 1941: 'People who are constantly asking "why" are like tourists who stand in front of a building reading Baedeker and are so busy reading the history of its construction, etc, that they are prevented from *seeing* the building.'[1]

Still, it would obviously be a mistake to suppose this could be avoided by, as it were, clearing one's mind of any sort of background knowledge in approaching a text or any artistic work. It would be an illusion to suppose that there *could* be a reader (viewer, listener, etc.) and a text (or picture, building, piece of music, etc.) without any presumptions at all. Unless the reader brings with him a great deal of knowledge and skill to the text, in an important sense there is no text for him to consider. A much earlier remark of Wittgenstein's (1914) in the same volume makes this same point: 'We tend to take the speech of a Chinese for inarticulate gurgling. Someone who understands Chinese will recognise *language* in what he hears. Similarly I often cannot discern the *humanity* in a man.'[2]

We need to be able to apply our knowledge and skill to a text in such a way that it does not come between us and the text, but brings the text to life. Another way of putting this same point would be to say that my judgement of a work must still genuinely be my judgement – and be also genuinely a judgement of the work before me – while yet being informed by the requisite knowledge of the work's surroundings. These surroundings will of course be very various in kind and indeterminate in extent. Critical judgements which have been made by others will frequently be an indispensable aspect of these surroundings.

However, such judgements (like the rest of the text's surroundings) may be viewed from different angles. They may be viewed from such an angle that they come between oneself and the work and prevent one from – or, as the case may be, allow one to avoid – making a judgement of one's own in the first person.

Here, as in many other philosophical contexts, the relation between first- and third-person judgements is of fundamental importance and a source of many difficulties.

1 *Culture and Value*, p. 40.
2 *Culture and Value*, p. 1. The remark is discussed further below, ch. 12.

George Eliot's depiction of Casaubon brings out the point in a masterly way. 'But do you care about them? ... They are, I believe, highly esteemed.... He is the painter who has been held to combine the most complete grace of form with sublimity of expression. Such at least I have gathered to be the opinion of conoscenti.' It is characteristic of Casaubon's replies to Dorothea (and characteristic of him) that they are actually grammatically in the third person. But this syntactical fact, though interesting, is inessential to the main point I want to make. We are all, I suppose, familiar enough with utterances which have the linguistic form of judgements made by the speaker but which betray, more or less evidently, their secondhand character.

Now it may at first seem as though such a substitution of other people's judgements for one's own is a gesture of self-effacement, a way of keeping oneself out of one's judgements. No doubt there is a sense in which that might be said, but it would be a great mistake to suppose that to be the whole story. In another sense it is precisely the other way round: a gesture of putting oneself into one's judgements when one doesn't belong there. This is brought out by George Eliot's comment on Casaubon: 'He had perhaps the best intention of acquitting himself worthily, but only of acquitting himself.' His attention wasn't on the frescoes on which he was supposed to be commenting, but on his own relation to other people's judgements of the frescoes. And in this respect his attitude was of course of a piece with his jealous fear of his fellow academics' opinion of his own pathetic and doomed scholarly work, 'The Key to all Mythologies'.

Casaubon is obviously something of a special case. (Though aren't we all special cases?) He cannot be made a model for all misuses of reference to context in the appraisal of works of art and literature. But one does not need to share his pusillanimous fear of the opinion of others in order to make the mistake of putting one's knowledge of the text's surroundings into the picture which one, as it were, draws of the text in one's critical judgement.

What is it to deploy knowledge of context so as to illuminate rather than obscure the text? What is it to make one's knowledge constitutive of one's judgement, rather than an element in it?

Let me ask a more general question about the relation of the subject – of the one who makes the judgement – to the judgement he makes. He, the judging, understanding, appreciative – or not, as the case may be – subject is a constant feature in all critical judgment. What is his role in its form?

In *Tractatus Logico-Philosophicus* sections 5.6–5.641 Wittgenstein compares the relation between the knowing subject and the world to the relation between the eye and the visual field. The eye is not a *part* of the visual field.

For the visual field does not have a form like this:

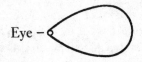

Simone Weil makes a very similar point in a way which makes clearer its relevance to my present concerns:

> A painter does not draw the spot where he is standing. But in looking at his picture I can deduce his position by relation to the things drawn.
>   On the other hand, if he puts himself into his picture I know for certain that the place where he shows himself is not the place where he is.[3]

'The place where he is' is obviously not to be construed *just* as a position in space. Casaubon, for instance, is to be located by reference to his relations with his academic colleagues, his attitude to his own work, to Dorothea and to much else. And his judgements show that *these* are what he is speaking about rather than the frescoes which are his ostensible subject matter.

If we speak, generally, of a relation between the subject and 'the world' – and there is of course danger in these rather grandiose philosophical phrases – the subject is to be located by reference to such contexts as these (and others). They are contexts which in a certain sense are constitutive of the way the world presents itself to the subject and by the same token they help to constitute the subject himself. For example, the way in which Casaubon's young wife, Dorothea, presented herself to him was determined by Casaubon's attitude of

> having made up his mind that it was now time for him to adorn his life with the graces of female companionship, to irradiate

---

3 *First and Last Notebooks*, p. 146.

the gloom which fatigue was apt to hang over the intervals of studious labour with the play of female fancy, and to secure in this, his culminating age, the solace of female tendance for his declining years.

We might compare *this* view of Dorothea with the various ways in which she presents herself to other characters in the novel – to her sister, her uncle, Will Ladislaw, Rosamund Vincy, etc. To make such a comparison one would have to go far beyond these people's different perceptions of Dorothea considered as it were in isolation. One would have, as George Eliot does, to depict their very different modes of life, their different postures towards the world – because what I am calling their different 'views of Dorothea' are different roles that she plays in their general perception of things.

This example illustrates another important point made by Simone Weil, closely connected with the remark I have already quoted from her notebooks. The world is not constituted for a human subject as a set of sensory impressions grouped together into meaningful situations by some mental act of interpretation. No, to use Simone Weil's language one 'reads' (more or less) intelligible situations as one reads sentences in one's own language. One is not conscious, for the most part, of the visual appearance of the words on the page in front of one; it is as though the sense of the sentences were the immediate object of one's awareness (compare the earlier quotation from *Culture and Value*). But it only makes sense to say this, of course, *given* the background of one's understanding of the language – and of much else besides: an understanding of the subject matter to which the passage one is reading makes a contribution, for example. These will not usually be objects of one's awareness, but they will help to constitute the sense, the meaning, of what *is* the immediate object of one's awareness.

If one applies this line of thinking more generally, as Simone Weil encourages us to do, we can say that, at every stage, the situations which one is aware of confronting, as one lives from day to day, are what they are by virtue of the place they occupy against the background of the rest of one's life. And the subject who confronts these situations and reacts to them in his own characteristic ways is revealed for what he is precisely in the structure which his life provides for the situations which confront him. An important corollary of this thought is that achieving a decent coherence as an individual human being can hardly be distinguished as a separate task from trying to make some decent sense of the situations which life brings one's way.

However, I am straying too far from my ostensible topic – the relation between a text and its context. It must, I think, be sufficiently evident that the line of thinking that I have been sketching has an important bearing on the nature of this relation. It implies in effect that to speak of studying a text in isolation from any context would be to speak nonsense. Outside any context whatever (if that phrase has any meaning) there would be no text to study.

That is so general a point that it is not much more than a platitude. But it can be taken a little further. Let us consider the distinction with which I began: between the critical approach to literature which seeks to respect a text's 'autonomy', and that which seeks to explain the meaning of a text by relating it to wider surroundings. The first sort of approach would, I suppose, concentrate on the internal structure of the text, the relations between the elements which make it up; the second would focus on the relations between the text and features external to it.

Now it would be impossible for anyone plausibly to deny that there is indeed a real difference in critical emphasis which these two descriptions indicate. But it would be a serious confusion to think that either approach could be made sense of in complete isolation from the other.

This becomes clearer if we ask how the internal elements of a text, the relations between which are the main object of attention in the 'autonomous text' approach, are supposed to be identified. Let's consider a simple example. Many years ago I was struck by a cartoon by Charles Addams in *The New Yorker*. It depicted, as from the stage of a theatre, an auditorium with rows upon rows of coarsely guffawing faces, as if at a rather vulgar vaudeville performance. In an unobtrusive position towards the back of the theatre, catching one's attention only after some scrutiny, was the face of Leonardo da Vinci's Mona Lisa, *La Gioconda*.

For my present purposes the interest of this cartoon is the way Addams exploits it, the capacity of a new concept to change our perceptions. You can perhaps imagine the startling effect of this juxtaposition of gross laughing faces with the familiar smile of Mona Lisa. The effect is sinister, rather than funny, and though one laughs at it perhaps, one does so rather nervously. Taken by themselves, neither the laughing faces nor Mona Lisa's smile are particularly sinister; they only become so when seen alongside each other in this way.

In saying this, I am clearly talking about the *internal* structure of
the cartoon, the relations between the elements that compose it. But
it is also surely obvious enough that I am able to talk in this way, and
you are able to understand me, because of our common familiarity
with many, many things *outside* the cartoon: with laughs and smiles
and the many different characters these can bear, with theatres, with
different human types, with art galleries and pictures, with
Leonardo's famous painting in particular and the kind of critical and
historical speculation there has been about it. I suppose that one of
the layers of meaning in Addams's cartoon is the bomb it detonates
under some of the more pretentious critical waffle about the
ineffability of the enigma of Mona Lisa's smile. I cannot but view
the cartoon in the context of a reservoir of knowledge of
indeterminate extent, and I have to use concepts embedded in that
knowledge in order to describe the internal structure of the cartoon
in the way I have done.

That the background knowledge is the source of the concepts that
I apply shows that, though indeterminate in extent, it is ordered, it
has a structure. And the cartoon itself exploits this structure,
suggesting hitherto unsuspected affinities and disrupting other,
familiar ones. For instance, smiles and laughs have many different
characters and they are more or less closely related to each other
according to the background against which one views them. There
are smirks and grins as well as smiles; and smiles can be both warm
and frosty. Besides 'straightforward' laughs there are chuckles,
chortles, guffaws, sniggers, titters and giggles, all of which can be
widely different in character. Their characters may also be
transformed by changes in context. I remember a story by Katherine
Mansfield in which a girl pushing a rather spoilt child in a swing in
the garden starts with rather studied jollity and almost imperceptibly
changes to extreme hysteria. Obviously Addams's effect is made
possible because there are relations and tensions of this sort that
can be exploited.

What I am describing is an example of a pervasive feature of our
thought and perception without which much art is hardly even think-
able. Think, for instance, of the exploitation of tonal values, of their
relations to other values, in music – so brilliantly exploited in its turn
in a literary form by Thomas Mann in *Dr Faustus*. Again, consider
the relations and tensions involved in social class and sexuality, a
particular English form of which is the theme of D. H. Lawrence's
Lady Chatterley's Lover. As a last example, think of the complex
affectionate and ironic allusions to the Cherubino of Mozart's *Le*

Nozze di Figaro embodied in the figure of Oktavian in Richard Strauss's *Der Rosenkavalier*.

These examples are all instances of what I would call 'internal' relationships – relationships which spring from, or even help to constitute, what the related terms essentially *are*. A simpler example will help to elucidate this notion. To say that red is darker than pink is to point to an 'internal' relation between those two characters; to say that one piece of material is darker than another, however, is to indicate an 'external' relation. Red is essentially darker than pink; it could not cease to be so without becoming a different colour. But a piece of material may at one time be darker than another piece and at another time lighter – perhaps because exposure to sunlight has made it fade – while remaining the same piece of material.

Mona Lisa's smile and the laughs of her companions in Addams's cartoon are *internally* related. They have the characters they have only by virtue of being seen in relation to each other. The businessmen's laughs are only sinister when seen in relation to Mona Lisa's smile.

This general point has an important bearing on the fears that I mentioned at the beginning – that attempts to interpret works of art and literature in terms of contexts to which they belong, psychological, sociological, historical, critical, etc., etc. must somehow be inimical to attempting to see the works for what they are in themselves. This is the fear that such enterprises must be 'reductivist', which amounts to saying that in the attempt to explain the significance of a work they succeed only in explaining it away, in submerging it in a sea of extraneous facts, as Casaubon did with the Roman frescoes.

I do not of course by any means want to deny that this can happen. But setting a work in a context can't, as I've tried to show, be avoided in any case; and it *need* not be reductive. Whether it is or not is closely connected with whether the contextual relations which are emphasized are 'internal' or 'external' in the sense I have sketched. To exhibit a text's *internal* relation to elements in its surroundings is not to submerge it in something extraneous; on the contrary, it is a contribution towards showing it for what it *is*.

Let me take an example. Suppose I learn that a certain piece of music, say, was composed in order to pay a debt. This may be interesting in all sorts of ways and may even explain why, let's suppose, the work is of poorer quality than most of its composer's work (though I'm not suggesting that would be a necessary consequence). But for the most part such a purely external relation to its context will not serve to illuminate the work's intrinsic characteristics; knowing about such a thing will be more or less irrelevant, aesthetically speaking.

Contrast that with the following case. Janáček's composition 'Diary of a Young Man who Vanished' displays the love of a young man for a gypsy girl, with whom he runs away. It is a work of delicate but very intense erotic feeling. I have read that Janacek composed this piece in his old age, at a time when he was himself very deeply involved in a relationship with a young girl. Now seeing the work against *that* background does, or so it seems to me, help to illuminate and bring into relief a desperately yearning character to its eroticism which one might otherwise not be aware of. This, I am suggesting, is because of the *internal* relation between the nature of the sexual attachment expressed within the work and the attachment of an old but still passionately emotional composer for a young woman. The two kinds of attachment – the composer's and the young man's for the gypsy girl – are, of course, quite different; but the very contrast between them brings something to light as does the contrast between Mona Lisa's smile and the laughing faces that surround her in Addams's cartoon.

The point is obviously related to the issues which exercise – or at least used to exercise – both critics and philosophers concerning the relevance of an artist's *intentions* to the aesthetic evaluation of his work. Those who have objected to reference to intention here have been, I suppose, worried that concern about how a work *came into existence* may distract attention from what the work *is*. (We might remember here Wittgenstein's reference to the tourists with their Baedekers in my earlier quotation.)

But the distinction between what something is and how it came to be (the Platonic distinction between 'being' and 'becoming') is complicated by the fact that *sometimes* how something came to be what it is is an essential aspect of what it is; but not always. And the notion of intention does straddle the two sides of the distinction between being and becoming. If you see me at the ticket office of the railway station you may ask me either 'What are you doing?' or 'Why are you buying a railway ticket?' and the reply 'I intend to travel to Helsinki' could be a response to *both* these questions. And, as my example of the Janáček composition and the other case of a composer's intention ('to make money') with which I contrasted it may serve to suggest, reference to an artist's intention can sometimes be illuminating about the aesthetic nature of his work, though it will not always be so.

II

I want now to turn to a rather different, though connected, question. I have so far been concerned, roughly, with Casaubon's failure – or refusal – to *look at* the frescoes he was showing Dorothea, his use of context to come between him and them. But his demeanour raises a further issue. The frescoes do not seem to mean anything to him; he makes no personal response. And now we may wonder what the relation is between seeing a work of art for what it is and responding to it in a way that is aesthetically appropriate to it.

One aspect of this relation seems clear enough. No response to a work will be, in any full sense, 'aesthetically appropriate' to the work, to the extent that it is not informed by some understanding of what the work is, of its real nature. Leaving aside difficulties which would compel me to make qualifications to this formulation, let me just say that, roughly speaking, understanding that work is a *necessary condition* of responding to it appropriately.

The question I want to consider is whether it is also a *sufficient condition*. That is, will someone who properly understands a work necessarily respond to it in an aesthetically appropriate way? Or, to ask the same question the other way round, is an aesthetically appropriate response a necessary condition of someone's under-standing it properly? And a related question is how an explanation of the nature of a work, of its own meaning, is related to an appropriate response. Does such an explanation, should it, aim at evoking such a response?

The difficulty of dealing with this question clearly has to do with a certain kind of complexity, even a certain indeterminacy, in the concept of 'understanding the real nature of a work of art': a complexity and an indeterminacy that affect the relation of this concept to that of an appropriate response.

There are other analogous cases where we feel that a certain kind of response is, as it were, necessarily required by a certain kind of object, so that anyone who understood the nature of that object would *have* to respond in that way. For instance Wittgenstein thought that ethics involved the idea of such a relationship and found this baffling. In his 'Lecture on Ethics' he wrote: 'the *absolute good*, if it is a describable state of affairs, would be one which everybody, independent of his tastes and inclinations, would *necessarily* bring about or feel guilty for not bringing about.'[4] But he went on to call the idea of such a state of affairs 'a chimera'. 'No state of affairs has, in itself, what I would like to call the coercive power of an absolute judge.'

The corresponding idea in aesthetics, with which I am now concerned, would be that a certain picture, poem, novel, play, etc. of its nature *compels* a certain response from anyone who properly understands its nature. And this is not intended as a psychological generalization so much as a metaphysical truth.

Let's look at this idea by returning to the case of a joke. The idea would be that a joke is, as it were, of its nature funny and that anyone who understands its funniness *has* to laugh at it. I want to discuss, quite briefly, how the explanation of a joke (which I suppose is meant to reveal its 'nature') is related to the disposition to laugh.

If I show someone the Charles Addams cartoon and he chuckles nervously at it, I take that as a sign that he had understood it, that he has 'seen the point'. If on the other hand he looks blank I take it he hasn't understood it. Suppose that, in that case, I take it upon myself to *explain* the joke to him. I say, perhaps, the sort of thing I have said about it here, and more. And suppose that, in reply to that he says, 'Well, yes, I see all that of course, and saw it from the beginning; but what is there in all that to make anyone laugh?' Let's suppose he is speaking sincerely. Has he understood the joke or not?

It's obvious enough, I take it, that an explanation of this sort – an explanation of why *I* laughed at the cartoon, isn't going to make someone else laugh (except perhaps politely) even though it is perfectly well understood. Why is this so? Well, for one thing a laugh is of its nature a spontaneous reaction, a sort of gesture of surprise – and a long explanation could hardly produce *that*. But in that case how can the explanation have been an explanation of why I laughed in the first place? It's true that laughing at a joke is a rather special case of an aesthetic response in that certainly not all such responses are gestures of surprise. But, still, I think one is inclined to say more generally that a response made at the end of an explanation is different from one made without such an explanation. I do not say better or worse – that would depend on circumstances – but different.

4 'A Lecture on Ethics', p. 7.

To say that the explanation (of the joke) is an explanation of why I laugh makes it sound too much perhaps as though in giving the explanation I am giving the reason for an action – and then if the explanation gives *you* the same reason as I *had*, why don't you act in the same way? To avoid this suggestion let me say that my explanation is rather an explanation of *the nature of my laugh*, an account of what sort of laugh it is. This explanation establishes a relation between my laugh and all those complex features of the Addams cartoon and, in so doing, it reveals an important dimension of my laugh. But perhaps someone could have such a relation to the cartoon and express it differently, otherwise, that is, than by laughing.

Here is another example. In Solzhenitsyn's *Cancer Ward*,[5] the following snatch of dialogue occurs between two patients (both of whom believe themselves to be dying). Kostoglotov ('Bonechewer') has been reading Tolstoy's *What Men Live By* and is deeply impressed by it. He says to Yefrem:

> "Yefrem ... that's enough of your whining – here, read this book."
> "Read, why should I read, we'll all kick the bucket soon."
> Bonechewer's bone twitched. "That's the point. If you don't hurry, you'll have kicked the bucket before you've read it! Here you are. Quick!"

That exchange makes, in concrete terms, the same point that Wittgenstein expresses in the *Tractatus* when he says that the world of the happy man is a different world from that of the unhappy man. It is not that Yefrem and Kostoglotov notice different things about their situation. Rather their situations make an entirely different sort of sense (or in Yefrem's case, lack of sense) to each of them. What are we to say: that their diametrically opposite reactions are equally manifestations of their having seen the same point?

If we do say that and try to say the same kind of thing about people who respond in radically different ways to a work of art or literature – or to a joke – then that may give the impression that one's aesthetic response is something quite arbitrary in relation to the features of the work, or joke, in question which are brought out in the critical explanation of it. If someone can see the features of a

5   Alexander Solzhenitsyn, *Cancer Ward*, Ch. 2.

joke, which are mentioned in an elucidation of why it's funny, and not find it funny, in what sense then, after all, has its funniness been elucidated?

One way of replying to this is to say that my laughter hasn't been shown to be *unrelated* to the features of the joke brought out in the elucidation. On the contrary, the nature of my laughter has been exhibited for what it is precisely by being put into relation with what is mentioned in the elucidation of the joke. If someone else laughs at it and then shows himself quite oblivious to and unperceptive of the features of the joke to which I am responding, then his is a different kind of laughter from mine; it doesn't have the same sense.

Putting the matter like this treats the explanation (of the joke, picture, play, etc.) as an account of the nature of possible responses to the work. And it's important to add that what responses *are* possible, conceivable, is internally related to the work responded to. Suppose, for example, that somebody were to say he found Bach's *St Matthew Passion* funny and laughed at it in the same way as he laughs as Rossini's *Barber of Seville*. Would that be intelligible? Does it even make sense to speak of 'laughing at' the *Matthew Passion*? (Laughing *at* something is not just a matter of uttering a sound like laughter in its presence.)

But there are cases where one may want to say something rather different: namely, that two people who respond quite differently to a work do *not* understand it in the same way. It's important to see that there's a certain indeterminacy about the distinction between a case describable like that and one describable as that of two people who understand the work in the same way but respond to it differently. An analogy may help to bring this out. (It's not intended to be used beyond the limited point that's here in question.) If, at a certain stage of my life, I lose my liking for chocolate, should we say that chocolate still tastes the same to me as it once did, but that while I used to find it pleasant, I am now indifferent to it? Or, should we rather say that it now tastes different to me? Well, there *are* of course cases where one could give a definite answer to this, one way or the other. But often, I think, we should be puzzled about what exactly was being asked. The very sense of the question would be unclear.

And this helps to bring out, by analogy, that the *distinction* between understanding a work (a text, etc.) for what it is and responding to it in an aesthetically appropriate way is by no means as clear as I may seem to have been assuming.

There are analogies with ethical cases too. When I'm horrified at the way somebody is behaving, at his cruelty to another person, say, I may sometimes say to him 'You can't behave like that' (which seems to assume that he does understand what he's doing). But in some cases I may address him differently and ask 'Don't you understand what you're doing?' That is, I may take his indifference to what he is doing as itself a criterion for his not understanding the nature of *what* he is doing. Remember Christ's moving words on the Cross (*Luke*, 23): 'Father, forgive them, for they know not what they do'.

It may perhaps sound strange that we should take something like that as a criterion for *not understanding*. But all I can say is that in many cases we *do* do this. And it may look less strange if we observe other familiar cases where the kinds of behaviour that we take as criteria for someone's understanding or not understanding turn out not to be what one might at the outset have expected when one approaches the question with big philosophical issues in mind.

4

Im Anfang war die Tat

I

Philosophers these days distinguish between the truth-conditions of a proposition and the conditions for asserting that proposition. It is often said that, whereas in the *Tractatus* Wittgenstein stressed the first of these notions, the later developments of his thought involved emphasis rather on the second. I do not think that this states the important changes in Wittgenstein's thought at all clearly and should like to consider why.

In *Tractatus*, 4.0312 Wittgenstein says that his fundamental thought is that 'the "logical constants" do not represent'. This reflects his concern to give an account of logical inference such that the validity of an inference should not be made to look as though it depended on an appeal to something's 'being the case'. His account was couched in terms of a system of truth-functions generated by repeated applications of the operation of negation on elementary propositions the essence of which was that they could be either true or false. The account therefore seemed to need a demonstration that there could and must be such elementary propositions. The idea of elementary propositions as pictures (*Bilder*) of possible states of affairs belongs to this demonstration. This idea has many ramifications which I must ignore, but one of its essential aspects is the thought that elementary propositions must be logically independent of each other: and this is important to the case I want to develop.

If elementary propositions were not logically independent there would be relations of logical dependence between propositions, not captured by the *Tractatus* account of truth-functions. (In his post-

Tractatus writings, of course, Wittgenstein very soon recognized that there are indeed such relations.)[1] Furthermore, it might seem that, without logically independent elementary propositions, we should be unable ever to assert anything at all. For if we are *ever* to be in a position to say that any proposition is true (or false) there must obviously be some propositions the truth (or falsity) of which we can determine without first determining the truth (or falsity) of some other.

But this leads to the doctrine of logically independent elementary propositions only because the *Tractatus* so austerely excludes those epistemological considerations which Wittgenstein later came to see as central to the discussion of such questions. That I can determine the truth or falsity of p independently of the truth or falsity of q does not require that p and q should be logically independent. I can see that this coat is blue (p) without questions about the truth or falsity of its being yellow (q) or red (r) entering into my reflections at all. Nevertheless p *can* only be true if q and r are both false.

The difficulty is dealt with (for instance in *Philosophical Remarks* and *Philosophical Grammar*) by substituting for the *Tractatus* view, that what we 'lay against reality' are individual elementary propositions, the view that what we lay against reality are *systems* of propositions. This move goes along with recognizing that there are countless such different systems, involving different understandings of what it is for a proposition to 'correspond with reality'; and hence with abandoning the attempt to give a single general account of what determining the truth or falsity of a proposition consists in. 'A proposition is everything that can be true or false' *looks* as though it determines what a proposition is, only because we mistakenly think we have some independent grasp of truth and falsity enabling us to determine what is and is not a proposition. Whereas all we can say is 'that we can only predicate "true" and "false" of what we call a proposition'.[2] Our understanding of how these terms are to be applied varies *pari passu* with our understanding of the propositions to which we apply them, and they cannot be used as points of reference for fixing the sense of the propositions.

The *Tractatus* had compared *Bilder* (and hence propositions) with measuring rods which we 'apply to reality' (2.1512). Wittgenstein's

---

1 See, for example, *Philosophical Remarks*, VIII, *Philosophical Grammar*, Part I, Appendix 4.

2 *Philosophical Investigations*, I, no. 136.

later emphasis on diversity of course robs this comparison of its central place. But the comparison itself was insufficiently thought through, as is brought out in a difficult and important discussion in *Philosophical Grammar*, part I, section VI, paragraph 79, which is worth looking at closely for the light it throws on confusions which seem to me still endemic in treatments of our topic. The passage raises the question whether we should write:

'*p*' is true (as in *Tractatus*)
or rather
p is true.

Shouldn't it be the latter? 'The ink mark is after all not *true*; in the way it's black and curved.' If we say that a *Satz* 'agrees with reality', *of what* are we saying this? Let us say:

p = This object is one metre long
and
'*p*' is true = This object has the length of this metre rule.

The second equation makes explicit the comparison of one thing with another which is supposed to be involved in the use of 'true'. The ruler must be taken here as standing in for the *Satz* '*p*'; it 'agrees with reality' if its ends coincide with those of the object. To operate the analogy we should have to say the rule 'says' that this object is one metre long; and that the correspondence of the ends of the ruler with those of the object 'says' that it is true that the object is one metre long. It's important that we're already in trouble here in trying to make the ruler and the correspondence of the ends 'say' anything. We have to imagine perhaps that I simply produce the ruler and approach the object with it; and perhaps to interpret *this* as my saying that the object is one metre long. But it is apparent that this interpretation already presupposes a background of technique and standards; and this is what Wittgenstein is getting at when he says the whole comparison is wrong because the phrase 'this metre rule' is a *description* and the phrase 'metre rule' the *determination of a concept*. In other words my laying this piece of metal against this object is no more than just that, not a case of *measuring* the object, except in so far as the piece of metal is being *seen as* a metre rule, which is possible only within the whole context of the practice of metric measurements. This context determines the concept, *metric rule*, and thus provides the possibility of describing the piece of metal as 'a metre rule'.

I put the ruler and the object together and their ends coincide. That is (within the context of metric measurement), I can say that the object is as long as the metre rule; which in terms of the comparison under examination, corresponds to the proposition ' "This object is one metre long" is true.' Wittgenstein's comment is: 'in " '*p*' is true" the ruler enters immediately into the proposition. "*p*" represents here simply the length and not the metre rule.' In other words, the piece of metal (which I describe as a metre rule) belongs to the method of applying the concept *one metre long*; it enters the picture simply as a *standard* of length. The ruler – Wittgenstein says – is here 'a purely geometrical appendage of the measured line'. We might say that I am measuring the object against the concept *one metre long*, not against the piece of metal, though the latter plays a role, as 'a purely geometrical appendage', in this application of the concept.

Wittgenstein's conclusion is:

> It can also be put thus: The proposition " '*p*' is true" can only be understood if one understands the grammar of the sign "*p*" as a propositional sign; not if "*p*" is simply the name of the shape of a particular ink mark. In the end one can only say that the quotation marks in the sentence "'*p*' is true" are simply superfluous.

We can now expand the equivalence of '*p is true*' and '*p*' in the following way. 'This object is as long as this metre rule' says the same as 'This object is one metre long,' while emphasizing that the result has been arrived at in a way appropriate for reaching such results. Analogously '*p* is true' says the same as '*p*', while emphasizing that '*p*' is being asserted on appropriate grounds; that is, it insists that I am justified in asserting *p*. And to say '*p* corresponds with reality' is just another way of insisting that we are justified (on appropriate grounds) in asserting *p*.

II

In the light of the foregoing, I want next to look at some things Bernard Williams and Michael Dummett have said about Wittgenstein.

Bernard Williams claims in his 'Wittgenstein and Idealism'[3] that Wittgenstein's view of the relation between truth and warranted assertion is either 'a triviality' or must have 'quite amazing consequences'. The amazing consequences are generated by the following argument scheme:

   (i) 'S' has the meaning we give it.
   (ii) A necessary condition of our giving 'S' a meaning is Q.
ergo
   (iii) Unless Q, 'S' would not have a meaning.
   (iv) If 'S' did not have a meaning, 'S' would not be true.
ergo
   (v) Unless Q, 'S' would not be true.

Williams comments: 'Since any number of substitutions for Q in (ii) which relate to human existence, language use, etc. make it true for any "S" one likes, and since (i) is supposedly true for any "S", and (iv) for any true "S", we can get the truth of any true "S" dependent on human existence, etc.; that is, prove unrestricted idealism.' As he concedes, the argument is unworrying if (v) is taken to mean 'Unless Q, "S" would not express a truth,' since that does not entail 'Unless Q, not S.' He thinks, though, that Wittgenstein's so-called 'theory of justified assertion' may prevent one from distinguishing 'between the sentence "S" expressing the truth, and what is the case if S'.

But Williams's phrase 'the sentence "S" expressing the truth' is confusing here. (He slides from 'expresses *a* truth' to 'expresses *the* truth'.) ' "S" expresses the truth' *sounds* like another way of saying 'S is true'. But in the context of Williams's argument it telescopes two expressions:

   (a) ' "S" expresses a proposition'
and
   (b) 'S is true'.

Given (a), quotation marks round 'S' are not necessary in (b), and if (a) does not hold then (b) is as senseless as 'S' itself. But if 'S' is senseless so, obviously, is the expression 'what is the case if S'. Williams is quite wrong in supposing that Wittgenstein's position allows us to 'get the *truth* [my italics] of any true "S" dependent on human existence, language use etc.' If we *do* (with Williams) express

3 *Understanding Wittgenstein*, pp. 93–4.

Wittgenstein's thought as being 'that the determinacy of reality comes from what we have decided or are prepared to count as determinate', it is imperative to remember that the 'determinacy' in question is one of *sense* not of *truth*. Whether this reduces Wittgenstein's position to a 'triviality' must be judged in the light of its role in his discussion of related questions.

This issue is quite central to any understanding of Wittgenstein's work, and I shall now pursue it further by discussing Michael Dummett's treatment of the dispute between 'realist' and 'anti-realist' conceptions of truth.[4] As Wittgenstein is the only alleged[5] anti-realist named, I shall treat the anti-realist arguments advanced in Dummett's discussion as intended to apply to Wittgenstein, even when this is not explicitly stated.

Let me start by considering Dummett's explicit attribution of certain positions to Wittgenstein. He refers to *Remarks on the Foundations of Mathematics*, Part I, Appendix I,[6] part of which runs as follows: 'So what does it mean to say a proposition "*is true*"? "*p*" is *true = p*. (This is the answer).' Presumably it is the remark in parentheses that leads Dummett to characterize Wittgenstein's view as being 'that the sole explanation that can be given of the notion of truth consists precisely in the direct stipulation of the equivalence thesis'.[7] However, the way Wittgenstein continues this passage makes it clear that is *not* what he is saying. His point is in fact very like that which Dummett himself makes earlier in the chapter when he comments on the unjustified optimism of those who think that the notions of truth and falsity will by themselves provide a sufficient basis for a theory of meaning. When Wittgenstein says: 'So perhaps what is being asked is: under what circumstances does one assert a proposition?' he cannot be taken as *contrasting* the question with: 'Under what circumstances is a proposition true?' For he has said that to call a proposition 'true' *comes to* asserting that proposition. His point is even clearer in *Philosophical Investigations* where he says that in one sense what a proposition is, is determined 'by the use of the sign in the language-game. And the use of the words "true" and "false" may be among the constituent parts of this game; and if so it belongs to our concept "proposition" but does not "*fit*" it.'[8] *On*

4 *Frege, Philosophy of Language*, ch. 13.
5 *Remarks on the Foundations of Mathematics*, 3rd edition, VI, no. 23. '*Nicht Empirie und doch Realismus in der Philosophie, das ist das Schwerste.*'
6 Wittgenstein, loc. cit., Part I, Appendix III.
7 Dummett, p. 458.
8 *Philosophical Investigations*, I, no. 136.

Certainty, section 200 reads: 'Really "the proposition is true or false" only means that it must be possible to decide for or against it. But this does not say what such a decision is like.' So far from claiming, as Dummett says, that 'the *whole* explanation of the word "true" ' as applied to a given *Satz* is given by the equivalence thesis', Wittgenstein is explicitly denying this. The equivalence thesis gives us all we can say *in general* about 'true', but the real work is done by a detailed examination of how it is applied in particular cases, and such an examination yields different results in different cases. In the examinations which Wittgenstein undertakes he places at least as much emphasis as does Dummett on what the latter calls the 'consequences' of accepting *p* (= accepting that *p* is true); and he *includes* in those consequences the possibility of applying the truth-functional calculus to it:

> And to say that a proposition is whatever can be true or false amounts to saying; we call something a proposition when *in our language* we apply the calculus of truth-functions to it. (*Philosophical Investigations*, I, section 136.)

Wittgenstein is emphasizing the dangers of looking at the matter the other way round; that is, of starting with the calculus of truth-functions, supposing that our ability to construct this calculus rests on an intuitive idea of what it is for a proposition to be true or false. We then come across various expressions which look like propositions and assume that they can be slotted without more ado into the calculus. We suppose that *therefore* we understand what it is to specify truth-conditions for the putative proposition. Then, because our attention has been distracted from the actual circumstances (if any) in which we regard someone as entitled to assert *p*, we are tempted into a mythological account of *p*'s truth-conditions. We find ourselves obsessed with a certain picture, but have no clear idea of what we are talking about when we speak of 'the truth-conditions of *p*'.

Dummett's realist plunges straight into such a mythology with his thesis 'that a thought can be true only if there is something in virtue of which it is true', a thesis which he thinks requires an 'ontological realm of facts to constitute that in virtue of which thoughts may be true'.[9]

9 Dummett, p. 464.

Read in one way the 'realist thesis' is perfectly in order: namely, if it means that we cannot simply assert anything at will. – In what sense 'cannot'? – Of course I can perfectly well arbitrarily utter certain words which, uttered in other circumstances, would constitute an assertion. But to the same extent as you thought I *had* uttered them arbitrarily, you would be disinclined to think I had made any assertion. Discussing a different, but closely related issue, Wittgenstein wrote: ' "*Can* that happen?" – Certainly. Just describe it in detail and you will then see that the procedure you describe can perfectly well be imagined, although you will clearly not apply such and such expressions to it.'[10]

Suppose I am walking with you down a familiar street and, out of the blue, point and say 'That house is made of *papier mâché*.' Asked to explain, I offer nothing that you (or anybody else) would for a moment accept as a reason for thinking the house is made of *papier mâché*. Being patient and concerned, you take me into the house and we feel the (perfectly normal) walls, doors, etc. I continue to utter my original words in the manner of one making an assertion. You wouldn't know *what* to make of my behaviour.

But was I not asserting something false? The question is whether I'm to be described as having 'asserted something' at all. Someone will object at this point that you must have understood my words as an assertion, since you took me into the house and did the things appropriate to testing such an assertion. But it isn't of course denied that my behaviour was in many ways *like* that of one making an assertion. Still, you could equally well, better, be interpreted as testing whether I really was making the assertion which in *some* ways I seemed to be making.

The point becomes clearer if we imagine a society in which people are constantly doing that sort of thing, though they *also* 'make genuine assertions' (that is, speak in circumstances similar to those in which we do normally take people to be making assertions). Could the members of such a society treat the cases which strike us as anomalies in the same way as they treat the 'genuine' cases? 'Could they?' That means, can we imagine their doing things which we should be willing to *count* as 'treating these cases in the same way', in respects relevant to what we understand by 'assertions'? For instance, when someone says of a perfectly ordinary house that it's made of *papier mâché*, they methodically demolish it, looking hard at

10   'Cause and Effect: Intuitive Awareness', p. 415.

the pieces of rubble and putting them alongside pieces of *papier mâché*; and at the end of all this they say, 'perhaps all the same it's made of *papier mâché*. Would *we* say they were 'investigating whether . . . etc.', and that they regarded the results as 'inconclusive'? Everybody must answer this for himself. My answer is that I shouldn't say this.

So the 'realist's' thesis that a thought can be true only if there is something in virtue of which it is true can be given a perfectly acceptable interpretation. It must be remembered that, on this interpretation, what this 'something' is has to be understood in the context of what we are willing to count as a case of exhibiting it, and that this will vary enormously for different kinds of case. The trouble with the 'realist', as is shown by his gesture towards an 'ontological realm of facts to constitute that in virtue of which thoughts may be true', is that he has a vague picture of an interpretation of quite a different sort – which does have an obvious application to some kinds of case, but not to problematic ones. What distinguishes him from his opponent is not, as Dummett claims, that *he* makes truth-conditions fundamental to meaning whilst his opponent doesn't, but rather that he tries to interpret 'truth-conditions' according to a certain model which he takes to be 'the most elementary level': that of 'observation-sentences'.[11] He wants to apply this picture across the board because he mistakenly thinks there is a certain kind of systematic connection between the various cases, exhibited by the calculus of truth-functions: overlooking the fact that there are *other* systems of operations which the truth-functional calculus does not capture, and which have to be presupposed before we can ever arrive at the necessary 'elementary' bases on which the truth-functional operations can be performed.[12]

Dummett himself thinks that 'our original grasp of there being something that makes a statement true derives from our use of basic forms of statement as reports of observations', and this provides us with 'a model for what it would be to recognize the sentences as true by the most direct means'. The 'realist' believes that a sentence the truth of which is recognizable, if at all, only 'indirectly' is one which 'contains expressions whose sense is given in terms of perceptual or mental operations which go beyond our capacities', for instance, one involving quantification over an infinite domain. We can understand

11 Dummett, pp. 466–7.
12 Cf. *Philosophical Remarks*, VIII, especially no. 76.

such a sentence 'by analogy with the finite case, even though we are subject to the limitation of only being able to carry out finitely many observations or tests within a finite time'.[13] Such an analogy can be developed via the postulation of 'some suitably placed hypothetical being with sufficiently extended powers'.[14]

This calls for several comments. In the first place, the contention that our original grasp of what it is for something to make a statement true derives from basic observation statements seems little more than an empiricist prejudice. 'Realism without empiricism in philosophy, that's what is most difficult.'[15] In any case, the passage from *Philosophical Grammar*, I, VI, section 79, which I discussed earlier, shows the complexity involved even in cases which we might be most inclined to call 'basic reports of observation'. And if the example of measuring length is considered insufficiently 'basic', it has to be remembered that to report anything at all we have to apply a concept which has been determined in some way,[16] namely, as Wittgenstein repeatedly argues, by a system of *practices*.

As to the idea that, where quantification over an infinite domain is involved, we can grasp the truth of what is said 'only indirectly', consider the following passage from *Philosophical Grammar*, Part II, II, section 10:

> But what makes a sign an expression of infinity? What gives the peculiar character that belongs to what we call infinite? I believe that it is like the case of a sign for an enormous number. For the characteristic of the infinite, conceived in this way, is its enormous size.
>
> But there isn't anything that is an enumeration and yet not an enumeration; a generality that enumerates in a cloudy kind of way without really enumerating or enumerating to a determinate limit.
>
> The dots in "I + I + I + I. . . ." are just the four dots: a sign for which it must be possible to give certain rules. (The same rules, in fact, as for the sign "and so on ad inf.".) This sign does in a manner ape enumeration, but it isn't an enumeration. And that means that the rules governing it don't

13 Dummett, p. 465.
14 Dummett, p. 467.
15 *Remarks on the Foundations of Mathematics*, VI, no. 23.
16 Cf. the discussion of 'seeing an aspect' in *Philosophical Investigations*, II, xi.

totally agree with those which govern an enumeration; they agree only up to a point.

There is no third thing between the particular enumeration and the general sign.

Wittgenstein's point would be missed by anyone who took him to be simply contradicting Dummett's realist. He is of course attacking the whole distinction between 'direct' and 'indirect' needed for expressing the 'realist's' case. The 'realist' thinks that 'I + I + I + I ...' is related to 'I + I + I + I' as is, say 'I + I + I + I + I + I + I + I', only, as it were, enormously more so – so much more so that it is (literally) beyond us to say how much more so. Whereas, though the expressions are indeed related, they are not related like that. The way in which we come to grasp the sense of the expression involving infinity is indeed difficult to describe (the difficulty springing from our not realizing when we should stop and simply say: that *is* the description). It is what Wittgenstein is describing in his discussions of *following a rule* and of the kind of training on which this rests. The response to the training *is* the grasping of the sense and not the taking of a hint about something that lies beyond.

Or let me put it this way: the response to the training is indeed a response – a movement beyond the training itself.[17] It consists in the adoption of a new concept, manifested in grammatical differences in the way the trainee talks. But the way he now talks is perfectly describable – differently of course from what fits the more 'primitive' way of talking out of which the new concept developed; but *completely* describable nonetheless. The appearance of incompleteness comes only from a faulty grasp of the relation between the new and the old way of speaking in which the new is seen as simply a fresh application of an existing concept instead of the expression of a *different* concept.

---

17 Cf. *Remarks on the Foundations of Mathematics*, VI, no. 10

You extract a theorem (*eine Lehre*) from the proof. So the sense of the theorem must be independent of the proof; for otherwise it could never have been separated from the proof.

Analogously I can remove the lines of construction from the drawing and leave the rest there.

So it as if the proof did not determine the sense of the proposition proved; and yet again as if it did.

But isn't it like that with every verification of every proposition?

The attempt by Dummett's realist to make his point by postulating 'some suitably placed hypothetical being with sufficiently extended powers' is bound to fail. For this being is conceived *entirely* in terms of his 'suitable placing' and 'sufficiently extended powers': and *the whole trouble* right from the start was that we were supposed not to be able to describe these. Postulating a being able to make infinitely many observations in a finite time is not like postulating, on a much larger scale, a being who lives long enough to experience the whole life-cycle of a redwood tree, from its germination to its withering. We can describe what it would be to make the latter observations, not the former: hence we cannot describe a being who can make the former. If we could, we should never have experienced our original difficulty.

I think the preceding discussion provides the means of answering the final objection offered by Dummett's realist:

> Replacement of the notions of truth and falsity, as the central notions for the theory of meaning, by those of verification and falsification must result in a different logic, that is, in the rejection of certain forms of argument which are valid on a classical, i.e., two-valued interpretation of the logical constants. In this respect, the linguistic practice which we actually learn is in conformity with the realist's conception of meaning: repudiation of realism as a philosophical doctrine entails revisionism about certain features of actual use.[18]

Dummett illustrates this objection with statements in the past tense. If such a statement is made, for instance from memory, then the present memory 'constitutes the verification of the assertion'. This, he says, makes the past-tense sentence 'undecidable', since what could decide it would only be a past observation of the event asserted to have occurred, and 'a verification cannot precede the making of the assertion verified.'[9]

However, 'the linguistic practice which we actually learn' does involve our saying in certain cases that we do *know* (from memory) that such and such a past event occurred. We do not look for further verification; or, in cases where we do, verification comes to an end

18 Dummett, p. 468.
19 Dummett, p. 469. For further discussion of this issue see *Philosophical Remarks*, V.

and at the end we say that the occurrence has been established. (Or, of course, that it has not: but it is not in dispute that we are often *in fact* unable to establish the truth about many matters.) Our linguistic practice does not consist in our saying that the past-tense statement *means the same* as the description of those present circumstances which we take as warranting the statement. Rather, *in* the present circumstances (which can of course be described) we do confidently make the past-tense statement and, beyond a certain point, we attach no sense to apparent 'expressions of doubt' as to whether it is true or not. Misled by a certain picture we may, when philosophizing, find it strange that we should have such a practice, and this appearance of strangeness can only be dissipated by closer attention to what the practice is. This is the very reverse of 'revisionism'.

Dummett's realist is particularly concerned about those cases in which someone remembered 'that either A or B without remembering whether A or not or whether B or not', concluding that such a disjunction cannot be interpreted 'in terms of a notion of truth for such sentences which coincides with the existence of a warrant for asserting them'.[20] Now Wittgenstein does not say that these 'coincide'. As we have noted, he says (amongst other things):

1   p is true $= p$.
2   To understand the use of 'true' and 'false' in connection with a given 'p', we should ask in what circumstances 'p' is asserted.
3   *One* feature of this use is the application to 'p' of the truth-functional calculus.

Applying this to Dummett's case we have:

1   'p or q is true' $=$ 'p or q'.
2   'p' or 'q' can be asserted when we can't assert 'p' or assert 'q'.
3   The truth-functional calculus has *already* been applied in the construction of 'p or q'.

If someone convinces me that not p and that not q, then I withdraw my original assertion. If he confirms that p (and/or that q)

---

20   p. 469. The discussion in *Philosophical Remarks*, IX is very relevant to the issue.

he confirms my original assertion. This is, as it were, part of the logical space to which my assertion belongs; there is certainly no departure from classical logic, no rejection of forms of argument 'valid on a . . . two-valued interpretation of the logical constants'.

Nor is there any revision of our actual use. It is a certain picture of the relation of that use to the truth-functional calculus which leads to 'revisionism'. Led by that picture to think that 'elementary' propositions must occupy a special place in our language, we may come to think that no one has a right to insist on the truth of p or q unless he has a right to insist either on the truth of p or on the truth of q. As Dummett is himself pointing out, the truth of p or q may stand firmer for someone than that of either of its disjuncts; and it may be added that in asserting p or q he need have absolutely no interest in *which* of the disjuncts is true.

'Truth-conditions' is a logician's term of art. Its use may already presuppose an approach to questions about meaning which Wittgenstein is rejecting. This does not imply that he is denying that the words 'true' and 'false' play an important role in our understanding of propositions. To say that he *replaced* 'truth-conditions' by 'assertion-conditions' (another term of art) in the 'theory of meaning' is misleading in its suggestion that he was offering an alternative theory of meaning. Whereas his point was that the notion of meaning and its connection with truth and falsity is not to be elucidated in terms of a general theory at all.

III

Close to the surface of all the issues I have been discussing lies the question of the kind of 'relation of language to the world' which is needed if we are to be able to *say* anything which is grounded in something independent. In the *Tractatus* the point of contact is located in the possibility of a direct 'comparison' between an elementary proposition and a *Sachverhalt*; and this possibility in its turn depends on the role of 'names' in the proposition whose meanings *are* their bearers; 'objects' which constitute 'the substance of the world'. Names and objects, however, are presented as a purely logical requirement, something which just has to be accepted. We cannot ask any questions about them, since to do so we should have to use those very names in our questions and presuppose that they do have meaning. Compare *Tractatus*, 3.263 which speaks of explaining primitive signs by means of elucidatory propositions containing those very signs, the meanings of which must therefore already be known before the 'elucidations' can be understood. Although Wittgenstein of course subsequently abandoned the misleading imagery associated with 'names' and 'objects', his insistence that 'the harmony of thought and reality is to be found in the grammar of our language' and on the 'arbitrariness' of grammar,[21] expresses an unremitting opposition to the idea that our ways of speaking can receive any justification from some sort of extralinguistic insight into the relation between words and things.

Many philosophers have, however, thought they could offer such a justification. Russell tried to do so in 'The Limits of Empiricism',[22] an article which stimulated Wittgenstein to develop, around 1937, some of his most thought-provoking ideas – ideas which prefigure much of what is central to his last writings, *On Certainty.*[23]

Russell argued that our words are causally connected with what we perceive and that this causal connection can itself be directly perceived, that is, it is not inferred from repeated past experience, even though it may be set up by the development of habits involving previous experience.

> But when I know that I said "cat" because there was a cat, I am not knowing that, in large numbers of similar instances, similar visual appearances have been followed by similar utterances . . . I am asserting something which I can know without going outside what is now happening. This is essential, since the knowledge is required for the connection of sensible occurrences with the verbal assertion of them.[24]

I think Russell's thought here is: if I had to 'go outside' what is now happening, the evidence might show that there is, after all, no causal connection between my words and the sensible occurrences. That would mean I was mistaken in what I thought I meant, perhaps even in supposing that I meant anything at all. And if I can't ever be sure beyond the possibility of refutation that I mean something, how can I ever be sure that I mean anything at all? Perhaps all my utterances

21 *Zettel*, no. 320.
22 Published in 1936.
23 'Cause and Effect: Intuitive Awareness'.
24 Russell, p. 136.

would turn out to be meaningless noises. So Russell's position is that our use of language must be based on an ultimate certainty, a knowledge *that something is so*, which is invulnerable to further falsification.

Wittgenstein agrees with Russell that we do often speak of one thing's being the cause of another without first establishing some general law by repeated observations or experiments. For instance, if I feel a tug on a cord which I am holding, look along it, and see someone pulling at the other end of it, I do not normally need further evidence to convince me that he caused the tug which I felt. The case is contrasted with that of a goat-farmer who experiments with various kinds of fodder to determine which is the cause of his goats' varying milk yield.[25]

On the other hand, our application of the word 'cause' in the first kind of case (and in Russell's examples) is not itself based simply on our immediate experience of the moment ('without going outside what is now happening'). Wittgenstein wrote in a pocket notebook (in about 1937):

> "I am immediately aware that my exclamation is caused by something." – So I'm immediately aware that the word "cause" fits this case? But remember that *words* are public property
> . . . .
> What if I said: The word "cause" fits my impression privately? – But "to fit" is a public word.
> Ask yourself: What do we make this noise of words for?[26]

These remarks are very damaging to Russell's position, the heart of which is that we understand what our words mean only because we see them to be caused by something extralinguistic; if this 'perception of the cause' is itself conceivable only *within* an established use of language, the foundation for language, which Russell thought he had provided, collapses. He is simply going round in a circle – *within* language.

The point might be put like this: *Given* an established use of the word 'cause', it is certainly possible to use it in cases where we have not conducted repeated observations and experiments to 'establish the causal connection'. Still, in calling A the cause of B we may be

25 'Cause and Effect: Intuitive Awareness', pp. 416–17.
26 'Cause and Effect', pp. 429–30.

right or wrong and our judgement is vulnerable to further evidence. (This does not mean that we cannot be completely – and justifiably – certain that our judgement will *not* be overturned. That our judgement is immediate and confident doesn't make it infallible.) 'It is just as if somebody claimed to have knowledge of human anatomy by intuition; and we say: "We don't doubt it; but if you want to be a doctor, you must pass all the examinations like anybody else." '[27]

So Wittgenstein's first point in response to Russell is this: there is such a thing as 'recognizing the cause of something immediately', but this is not an infallible, self-authenticating 'knowing'. At the same time, however, he recognizes that Russell is close to something important in believing that our use of language fundamentally involves an unhesitating response to situations on our part concerning which it cannot intelligibly be supposed that we 'might be wrong': not because we are infallibly *right*, but because 'the point is that there is no *right* (or wrong) about it. (And of course no one would say: "I'm sure I'm right that I have pain.")'[28] I shall return to this later, but first I want to explore Wittgenstein's reasons for agreeing that an unhesitating 'certainty' is fundamental to language.

> The *basic form* of our game must be one in which there is no such thing as doubt. – What makes us sure of this? It can't surely be a matter of historical certainty.
>
> 'The basic form of the game can't include doubt.' What we are doing here above all is to *imagine* a basic form: a possibility, indeed a *very important* possibility. (We often confuse what is an important possibility with historical reality.)[29]

So Wittgenstein describes various possible ways in which people might act and speak, where it might seem possible to say that hesitation, or doubt as to whether something is or is not the case, is, as it were, their point of departure. For instance:

> So imagine a mother whose child is crying and holding his cheek. *One* kind of reaction to this is for the mother to try and comfort her child and to nurse him in some way or other. In this case there is nothing corresponding to a doubt whether the

---

27 'Cause and Effect', p. 419.
28 'Cause and Effect', p. 430.
29 'Cause and Effect', p. 411.

child is really in pain. Another case would be this: The usual
reaction to the child's complaints is as just described, but
under some circumstances the mother behaves sceptically.
Perhaps she shakes her head suspiciously, stops comforting
and nursing her child – even expresses annoyance and lack of
sympathy. But now imagine a mother who is sceptical right
from the very beginning: If her child cries, she shrugs her
shoulders and shakes her head; sometimes she looks at him
inquiringly, examines him; on exceptional occasions she also
makes vague attempts to comfort and nurse him. – Were we to
encounter such behaviour, we definitely wouldn't call it
scepticism; it would strike us as queer and crazy. – "The game
can't begin with doubting" means: we shouldn't call it
"doubting" if the game began with it.[30]

To say, of the first of the cases described, that 'there is nothing
corresponding to a doubt', is to warn us against the temptation to
think the mother is making an 'unquestioning assumption' or 'knows
something intuitively'. There is no question of her assuming or
knowing anything; she just unhesitatingly *acts* in certain ways. *Given*
such a background of unhesitating reactions, we can *then* imagine, as
in the second case, forms of behaviour which we could regard as
expressing doubt. But if she were to exhibit that sort of behaviour
without such a background, as in the third case, we should not want
to call it 'the expression of doubt': 'As things are, the *reasons* for
doubting are reasons for leaving a familiar track', and 'Doubt is a
moment of hesitation and is, *essentially*, an exception to the rule.'[31]
How is this discussion related to the issues I raised earlier
concerning the true–false 'bipolarity' which belongs to our idea of a
proposition? We *use* the terms 'true' and 'false' in contexts, for
instance, where we are wondering or investigating whether
something is so or not, hesitating whether we should accept that
something is so, manifesting doubt as to whether something is so, or
insisting that something is so in the face of scepticism: contexts
involving the contemplation of two mutually exclusive possibilities.
Without these human phenomena the words 'true' and 'false' would
not have the sense they do have for us. That these phenomena are

30 'Cause and Effect', p. 414.
31 'Cause and Effect', p. 412.

fundamental to the lives we lead has much to do with our preoccupation with 'exploring the nature of things' or 'finding out how things are'. Hence it is very natural – and perfectly proper – that we should want to make the distinction between truth and falsity central in trying to account for the kind of harmony that obtains between our thought (and our language) and the world. Carefully investigating what is true and what is false *is* the process of, as it were, achieving a close fit between our thoughts, beliefs and the way things actually are. But although the distinction between truth and falsity is indeed, in this sense, fundamental to the link between what we say and the way things are, it is not *the* 'primitive' link. Wittgenstein's discussions show this by demonstrating that the phenomena of human behaviour to which the use of 'true' and 'false' belongs would not have the sense they do have – would not be regarded as manifestation of doubt and questioning – without the background of a pattern of unquestioning responses: responses which are 'unquestioning' in the sense that the contexts in which they occur do not make any room for the idea of a question's being asked. As Wittgenstein puts it, within the practice of investigating something (for example the cause of something):

> something that we call doubt and uncertainty plays a role, but this is a second-order feature. In an analogous way it is characteristic of how a sewing machine functions that its parts may wear out and get bent, and its axles may wobble in their bearings, but still this is a second-order characteristic compared with the normal working of the machine.[32]

And again:

> Language – I want to say – is a refinement, *im Anfang war die Tat* ("in the beginning was the deed").
> First there must be firm, hard stone for the building and the blocks are laid rough-hewn one on another. *Afterwards* it's certainly important that the stone can be trimmed, that it's not too hard.[33]

Goethe's '*Im Anfang war die Tat*' of course has considerable

32 'Cause and Effect', p. 420.
33 'Cause and Effect', p. 420.

resonances. On the whole, the best thing to do with resonances is to leave them alone to resonate. However, Wittgenstein's quotation of the line reverberates through many different corners of his philosophy, and I should like to conclude by just gesturing in the direction of some of them. Goethe was drawing attention to the *creative* role of 'the deed', and in Wittgenstein this is expressed in the importance ascribed to certain primitive human actions and reactions for *concept-formation*. This gets its most general form of treatment in the pervasive discussions of what is involved in learning and following a rule. Again, in his discussion of the role of ostensive definition in the conferring of names on objects, he draws attention to the fact that when I see someone point with his finger, I characteristically don't look *at* his finger, but *away* from it in what I call 'the direction in which he is pointing' – and I *have* this latter concept only by virtue of the fact that I *do* naturally, along with everyone else, react to his outstretched arm and finger in that way. In the 1937 notes to which I have been referring, Wittgenstein emphasizes the importance for our concept of causality of a certain typical reaction of people towards states of affairs they want to get rid of.

> *We react to the cause*
> Calling something "the cause" is like pointing and saying: "He's to blame!" We instinctively get rid of the cause if we don't want the effect. We instinctively look from what has been hit to what has hit it. (I am assuming that we do this.)[34]

Simone Weil makes a closely analogous point in the emphasis she places on *methodical ways of working* in our dealings with nature, as what brings to birth the concept of natural necessities. If, for instance, we want to lift a stone that is too heavy for is, we, as it may seem paradoxically, direct our immediate attention away from the stone and look for something we can use as a lever. Simone Weil also speaks of the relation men have to physical objects, which makes it possible for them to distinguish their various properties, as a sort of 'dance':[35] and she means, quite literally, a pattern of movements of people's *bodies*, involved, for example in distinguishing an object's weight, shape, texture, flexibility and so on. These patterns of movement don't *follow* a prior recognition of such

34 'Cause and Effect', p. 410.
35 Simone Weil, *Lectures on Philosophy*, p. 52.

properties, they belong to the formation and application of the concepts of the properties in question. The point Simone Weil is making here is closely akin to Wittgenstein's. Something similar is involved in the way Wittgenstein treats our reaction to a man's groans and writhings in relation to the concept of pain and even to the concept of a human being: 'How am I filled with pity *for this man*? How does it come out what the object of my pity is? (Pity, one may say, is a form of conviction that someone else is in pain.)'[36] It is instructive to reflect on the contrast between Wittgenstein's treatment of this subject and Strawson's.[37] Strawson's starting point is the *statement* in which a predicate is ascribed to an identified subject; Wittgenstein's is the primitive *reaction*. Not, of course, that Wittgenstein denies that we can make true and false assertions about persons: his point is that these assertions make use of a concept which is the creation of a mode of acting to which the true–false bipolarity does not apply. 'The deed' now fills the role taken in the *Tractatus* by the relation of 'name' to 'object'. One important difference is that deeds, unlike 'objects' can be described; another is that emphasis on the deed opens the door to an understanding of how *new* concepts can be created and to a way of grasping concepts and ways of thinking very different from our own. And just because there is no application for the true–false polarity at the level of the deed, this is *not* to open the door to 'idealism' or 'relativism'.

36 *Philosophical Investigations*, I, no. 287. For further discussion see below, ch. 10.

37 P. F. Strawson, *Individuals* (chapter on 'Persons') – though his essay 'Freedom and Resentment' contains suggestions of a position closer to Wittgenstein's.

5

Facts and Superfacts

The previous chapter, *Im Anfang war die Tat*, is a revised version of a contribution to the Wittgenstein Colloquium held in London, Ontario in 1976.[1] Coincidentally, the original lecture on which Saul Kripke based his influential book on Wittgenstein[2] was delivered at the same colloquium. Kripke's book is an outstanding example of the reading of Wittgenstein against which my paper was directed.

The first paragraph of Part I, section 201, of *Philosophical Investigations* provides Kripke with his starting point: 'This was our paradox: no course of action could be determined by a rule, because every course of action can be made out to accord with the rule. The answer was: if everything can be made out to accord with the rule, then it can also be made out to conflict with it. And so there would be neither accord nor conflict here.'

Kripke thinks that Wittgenstein is propounding a 'sceptical problem' about rule-following analogous to Hume's problem about causation; and he thinks that the 'private language argument' belongs to a 'sceptical solution' (a phrase which again deliberately echoes Hume) which Wittgenstein provides to his problem. In order to get a clear view of what Kripke thinks Wittgenstein was sceptical about, we have to attend to his own understanding of rule-following. Using the elementary addition rule as his example he explains himself as follows on page 7:

> I, like almost all English speakers, use the word "plus" and the symbol "+" to denote a well known mathematical function,

1 See Irving Block (ed.), *Perspectives on the Philosophy of Wittgenstein*.
2 Saul A. Kripke, *Wittgenstein on Rules and Private Language*.

addition. The function is defined for all pairs of positive integers. By means of my external symbolic representation and my internal mental representation, I "grasp" the rule for addition. Although I myself have completed only finitely many sums in the past, the rule determines my answer for indefinitely many new sums that I have never previously considered. This is the whole point of the notion that in learning to add I grasp a rule: my past intentions regarding addition determine a unique answer for indefinitely many new cases in the future.

I think it is important that Kripke shows no sign of regarding this characterization of what is involved in grasping and applying a rule as in any way philosophically tendentious or questionable. It is supposed to express the common understanding of what following a rule is. This is an essential element in his thesis that 'Wittgenstein's main problem is that it appears he has shown *all* language, *all* concept formation to be impossible, indeed unintelligible' (p. 62).

What features of rule-following, thus understood, does Kripke think that Wittgenstein's 'scepticism' is directed against? His text suggests three different answers to that question.

On pages 8 to 9 he writes that a person who has been taught to add by reference to a finite number of examples and who now applies the rule (as he thinks) to a new example, say 68 + 57, and gives the answer 125, may be 'misinterpreting [his] own previous usage' which was consistent with quite different rules, for instance that defining the 'quus' function (an invention with which Kripke has much fun, the details of which, however, must not detain us here). It is of course clear even from the few sentences of *Philosophical Investigations* section 201 already quoted that this does *not* state Wittgenstein's 'paradox', which was not that I may be *wrong* about the rule I was following in my treatment of past examples, but that there is really no question of being either right or wrong about it ('neither accord nor disaccord').

Later, on page 21, Kripke comes to insist that the problem is not the epistemological one first suggested. It is rather that 'there is no fact about me that distinguishes between my meaning plus and my meaning quus. Indeed there is no fact about me that distinguishes my meaning a definite function by "plus" (which determined my response in new cases) and my meaning nothing at all'. So Wittgenstein's scepticism, it seems, is to be taken as a scepticism about whether, when we say of someone that he means something or other by what he says, we are ever stating a genuine fact about him. This reading of Kripke is reinforced by the emphasis (sometimes actually registered by italics) that he places on the word 'fact' in passages like that just quoted. I will return to this reading of him shortly.

The parallel with Hume that Kripke wants to draw requires a different emphasis, however. Both Wittgenstein and Hume 'develop a sceptical paradox, based on questioning a certain *nexus* from past to future. Wittgenstein questions the nexus between past "intention" or "meanings" and present practice: for example: between my past "intentions" with regard to "plus" and my present computation "68 + 57 = 125" . . .' (p. 62). From this it seems that Wittgenstein is not sceptical about whether there is such a thing ('fact') as meaning something but whether, rather, there is really any 'nexus' between someone's meaning something on a particular occasion and whatever he may do subsequently. *Prima facie* that question could only arise if on some occasions people did mean something by what they said or did (and if, therefore, it were sometimes a fact that someone meant something).

These two apparently different interpretations are brought together through the conception of an 'act of meaning' as a superlative fact' (*übermässige Tatsache*: see *Philosophical Investigations* section 192) such that 'The steps are *really* already taken, even before I take them in writing or orally or in thought. And it seemed as if they were in some *unique* way predetermined, anticipated – as only the act of meaning can anticipate reality' (section 188). That is to say, the idea of a peculiar nexus between meaning such and such by a word and applying it in such and such a way in the future goes hand in hand with the idea of meaning as a superlative fact. To be sceptical about the one is to be sceptical about the other.

Here we have to ask how Wittgenstein's critique of the temptation to use such a 'philosophical superlative' is related to the understanding of rule-following that is manifested in our actual practices of acting, speaking, counting, calculating, etc. Wittgenstein takes very great pains to distinguish his critique from any rejection of our ways of using the problematic expressions in the context of our normal practice. Kripke is cool about this aspect of his thought. He compares it with Berkeley's insistence that his denial of 'material substance' involves no rejection of anything believed in by the vulgar; and with Hume's remark that "'tis in vain to ask, *Whether there be body or not?* That is a point, which we must take for granted in all our reasonings'.[3]

There are undeniable parallels here which are important not only historically but as indications of the underlying philosophical pressures which have led such people to write in this vein. But there are big differences too and Kripke takes little account of these. 'Personally I think such philosophical claims are almost invariably suspect', he proclaims in his bluff, comprehensive way (p. 65). He does not notice for instance that the distinction Wittgenstein emphasizes is not so much that between 'philosophical' and 'common sense' *statements* about what rule-following consists in, as that between our ordinary *practice* of rule-following and the philosophical *explanations* we are inclined to give of that practice. What Kripke calls 'common sense philosophy' is an *interpretation* of our practice just as much as is, say, scepticism; and our practice is prior to any interpretation. Of course the use of certain linguistic expressions is often an essential element in our practice and there is a standing danger that when we are not actually involved in the practice we shall misconstrue the relation of our use of such expressions to it.

The point is right at the heart of Wittgenstein's philosophy. It seems to me that Kripke consistently fails to see its importance and that this failure distorts his whole account. A striking illustration of this is the fact that the passage quoted from section 201 of *Philosophical Investigations* with which Kripke starts his exposition of Wittgenstein's 'scepticism' is in fact only a preparation for the main point Wittgenstein makes in that section. Having pointed out that it will be impossible to distinguish accord and disaccord with a rule if we suppose that any course of action can be interpreted as being in accord with it, Wittgenstein *then* goes on to say that this whole argument rests on '*a misunderstanding*' (my italics). The misunderstanding consists in failure to see that 'there is a way of grasping a rule which is *not* an *interpretation*, but which is exhibited in what we call "obeying the rule" and "going against it" in actual cases.'

To convince ourselves that Wittgenstein is not attacking a straw man we need look no further than the passage from page 7 of Kripke's book that I quoted earlier, where it is said that I grasp a rule 'by means of my external symbolic representation and my internal mental representation'. Here, in the very identification of

3   David Hume, *A Treatise of Human Nature*, Book I, Part IV, Section 2.

what is under discussion, we find the misunderstanding Wittgenstein
characterizes by saying that 'we give one interpretation [read
'representation'] after another; as if each contented us at least for a
moment, until we thought of yet another standing behind it' (section
201).

When Kripke writes of Wittgenstein as denying that there is
any nexus between somebody's having meant something in the
past and what he does now, he is presumably alluding to what
Wittgenstein says about the steps involved in applying a rule as
being 'determined' (*bestimmt*) by an 'act of meaning'. In section 189
Wittgenstein responds to the question whether he is *denying* that the
steps are determined by the formula by saying (with an emphasis
that is unusual for him): 'The question contains a mistake'. He goes
on to explain in some detail what Kripke says on page 70 he is
'cagey' about – '*what* "erroneous interpretation" [his] opponent is
placing on ordinary means of expression'. According to Wittgenstein
there is a confusion between the use of the word 'determine' (a) to
describe a people who are so trained 'that they all work out the same
value for y when they substitute the same number for x'; and (b) to
specify a formula of a particular mathematical kind: one which
determines a number y for a given value of x. Is Kripke, in the
quoted passage, using the word 'determine' to characterize the kind
of arithmetical function addition is or, rather, to describe the
practice of someone who has had a certain sort of training in the use
of '+'? The answer must be, I think, that he is conflating the two
uses in just the sort of way Wittgenstein calls a 'mistake'. Thus, on
page 8, Kripke writes that '"plus" as I intended to use that word in
the past, denoted a function which, when applied to the numbers I
called "68" and "57", yields the value 125.' The idea seems to be
that my past use was based on a particular interpretation (it 'denoted
a function'); that function determines a particular value of z when
given values are substituted for x and y in the formula '$x + y = z$';
because my past use involved an intention to denote that function,
my answer to the question '68 + 57 = ?' is similarly determined. It
is as though the arithmetical determination takes on a certain causal
efficacy when incorporated into my intention. But we can only think
like this as long as we do not appreciate the ambiguity in words like
'determine' to which Wittgenstein points. And failure to appreciate
this is fostered by the sort of 'misunderstanding' Wittgenstein
alludes to in that part of section 201 which Kripke does not quote.

The foregoing illustrates how inextricably interwoven are the details of Wittgenstein's treatment of these questions and his insistence that 'It is not our aim to refine or complete the system of rules for the use of our words in unheard-of ways' (section 133). For this reason there seems to me to be a massive misunderstanding in Kripke's following remark, which is central to his conception of Wittgenstein as a sceptic à la Hume: 'had Wittgenstein . . . stated the outcome of his conclusions in the form of definite theses, it would have been difficult to avoid formulating his doctrines in a form that consists in apparent sceptical denials of our ordinary assertions' (p. 69). But if Wittgenstein *had* written in the mode Kripke plainly thinks would have been more candid, he would have been saying something of a quite different, and much less interesting, kind than what he in fact did say. Kripke quite explicitly rejects this. '. . . I choose to be so bold as to say: Wittgenstein holds, with the sceptic, that there is no fact as to whether I mean plus or quus' (pp. 70–1).

This way of putting things goes with Kripke's view (which he shares with Dummett) that Wittgenstein tried, in the *Tractatus*, to explain the meanings of sentences in terms of their truth-conditions, but replaced this view, in *Philosophical Investigations*, with 'a picture of language based . . . on *assertability conditions* or *justification conditions*: under what circumstances are we allowed to make a given assertion?' (p. 74).

So fundamental is this to Kripke's interpretation that it is surprising he should discuss in such a perfunctory way (on p. 86) Wittgenstein's most explicit treatment of the way in which the notions of truth and falsity are related to that of a proposition in sections 134–42 of *Philosophical Investigations*. Kripke misidentifies the scope of this discussion as falling between sections 134 and 137, which is symptomatic of his having missed the main point: namely the misleading picture suggested by saying that 'what fits the concept "true", or what the concept "true" fits, is a proposition'. The word '*fit*' is said to be the main source of this picture and this is what is examined in the sections up to 142 which Kripke overlooks. What makes us suppose that we have 'a concept of true and false, which we could use to determine what is and what is not a proposition' is that a certain form of words may conjure up an immediate picture (a picture, as it were, of the truth-conditions) the having of which we take to constitute our understanding of the words in question; and we overlook the complexities in our use of the words which have to be attended to if we are to know in what

circumstances we are in fact entitled to say that the truth-conditions
are or are not satisfied.

How accurate this diagnosis is should be evident to anyone who
will study the classic symptoms of the disease exhibited, for instance,
on page 72 of Kripke's book: ' "the cat is on the mat" is understood
by those speakers who realize that it is true if and only if a certain
cat is on a certain mat; it is false otherwise'. Well yes, of course, and
that Tarskian formula can be adapted for any sentence to which it
makes sense to attach the words 'is true' and 'is false' – for example,
'He meant addition when he used the word "plus" ' or (to take a
different sort of case from Kripke's Postscript on 'Wittgenstein and
Other Minds') to 'He has a headache'. But such a formula is going
to be helpful as an explanation of the meaning of the expression in
question only to extent that the person to whom it is addressed
knows when it is correct to say that those truth-conditions are
satisfied: when, that is to say, he masters the use of the words in
which the obtaining of the truth-conditions is stated. Wittgenstein's
point is not, as Kripke seems to think (on p. 136 for instance), that
when we say of someone else that he has a headache there are no
'corresponding facts', the obtaining of which makes my statement
true and the non-obtaining of which makes it false. His point is
rather that there is no short cut to understanding what these facts
are which by-passes an understanding of how expressions like 'He
has a headache' are used.

Incidentally, to ask how an expression is used is not to ask 'What
use is it?' or 'What is its utility?' as Kripke on several occasions
assumes. Wittgenstein quite emphatically rules out this interpretation
in, for example, *Zettel* no. 320, where he contrasts rules of grammar
and rules of cookery. The latter specify the best way to attain an end
which can be described independently of them; but to talk about a
certain state of affairs *is* to follow the rules of grammar which
constitute talk about such states of affairs; there is no other way of
talking about them. This is also part of the point made in
Philosophical Investigations nos 295–301, which Kripke discusses on
p. 138 of his book but misconstrues, partly because he is
understandably misled by Professor Anscombe's translation of
'*Vorstellung*' as 'image'. I will give my own rendering of no. 300:

Consider the language game with the words "He is in pain".
To it – one would like to say belongs not merely the picture of
behaviour, but the picture of pain too. Or; the paradigm not

merely of behaviour, but of pain too. – To say "the picture of pain is introduced into the language game with the word 'pain' " is a misunderstanding. Pain is not represented through a picture, nor can anything be substituted for *this* representation that we could call a picture. It is true that in a sense the representation of pain enters the language game; but not in the form of a picture.

A representation is not a picture, but a picture can correspond to it.

If *'Vorstellung'* is rendered as 'image', as in the official translation, the *contrast* with 'picture', which is the whole point of the paragraph, gets lost. When Wittgenstein says that the representation of pain enters the language-game he means roughly, I take it, that the language-game is informed by, or expressive of, the notion of pain as well as the notion of behaviour. But the important point is that there is no *other* place to seek the representation of pain than in the language-game. (It is of course important to remember in this connection that the language-game and its rules of grammar include the *application* of the words that belong to it, an application which is what it is by virtue of the position which it occupies within the lives of those who play the language-game.)

In just the same way (see section 297) there is no other way in which *the picture represents a boiling pot* than the way it is used; it does not do so by virtue of there being something boiling in the picture of the pot. The picture is *of* a boiling pot; that is, the *representation* of something boiling in the pot is achieved by the picture, but not by way of *a picture of something boiling in the pot.*[4]

We should not suppose, then, that our understanding of the statement 'He is in pain' rests on a picture of his pain, this being a picture of the truth-conditions of that statement. But in this respect there is no contrast with the statement 'The cat is on the mat'; for though someone may have a picture of a cat on a mat when he hears or says this sentence, that is neither necessary nor sufficient for him to be said to understand it. In the one case as in the other, understanding goes with correct use. Making these points provides no reason for saying that the statement 'He is in pain' cannot be true or false; although, of course, knowing when it is true that he is in pain is no different from knowing when he is in pain. Our

4   See below, pp. 76–8 for further discussion of this passage.

understanding of what the truth-condition is is not something
separable from our understanding of when we are in a position to
assert that he is in pain. This is not to replace talk of truth-
conditions by talk of assertability conditions in the explanation of
meaning; it is to comment on the grammar of the expression 'truth-
conditions'.

With these considerations in mind I return to Kripke's account
(p. 77) of 'Wittgenstein's sceptical conclusion: no facts, no truth
conditions correspond to statements such as "Jones means addition
by '+' " – 'Now if we suppose that facts, or truth conditions, are the
essence of meaningful assertions, it will follow from the sceptical
conclusion that assertions that anyone ever means anything are
meaningless.' But the view of *Philosophical Investigations*, he says, is
rather that all that is needed to 'legitimize' assertions is that
conditions for such legitimate assertion be specifiable and that 'the
game of asserting them under these conditions has a role in our
lives. No supposition that "facts correspond" to those assertions is
needed'.

What *is* the supposition that 'no truth conditions correspond' to
the statement in question? Kripke acknowledges (p. 69) that
Wittgenstein would recognize the perfect propriety of saying, in
suitable circumstances, things like 'It's true that, or a fact that, Jones
meant addition when he wrote "+" '. We may add, given
Philosophical Investigations section 136, that Wittgenstein would say
that '*in our language* we apply the calculus of truth-functions to it'.
We can do this perfectly well in a way that will enable us to apply
the truth-functional calculus: and there is nothing in *Philosophical
Investigations* to say we cannot. Furthermore there is no reason at all,
as far as I can see, to take Wittgenstein to mean that our application
of the calculus of truth-functions to what we call a proposition is
incidental, or inessential to what we understand a proposition to be.
On the contrary, its being essential is one of the main sources of our
temptation to give it the wrong sort of emphasis.

Kripke plainly regards such an argument as this as weaselling. He
seems to think that however much Wittgenstein may protest that of
course it's perfectly all right for anyone to *say* that a statement of the
problematic sort is true or false, he's still not really admitting that
such a statement states a genuine fact. But what are we to
understand as a *genuine fact*, if not what is stated by a statement we
take to be true? Kripke, I think, gives no other acceptable
explanation. And it should be noted that the *Tractatus* does not

suggest any other interpretation of the T/F notation than the distinction between truth and falsity as it is ordinarily understood. To be sure, the *Tractatus* has virtually nothing to say about what is involved in deciding between truth and falsity in particular cases, whereas *Philosophical Investigations* makes this a central issue. That shift does bring with it a fundamental change in the appearance of the whole landscape, such that the way Kripke uses the word 'fact' inevitably prompts the question: 'if you are using words like "fact", "truth", etc. in some way such that understanding them does *not* depend on understanding how to apply the sentences to which they are attached, what is it?' An answer to this question is required if we are to take seriously the suggestion that Wittgenstein was a sceptic. But I do not believe that Kripke offers an answer.

6

Wittgenstein: Picture and Representation

In his philosophical thinking about religious belief Wittgenstein devoted a lot of attention to the role of what he called 'pictures' in the life of a believer. People sometimes write as though he had a theory of religious concepts as pictures of a certain sort. But this seems to me far from the truth. Wittgenstein did, certainly, hold that a certain sort of religious believer is distinguished by the fact that his life is dominated by certain pictures (for instance, a picture of the Last Judgement). And it's also true that he opposed an 'reductive' account of religious belief of a kind that would attempt to eliminate the believer's 'picture' as inessential and talk simply about him as having a certain 'attitude'.

Consider, for example, his response to Casimir Lewy during the following exchange after one of his lectures on religious belief.

> Suppose, someone, before going to China, when he might never see me again, said to me: "We might see one another after death" – would I necessarily say that I don't understand him? I might say [want to say] simply, "Yes. I *understand* him entirely."
>
> *Lewy* "In this case, you might only mean that he expressed a certain attitude."
>
> I would say "No, it isn't the same as saying 'I'm very fond of you' " – and it may not be the same as saying anything else. It says what it says. Why should you be able to substitute anything else?[1]

1 Wittgenstein, *Lectures and Conversations on Aesthetics, Psychology and Religious Belief*, pp. 70–1.

I once had an actual encounter which perhaps expresses Wittgenstein's point more forcibly than this imaginary example. I was staying in the house of a couple one of whose young children was suffering from a terrible degenerative disease of the nervous system. The child was in constant distress, incontinent and already virtually without the normal functions of human intelligence and perception. The child was certainly going to die within a very few years. I had a moving conversation with the child's mother in which she said to me that she firmly believed that one day, after death, the whole family would be together again and that her afflicted child would be there as a whole, normal human being – in full possession of the developed faculties which he had never had and never, in life, would have.

The difficulties in understanding the application of any picture of things I will do 'after death' are enhanced in this case. After infancy the child had never been a person with sound human faculties. Yet it was crucial to what his mother was saying that she would be reunited with *this child with normal human faculties*. But since the child had never existed as a normal human being, it is unclear what it would mean to meet *him* as a normal human being – with no possible conception of how he might have become one. Such a possibility is cut off by death, quite apart from the purely *medical* impossibility of recovery in such a case.

I think it is important to notice that difficulties such as these *would* arise and have to be dealt with on a certain way of trying to understand the mother's thought. But it is even more important to realize that if one *does* think one has to deal with these difficulties one is *misunderstanding* her thought.

It will help to explain what I mean if I compare this case with that which I discuss in the next chapter. In the story by Isaac Bashevis Singer that I comment on there, the disappearance of the shed is narrated by the storyteller within Singer's story as something that had actually happened, rather than as a fantasy. I try to bring out the conceptual problems *we* would encounter in trying to respond to the narrative in such a way. This is a relevant issue to raise in that case, precisely because the disturbing force of Singer's story derives largely from the tension produced in the reader by its artful construction: the device of having it narrated by a storyteller within the story induces the reader to take it in that factually narrative way, as an account of something that had actually happened. I do not of course mean that the reader is induced to *believe* it; he is induced to *understand* it as something which canvasses his belief.

I have claimed that it would be a misunderstanding to try to respond to the words of the sick child's mother in that way. But this claim is not easy to justify. One can say of course that she was not offering a prediction of something she was going to experience in the course of her life. And that is perfectly true, since she was speaking of her confident hopes for what would come 'after death'. But did she not think of the reuniting in death as completely analogous to a reuniting in life? How am I to answer that? What decides it?

A remark made by Wittgenstein in a different context is relevant here. 'The most important thing here is this: there is a difference; we notice the difference, "a categorical difference", without being able to say what it consists in. It is in cases like this that we usually say that we recognize the difference by introspection.'[2] Nowadays the jargon has it that we 'have an intuition' of the difference. That is just about as helpful.

The child's mother was not a philosopher and her faith in her being reunited with her son after death was certainly not a philosophical conviction, arrived at by any process of reasoning. Equally, she was not interested in analysing philosophically what her faith amounted to. In fact she quite explicitly rejected any such analysis as irrelevant to her concerns. I asked earlier whether she did not, all the same, think of this reuniting as something completely analogous to the reuniting of a family in life. I would now answer that question by saying she had never put the matter to herself like that. What *is* the case is that she was unselfconsciously using an expression ('reunited with my son') which she would also have used in speaking, say, of something about to happen in a certain town next week. By 'unselfconsciously' I mean, approximately, without raising any questions concerning the way she was using it or its relation to other ways of using it. We all do the same: for example in reporting our dreams, without being committed to any sort of philosophical interpretation of what a dream is. Just as little was this mother committed to any philosophical interpretation of life after death.

Her words are, of course, an expression – a wonderful expression, it seems to me – of her love for her son. They are the words she needed to express her relation to him and his terrible condition.

2   *Zettel*, no. 86.

And *my own response to her words* is a response to the unbearable poignancy of that love; and part of my response is the conviction that it would be an obscene misunderstanding to treat her words as I treat Singer's story. It is not that I first see that she is using the words differently and from that conclude something about the proper and improper ways of treating them. No, my response is the primary thing. My understanding of the words is revealed in my response. And if I now want to be clear about *how* I am understanding them, I must be clear about the character of my response.

I am not saying that her words are *reducible* to anything like 'I love him from the depths of my heart'. Such an utterance would not have 'meant the same'; and of course the impact of the words she in fact used derives in part from their relation to other uses to describe reunitings between human beings after painful separations. But that does not mean that the words here 'mean the same' as words used in those other circumstances. It is not that my understanding of her love helps me to understand her words; on the contrary, it is in understanding her words (*these* words *so* used in *this* context) that I see something of the nature of her love.

It would be a misunderstanding for someone to ask me, at this stage: 'Well, how *do* you understand them then?' For that is precisely what I have been explaining! And it seems to me that the difficulties I have been discussing are at the heart of what Wittgenstein wrote about the use of pictures in such cases. Of a different sort of case ('God's eye sees everything') he says – still, I think, with Lewy's intervention in mind – the following:

"He could just as well have said so and so" – this [remark] is foreshadowed by the word "attitude". He couldn't just as well have said something else.

If I say he used a picture, I don't want to say anything he himself wouldn't say. I want to say that he draws these conclusions.

Isn't it as important as anything else, what picture he does use?

Of certain pictures we say that they might just as well be replaced by another – e.g. we could, under certain circumstances have one projection of an ellipse drawn instead of another.

[He *may* say]: "I would have been prepared to use another picture, it would have had the same effect. . . ."

The whole *weight* may be in the picture.[3]

Wittgenstein insisted that the believer must be taken to mean just what he says when he speaks in terms of the picture; that indeed, he claimed, is what distinguishes him as the kind of believer he is.

But on the other hand, both in the *Lectures* and elsewhere in his writings Wittgenstein was at pains to bring out that the way in which a picture may enter into our thinking (in religious, *and also in other*, contexts) raises a *problem* for philosophy. It will seldom constitute the *solution* to any philosophical problem about meaning. To say of the speaker that he means just what he says when he speaks in terms of his picture is not to say anything about what, in the problematic cases, is involved in 'meaning what one says'. It is to *raise the question* of what is so involved.

To see this matter in perspective it will be well to remind ourselves of the great change in the way Wittgenstein thought of the role of pictures in language between the *Tractatus Logico-Philosophicus* and the mature philosophical position which he started to develop in the early thirties.

According to the *Tractatus* a proposition *is* a picture of a possible state of affairs. Of course in developing this position Wittgenstein used the word 'picture' in a very broad, and perhaps extended, sense. It was, however, no accident that the word he used in this connection, '*Bild*', is cognate with words like '*abbilden*', '*Abbildung*', which have a specialized use in geometry ('to project', 'projection'). His idea is that a proposition pictures a possible state of affairs by way of a certain 'law of projection', in the way in which maps depict the Earth's surface by means of a definite law of projection, or in the way in which one geometrical figure may be a projection of another. Of course Wittgenstein was in a sense perfectly well aware that in his usage 'law of projection' has a sense wider than the strictly geometrical one; but his explanations of how pictures relate to the facts usually involve an appeal at the crucial point to a sort of analogy with geometry which is never closely examined or worked out in detail.

We could perhaps get a grasp of the way the *Tractatus* conceives things by the following analogy, itself suggested by the language of the *Tractatus*. Imagine a cinema projector which projects an image on to a screen. This image represents a possible state of affairs; it

3   *Lectures and Conversations*, pp. 71–2.

corresponds to the *Tractatus* proposition. Now suppose that the screen on which this image is projected is itself painted; sometimes what is painted on the screen will coincide exactly with the image cast by the projector and sometimes it will not. When there is such coincidence this corresponds to the proposition's being true; when there is not, to the proposition's being false.

It has been claimed, for instance by Anthony Kenny – but also by others – that this *Tractatus* account of propositions survives, though more or less concealed, in Wittgenstein's later thought, but is supplemented with accounts of other uses of language, of a non-'fact-stating' sort, which were ignored in the *Tractatus*. This is catastrophically misleading. For one thing, I do not see how the *Tractatus* account of propositions as pictures can be dissociated from the special use made of concepts like *name, object, substance, elementary proposition, simple, truth-functional analysis* in that work. These notions were introduced in the way they were precisely in order to give the 'picture' account determinate structure. And they are subjected to witheringly destructive *criticism* in the early sections, for example, of *Philosophical Investigations*. These criticisms, it should be noted, are only *partly* aimed at the pretensions of the 'picture theory' to elucidate 'language' *tout court*, rather than quite particular uses of language which exist alongside many others. They are also aimed at the claims of the 'picture theory' to account for those very uses of language which it has mainly in view: 'fact-stating propositions'. Indeed they were designed to undermine the very assumption that there *is* a determinate class of expressions that can be usefully so designated. The author of such criticisms can hardly be held to have *retained* the original theory in any real sense, even with appropriately reduced scope.

As I said earlier, Wittgenstein often does, in his later work, emphasize the power and importance which the pictures associated with, or involved in, certain forms of expression have for us in various contexts. And he is by no means reductive in his attitude to them. 'The picture is *there*; and I do not dispute its *correctness*. But *what* is its application?'[4] For Wittgenstein at this stage of his work the interesting cases are not cases where reference to a picture constitutes the *solution* of any problem; on the contrary, it is a major *source* of the problem. 'The picture is *there*. . . . But *what* is its application?'

4 *Philosophical Investigations*, I, no. 424.

In the discussion to which this remark belongs Wittgenstein distinguishes between cases in which 'we exert ourselves to find a picture and once it is found the application as it were comes about by itself' (cases which seem congenial to his *Tractatus* account of propositions) from others in which we are already gripped by 'a picture which forces itself on us at every turn, but does not help us out of the difficulty, which only begins here'.[5] He gives as an example of the first kind of case a pictorial explanation of how a certain mechanism fits into a box: 'You see, it goes in like *this*'. The picture immediately conveys to us the road we have to take.

But in the other sort of case, such as the expression: 'While I was speaking to him I did not know what was going on in his head', the picture suggested by the words is of a road which 'we cannot use . . ., because [it] is permanently closed'. 'In the actual use of expressions we make detours, we go by side-roads'.[6] The only ways of finding out what is going on in his head are the ways in which we *do* (when we do) find out what another person is thinking. This is not, as it were, an *indirect* method. When Wittgenstein says 'We see the straight highway before us, but of course we cannot use it, because it is permanently closed', he does not mean that there *is* such a permanently closed highway, but rather that when we philosophize about such expressions they induce us to picture such a highway to ourselves. It is when we concentrate on this picture rather than on the actual use of the expression which gave rise to it, that we arrive at the idea of its being 'permanently closed' and of the routes we in fact take to reach our destination being 'detours'.

I want to reiterate here that Wittgenstein is not reductive about such pictures. He is not suggesting that they could be dispensed with, leaving everything substantially the same. Because although they may cause us problems when we philosophize, they are also essential to the way we represent things to ourselves. 'I should like to see inside his head' belongs with many other, often non-linguistic, expressions, for instance gestures, postures, facial expressions. I gaze into a person's eyes; that is connected with the idea that I am 'trying to see into his soul'. And so I am! But that is a different use of the words 'see into' from that in which we speak of trying to see into a darkened room, a use, however, which essentially characterizes an important aspect of our relations with each other.

5   No. 425.
6   No. 426.

As we shall see, Wittgenstein does not think that the representation of the state of a person's mind *is* a pictorial representation: a picture can be an essential aspect of a form of representation without itself *constituting* the representation.

A representation is not a picture, but a picture can correspond to it.[7]

I want to say: we have the vivid picture and that use which seems to contradict the picture and expresses the phychical.[8]

Although in the last sentence quoted the singular verb ('expresses') makes it sound as though it is only the use (which happens to contradict the vivid picture) which 'expresses the psychical', I think the thought of the whole passage is that it is precisely the tension between the picture and the use that does so. Why, otherwise, would Wittgenstein say that the picture of 'seeing what is going on in his head' is to be taken seriously? If it contributes nothing but confusion, would it not be better to be rid of it? But it is not Wittgenstein's view that the picture contributes nothing but confusion. It plays an essential part in our representation of the psychical; it is the complexity of that representation which creates the confusion for the philosopher, who would like to be able to give a much simpler account. But Wittgenstein thought that such a 'simpler' account would miss out much that is of genuine substance.

Philosophical Investigations, I, no. 427 characterizes the use as *essentially* seeming to contradict the picture. Thus, a use that seems to contradict such a picture (a picture to which, nevertheless, we are strongly attached) is precisely what we need for what we want to express. (The word 'contradict' in this context plainly does not mean what a logician means when he speaks of one proposition as contradicting another.)

With all this in mind let us now return to some things Wittgenstein said about religious belief.

His attitude towards the acceptance of pictures involved in religious belief was not a settled one; and this is one reason for not regarding what he says as constituting a theory. He treats different cases differently and his reactions to particular cases are avowedly

7 No. 301.
8 No. 428.

very personal sometimes. (I am reminded here of the remark in his *Lecture on Ethics* that on certain matters he has to 'speak for himself'.) A look at this point may help us to understand better what is at issue. Here is a passage from one of his notebooks, written in 1937:

> Religious similes can be said to move on the edge of an abyss. Bunyan's for example. For what if we simply add: "and all these traps, quicksands, wrong turnings, were planned by the Lord of the Road and the monsters, thieves and robbers were created by him"? Certainly, that is not the sense of the simile! But such a continuation is all too obvious! For many people, including me, this robs the simile of its power.
>
> But more especially if this is, as it were, suppressed. It would be different if at every turn it were said quite honestly: 'I am using this as a simile, but look: it doesn't quite fit here.' Then you wouldn't feel you were being cheated, that someone was trying to convince you by trickery. Someone can be told for instance: "Thank God for the good you receive but don't complain about the evil; as you would of course do if a human being were to do you good and evil by turns." Rules of life are dressed up as pictures. And these pictures can only serve to *describe* what we are to do, not *justify* it. Because they could provide a justification only if they held in other respects as well. I can say: "Thank these bees for their honey as though they were kind people who have prepared it for you"; that is *intelligible* and describes how I should like you to conduct yourself. But I cannot say: "Thank them because, look, how kind they are!" – since the next moment they may sting you.
>
> Religion says: *Do this! – Think like that!* – but it cannot justify this and once it even tries to, it becomes repellent; because for every reason it offers there is a valid counter-reason. It is more convincing to say: "Think like this! however strangely it may strike you." Or: "Won't you do this? – however repugnant you find it."[9]

Wittgenstein came back to the case of Bunyan in 1948 and expressed himself somewhat differently about it.

9 *Culture and Value*, p. 29.

Just look at an allegory like "The Pilgrim's Progress" and notice how nothing is right – in human terms. – But isn't it right all the same? I.e.: can't it be applied? Indeed, it has been applied. (On railway stations there are dials with two hands; they show when the next train leaves. They look like clocks though they aren't; but they have a use of their own.) (It ought to be possible to find a better simile.)

If anyone gets upset by this allegory, one might say to him: Apply it differently, or else leave it alone! (But there are *some* whom it will confuse far more than it can help.)[10]

There is one important difference between Wittgenstein's treatment of this case and his treatment of the role of pictures in our 'concept of the psychical'. In the later case he writes as though the picture ('I wish I knew what is going on in his head') is likely to produce confusion only when we *philosophize*; but that we do not find any difficulty in our actual application of the picture in our ordinary dealings with each other. In his first discussion of Bunyan's *The Pilgrim's Progress* on the other hand the suggestion is that Bunyan's picture may actually produce *religious* confusion; that is to say it may introduce confusion into the religious life of the believer. He emphasizes that whether this happens or not will depend on the particular believer concerned; and this emphasis is increased in the later passage, where he points out that Bunyan's picture can be (and has been) applied by some without trouble. His attitude to this is quite pragmatic: if such a picture gives you trouble, abandon it; otherwise use it. Of course that does not rule out the possibility that someone who *is* troubled by the picture may come to think his misgivings misconceived, to think that he was failing to see something important. And it is equally possible for someone who once did apply the picture without qualm later to think that this had been possible only because he had failed to think about certain matters rigorously enough. There are no general rules in all this which philosophy somehow has the authority to prescribe.

There is a temptation (I feel a temptation) to express the point through a distinction between 'philosophical' confusion and other sorts of confusion. But that smacks too much of a theoretical distinction for me to be happy about ascribing it to Wittgenstein. And in fact such a distinction would not be clear. Somebody might well be led into religious doubt through philosophical reflection on

10 *Culture and Value*, p. 77.

something like Bunyan's allegory. Where does philosophy end and religion begin in such a case? That is a question better not asked. The important question will be whether a particular picture is one that furthers or stands in the way of my religious life. I do not mean that this is a question easily answered; for there is always the possibility that I will not notice (through laziness or inattention for example) that a particular image is in fact impeding me religiously. But in any event it is a question the force of which will only be apparent within the life of the believer; it is not one to which the philosopher can give any general theoretical answer.

There are, however, certain questions which are more naturally thought of as philosophical questions concerning the role of pictures in religious understanding rather than as questions concerning the religious appropriateness of this or that picture. And these are the questions with which Wittgenstein is most concerned in the lecture on religious belief.

There is a well-known passage in *Lectures and Conversations* (p. 63) where Wittgenstein speaks of Michelangelo's depiction of the creation of Adam. Those who discuss this seem to me frequently to miss the all-important irony in some of the things he says. The train of thought in the passage runs roughly as follows. 'In general there is nothing which explains the meanings of words so well as a picture.' So let us look at as clear an example as possible of a picture used to exhibit a religious concept. Michelangelo painted a picture of God creating Adam and we can look at this picture as an attempt to explain what it means to say that God created Adam. After all, we are not likely to find a *better* picture for our purpose than one painted by Michelangelo, who 'was as good as anyone can be and did his best'.

Wittgenstein by no means *denies* that Michelangelo's painting may be used in an explanation of what talk about the 'creation of Adam' means. 'You could imagine that religion was taught by means of these pictures', he says. But this solves no philosophical puzzles. For how does such an explanation work? Not in the way a drawing of Noah's ark might explain to someone what the word 'ark' means in this context. (The latter case is analogous to the one discussed earlier: that of using a picture to show someone how a mechanism fits into a box.) 'If we ever saw this [*sc.* Michelangelo's *Creation of Adam*], we certainly wouldn't think this the Deity. The picture has to be used in an entirely different way if we are to call the man in that queer blanket "God", and so on.' What is important in the explanation by means of the picture is 'the technique of using this picture'.

The notion of a 'technique' of using the picture replaces that of a 'rule of projection' on which the *Tractatus* had relied. ' "The connection between the picture and what is pictured" is what we might call the lines of projection; but so too might we call the technique of projection.'[11] The geometrical model itself involves a picture of lines drawn from one figure to another; but the lines only show the sense in which one figure is a projection of the other in so far as we are familiar with the technique according to which those lines have been drawn. It is better to concentrate on the question of *technique* if we are not to be misled.

We shall then see that there are techniques of application in the context of which talk of 'projection' is out of place. We see Wittgenstein making this step in the following remark from 1944. In my original 'official' translation of this remark in *Culture and Value* (p. 44e) I regrettably missed the importance of Wittgenstein's use of the word '*Abbildung*' and translated it with 'representation'. I will give the original German and a fresh translation.

Wenn etwas an der Freudschen Lehre von Traumdeutung ist; so zeigt sie, in wie *komplizierter* Weise der menschliche Geist Bilder der Tatsachen macht.

So kompliziert, so unregelmässig ist die Art der Abbildung, dass man sie *kaum* mehr eine Abbildung nennen kann.

If Freud's theory of dream interpretation has anything to it; it shows how *complicated* is the way in which the human mind makes pictures of the facts.

So complicated, so irregular, is the method of projection, that it can *barely* be called a projection any longer.

This crucial change of emphasis leads Wittgenstein in his mature writings to ask questions which he would, perhaps, have thought philosophically inessential at the time of the *Tractatus*: there, reference to a 'rule of projection' is thought enough. Of course the *Tractatus* showed awareness that there were *different* rules of projection for different sorts of expression, but there was nothing like Wittgenstein's later sensitivity to the extraordinary variety and to the philosophical importance of this variety.

Wittgenstein's stress on the technique of application in the

11 *Zettel*, no. 291.

lectures on religious belief addresses itself to the puzzlement we may feel about how the conception of the *divine* enters into Michelangelo's picture. If we leave this conception out, we seem to be left with a picture of two human beings in certain peculiar postures vis-à-vis each other. Putting the matter like this suggests an analogy with another important point which Wittgenstein makes in his discussion of our knowledge of each other's thoughts and feelings. There is a crucial passage in his treatment of the relation between the thought that another person is behaving in a certain way and the thought that he is in pain; a passage in which he uses the concept of a *picture* in order to bring out the difference between these thoughts. I am thinking of *Philosophical Investigations* Part I, nos 300–1. I will quote this first in German, since a difficulty in the standard (Anscombe) translation has been responsible for much misunderstanding:

> Zu dem Sprachspiel mit den Worten "er hat Schmerzen" gehört – möchte man sagen – nicht nur das Bild des Benehmens, sondern, auch das Bild des Schmerzes. Oder: nicht nur das Paradigma des Benehmens, sondern auch des Schmerzes. – Zu sagen "Das Bild des Schmerzes tritt ins Sprachspiel mit dem Worte 'Schmerz' ein", ist ein Missverständnis. Die Vorstellung des Schmerzes ist kein Bild, und diese Vorstellung ist im Sprachspiel auch nicht durch etwas ersetzbar, was wir ein Bild nennen würden. – Wohl tritt die Vorstellung des Schmerzes in einem Sinn ins Sprachspiel ein; nur nicht als Bild.
>
> Eine Vorstellung ist kein Bild, aber ein Bild kann ihr entsprechen.

The sense of this passage hangs on the *contrast* between the words '*Bild*' and '*Vorstellung*'. Miss Anscombe translates '*Bild*' as 'picture' and '*Vorstellung*' as 'image': a word which itself has overpoweringly pictorial associations. Not unnaturally, readers of her translation have been puzzled as to just what contrast Wittgenstein can have had in mind: and some strange suggestions for solving this puzzlement have been made from time to time. (See my discussion of Saul Kripke above, pp. 60–61.) It is certainly true that '*Vorstellung*' can in *some* contexts be rendered as 'image', but it is a versatile term which can often be rendered by the (pictorially neutral) 'conception' or 'representation'. (I was formerly inclined to favour 'conception'; but David Shwayder has persuaded me of the superior merits of 'representation'.) With this in mind I will now give my own version of the whole passage.

> Consider the language game with the words "He is in pain". To it – one would like to say – belongs not merely the picture of behaviour, but the picture of pain too. Or; the paradigm not merely of behaviour, but of pain too. – To say "The picture of pain is introduced into the language game with the word 'pain' " is a misunderstanding. Pain is not represented through a picture, nor can anything be substituted for *this* representation that we would call a picture. It is true that in a sense the representation of pain enters the language game; but not in the form of a picture.
> A representation is not a picture, but a picture can correspond to it.

What is it for a representation, or conception, to correspond to a picture without itself being a picture? Let me consider this, first, for the case of pain.

Suppose I hear that my friend has been severely injured. I am filled with pity for the terrible pain he must be suffering. I picture him tossing, turning and groaning on a hospital bed, his face contorted and covered with sweat. I am representing him to myself as in pain, representing his pain to myself. To this *representation* corresponds the *picture* of his behaviour that I have just described. The same picture could correspond to quite a different representation. Perhaps my friend is an actor on tour in a role that requires him to enact just the scene I have described. I admire his powerful acting technique and picture him on stage behaving as described. This picture does *not* correspond to the representation of him as in pain, but to the representation of him as acting a part. What marks the contrast between the two cases is, in the first instance, the difference in the contexts in which the pictures occur: a difference already lightly sketched in my descriptions. I say 'in the first instance' because of course behind that difference, and making it the difference it is, lies the whole immense contrast between the significance of suffering and of acting in our lives. (This is the most important dimension of all in Wittgenstein's account and it is one which is systematically undervalued by those who still think of him as some sort of 'behaviourist'.) It is this contrast which makes it possible for one and the same picture to 'correspond' to two entirely different representations. There does not have to be a different picture corresponding to each different representation (in this case, a picture of the behaviour and a picture of the pain lying behind the behaviour). Of course, Wittgenstein has *further* arguments to show the difficulties in putting the matter in this latter way, but it would take me too far away from my main subject to discuss these arguments here. For my purpose, what is important is the distinction between my thinking about something and my forming a picture of what I think about.

I return now to the case of Michelangelo's picture of God creating Adam.

It would have been possible, though no doubt not the way things actually happened, for Michelangelo to have had two human models for his painting, for him to have arranged them in front of him in somewhat the way God and Adam are arranged in the picture – difficult of course, but perhaps not impossible – and for him then to have painted his picture 'from the life'. In one sense he would then have been painting the two men in front of him; in another he would have been painting God creating Adam. Compare that with the following case. An artist who had been at the Battle of Waterloo subsequently paints a picture of Wellington, as he had seen him at the battle. To assist him in the painting he uses a model, dressed as Wellington was dressed, though facially different. In this case we might say that the representation of Wellington at Waterloo enters into what the painter is doing *partly* in the form of a picture (in his mind's eye); and this fact is relevant to our calling the painting he makes (in one sense) of the model a picture of Wellington at Waterloo. But in the case of Michelangelo painting the Creation of Adam (in my fantasy, 'from the life') though the representation of God enters into what he is doing, it does not do so 'as a picture' in the way Wellington did in my contrasting example.

As in the case of the representation of pain, we must seek an account of the matter in 'the use to which the picture is put'. This includes not only the ways in which subsequent viewers of the picture use it, but also what it was for Michelangelo, that is to say, its connection with things of importance in Michelangelo's life: the interests and concerns of his life that he tried to express in painting it. We must also not forget the dependence of those interests and concerns on the historical traditions within which he was working and his own relation to them. It is fairly clear that the picture represents the majesty of God the Creator. One of the most striking things about it from this point of view is that 'majesty' should be represented by (in Wittgenstein's phrase) 'the man in that queer blanket', rather than by the traditional paraphernalia of kingship. It throws light on our present difficulty to raise the further difficulty of how it was at all possible to represent God's majesty in this way. The answer that Michelangelo's picture immediately suggests is that God's majesty as expressed in the creation of man is the majesty of love, not at all the majesty associated with worldly power. And of course the phrase 'the majesty of love' has all sorts of reverberations within the Christian tradition. By this I mean in part the emphasis on love in (certain parts of) The Scriptures, but also practices and traditions of worship and prayer, the role of Scripture in these, and many other matters. The Christian tradition is certainly not all of a piece, it comprises mutually antagonistic currents. It was Michelangelo's position in the historical situation of his time in respect of that network of traditions that made it possible for him to represent the Creation as he did, which gave such a representation *point* – in opposition to other ways of conceiving God's majesty.

What I have said in the last paragraph is intended only to provide sketchy examples of the *kind* of material we need to appeal to if we want to give an account of how Michelangelo's picture involves a 'representation of the divine'. *This* representation does not itself come in the form of a picture: Michelangelo was not making an inspired guess as to what the creation of Adam truly looked like (as an artist might do for the Battle of Waterloo). In other words, what makes the picture a religious picture is not its pictorial relationship to some event. If it is said that it is a relationship to a *supernatural* event, that of course makes a difference: but the chances are that in this context the speaker will be conceiving the 'supernatural' event as a weird sort of *natural* event. So it is better to leave aside talk about 'a relationship to an event' altogether.

Here again a remark made by Wittgenstein in his discussion of the representation of pain is apposite. 'Certainly when the water in the pot is boiling, steam rises from the pot, and a picture of steam too rises from the pictured pot. But what if someone wanted to say that there must be something boiling in the picture of the pot too.'[12] The picture of the steam rising from the pictured pot represents the

12 *Philosophical Investigations*, I, no. 297.

water boiling in the pot. But, in the sense in which we can speak of 'the picture of the steam', there is no picture of the boiling water. On the other hand, the picture of the steam rising is essential to the representation of the boiling – at least in *this* form of representation.

In this case of course other forms of representation are possible, including one which does involve a picture of the water boiling in the pot. Nothing of the sort is possible in the representation of the divine (or of the physical); and this is a feature of what we understand by 'representation' in these cases. Certain pictures of Christ on the Cross show him with his eyes raised towards his divine Father in Heaven. In that sense the notion (*Vorstellung*) of God the Father is an essential feature of their representation. But *He* is not pictured. We may want to say that the situation is different in Michelangelo's picture of the Creation of Adam and that here God the Father is pictured pictorially. We can say that if we like. But let us not overlook the fact that what makes the picture a representation of God the Father (rather than of a man in a queer blanket) is not itself something pictorial. In just the same way, what makes the picture of the steam rising from the pot a representation of water boiling in the pot is not something pictorial.

7

Ceasing to Exist

In his Third Meditation Descartes argues that finite substances depend on God's creative power not merely in respect of their origin, but equally in respect of their continuing existence.

> For all of the course of my life may be divided into an infinite number of parts, none of which is in any way dependent on the other; and thus from the fact that I was in existence a short time ago it does not follow that I must be in existence now, unless some cause at this instant, so to speak, produces me anew, that is to say, conserves me. It is a matter of fact perfectly clear and evident to all those who consider with attention the nature of time, that, in order to be conserved in each moment in which it endures, a substance has need of the same power and action as would be necessary to produce and create it anew, supposing it did not yet exist, so that the light of nature shows us clearly that the distinction between creation and conservation is solely a distinction of reason.[1]

I shall not discuss the notion of creation here. I will just remark in passing that, though I agree with Descartes that the relation of the world to God expressed in the idea of creation must be a *continuing* relation of dependence, it does not seem to me something to be established by the sort of metaphysical reasoning Descartes offers, or to be the sort of relation which that reasoning suggests. What I have to say will, though, have a bearing on Descartes's conception of the existence of finite things and, in particular, on his implied claim

1 *The Philosophical World of Descartes*, trans. Haldane and Ross, Vol. 1, p. 168.

that there is nothing in the nature of any such thing considered in itself which supports any presumption that it will continue to exist from one moment to the next.

Descartes is not, of course, speaking of some power which counteracts the natural processes of decay or combats natural agents of destruction. What he says has nothing to do, for instance, with the speed with which my car rusts or the resistance of warships to Exocet missiles. Given as much decay and destruction as you like to imagine, Descartes would still think some explanation necessary for us to conceive of any such processes as decay and destruction at all. He is concerned with the bare distinction between existence and non-existence; his contention is that there is nothing in the conception of a thing's existence at a given moment that implies anything at all about its existence at any other moment. If something does continue to exist from one moment to another, that needs explaining in terms of some external power.

It seems to be a presupposition of this claim that it is perfectly conceivable that anything should cease to exist, from one moment to the next, just like that. That is the claim I want to investigate.

I am assuming that Descartes's contention does not, at this point, bring into play any special considerations relating to *substances* in his quasi-technical sense of that term, but that it is meant to apply to the existence of finite things in an ordinary non-technical sense. The fact that his argument rests purely on considerations about the nature of time seems to me to point to its applicability to any temporal existent. But certainly the point of interpretation is controversial.

I hope that the reference to Descartes will establish my subject as one of serious philosophical concern. I say this because my next quotation, which I shall spend a good deal of time discussing, may strike some as frivolous. It is from a story by Isaac Bashevis Singer called 'Stories from Behind the Stove'.[2] In it Zalman the glazier is starting to tell a tale in the Jewish study house in a Polish village.

> "People do vanish," he said. "Not everyone is like the Prophet Elijah, who was taken to heaven in a fiery chariot. In the village of Palkes, not far from Radoshitz, a peasant was ploughing with an ox. Behind him walked his son, sowing barley from a bag. The boy looked up and the ox was there but his father

2   Isaac Bashevis Singer, 'Stories from Behind the Stove' in *A Friend of Kafka*.

had gone. He began to call, to scream, but there was no answer. His father had disappeared in the middle of the field. He was never heard from again."

"Perhaps there was a hole in the earth and he fell in?" Levi Yitzchock suggested.

"There was no hole to be seen – and if there had been a hole, why didn't the ox fall in first? He was in the lead."

"Do you mean that the demons carried him away?"

"I don't know."

"Perhaps he ran away with some woman," Meir the eunuch suggested.

"Nonsense, an old man of seventy – maybe more. A peasant does not run away from his earth, his hut. If he wants a woman, he goes with her into the granary."

"In that case, the Evil Ones took him," Levi Yitzchock said judiciously.

"Why just him?" Zalman the glazier asked. "A quiet man, Wojciech Kucek – that was his name. Before the Feasts of the Tabernacle, he used to bring branches for covering the Sukhoth. My own father bought from him. These things do happen. . . ."[3]

The conversation is presented in the form of an argument in which, by appealing to an example, Zalman apparently seeks to convince his audience that a certain kind of event, which they believe never happens, does sometimes happen. The effrontery of his arguments is of course intentionally comic. I apologize in advance to Mr Singer for spoiling the joke by subjecting them to rather solemn analysis. But, as so often, a good joke conceals a deep philosophical point and I know no way of making that explicit without losing the joke.

My own purpose at this point in my argument is not to argue either for or against the truth of Zalman's claim. I have a perhaps more fundamental worry. I am not sure that I understand the claim, what it means. That does not mean that I fail to understand Singer's story. I understand that in somewhat the way I understand Escher's drawings of impossible situations and objects. And to that extent I understand the sense of Zalman's claim, 'People do vanish', too: I understand it as it occurs in Singer's story. But were I to be confronted with someone

3 'Stories from Behind the Stove', pp. 61–74.

like Zalman who apparently tried to convince me in earnest that 'people do vanish', I do not think I should understand *what* he was trying to have me believe. I should like to suggest too that there are quite far-reaching considerations which ought to give pause to anyone who believes the sense of such a claim to be quite obvious.

Let me spend a little time examining the form of the argument between Zalman and his audience. Zalman wants to convince them of the general proposition that people (and things) do vanish. That is the *conclusion* of the argument. (It is quite important to remember that.) By 'vanishing' Zalman appears to mean just going out of existence, not as a result of any describable process of destruction or decay or disintegration or dissolution, etc. Not even, necessarily, as the result of supernatural intervention – though conceptions of the supernatural are not far away in Singer's story. At one moment the object in question exists, at the next moment not; and that is all. The form of the argument is to offer a case (and later another one) of something or someone's vanishing.

In that respect the argument is very reminiscent of that used in one of the most notable philosophical lectures ever delivered to the British Academy: G. E. Moore's 'Proof of an External World', in which he held up his two hands, said 'Here is one hand and here is another' and claimed to 'have proved *ipso facto* the existence of external things'.[4] The comparison is instructive, because just as those who found difficulty with Moore's conclusion found equal difficulty in accepting the cases he offered them as cases of the existence of external objects; so those who find difficulty with Zalman's conclusion in Singer's story will find equal difficulty in accepting that he has offered them a genuine example of a person's vanishing. But there is an obvious difference between the two cases as well. Whereas Moore claimed, at least, actually to confront his audience with a case of an external object, neither we, the readers of Singer's story, nor the hearers of Zalman's, are actually confronted with anyone or anything that vanishes. We are confronted with words; and our primary problem is to be clear what sort of sense we can attach to those words. Specifically, can we make sense of envisaging ourselves raising a serious question about their truth and falsity? I apologize for this cumbersome formulation of the question. The reason for this should become apparent as I go on.

In the story itself Zalman's interlocutors resist his account of what

4   G. E. Moore, 'Proof of an External World', *Philosophical Papers* p. 146.

happened. They suggest various naturalistic explanations, explanations of just the sort which are characteristically offered when someone disappears from view in the way people uncontroversially do. He counters these suggestions in a way which is again familiar and telling enough, in uncontroversial cases. There was no hole; if there was, why didn't the ox fall into it? Peasants of seventy don't abandon their home and land to run after a woman. In the circumstances in which such rebuttals are familiar to us, their point is to pave the way to better explanations. The rhetoric of Zalman's persuasion exploits this, but in a way that is sheer effrontery. The rebuttals are of the form 'Things don't happen like that' and his listeners are supposed to conclude, 'So he vanished, went out of existence'. But it could only be reasonable of them to reach this conclusion if, *prior* to the argument, 'People do sometimes vanish' were *more* acceptable to them than, for example, 'Peasants of seventy do sometimes abandon everything for a woman'. Otherwise the argument can exert no logical leverage on them. But in that case the argument would be superfluous, since 'People do sometimes vanish' is supposed to be its *conclusion*, is supposed to be what the argument is to convince them of.

A connected point is this. We have methods of investigating whether there are holes and whether people or animals have fallen down them; whether men have run away with women, etc. We understand and can evaluate claims that something of the sort has happened in a particular case in the context of our familiarity with these methods. Such a claim has logical force in the context of arguments like that in Singer's story just because there are means of assessing its acceptability *outside* the particular context of the argument. The situation is quite otherwise with the claim 'He vanished'. We do not have any general methods of investigating whether people have vanished. At best 'he vanished' is something we're driven back on: to say when we despair of finding any other explanation.

But I should not say, as I just did, 'any *other* explanation', since precisely because of the considerations I have been rehearsing, 'It has vanished' is not an explanation at all. It is just an expression of despair at the prospect of finding an explanation. So far, at least, I have uncovered no other logical force that it has. And if it *has* no other logical force, it seems to me clear that it cannot, as it is supposed to do by Zalman, support the general conclusion, 'People do vanish'. At best that would be a resigned admission that there are occurrences of a sort for which we cannot hope to find an explanation.

But occurrences of *what* sort? *Not* occurrences of the sort: people vanish! For to say that would precisely presuppose that we had fixed a use for this expression other than as an expression of resignation about the finding of explanations. And of course, were we to find a common or garden naturalistic explanation for the phenomenon that had been puzzling us, we could *cease* calling it a case of someone's vanishing (in the strange sense in which Zalman would like to have us understand that expression).

So the provisional and so far tentative conclusion I have reached is that when Zalman says of Wojciech Kucek, 'he vanished', this can be taken *neither* as an expression of the explanans *nor* as a description of the explanandum. What status it has is still obscure.

Perhaps it will be thought perverse of me to link so closely the issue of what sense we are to attach to the claim 'he vanished' with the issue of what logical role it plays in an argument such as is displayed in Singer's story. For, it will be said, the sense of 'he vanished' is evident enough in itself quite apart from any role it may have during argument etc. All we have to do is to specify the truth-conditions, isn't it, and isn't that easy enough?

Let's try it with the second example cited by Zalman in Singer's story, in which such truth-conditions seem to be cited in some detail. 'Near Blonia there lived a man, Reb Zelig the bailiff. He had a stove and a shed where he kept kindling wood, flax, potatoes, old ropes. He had a sleigh there too. He got up one morning and the shed was gone.'

Zelig thinks he is mad. But everyone else confirms that the shed is no longer there. It has left no trace, the grass is growing high in the place where it was. A group of 'enlightened' sceptics dig a six-foot-deep ditch in the place. 'The earth was full of roots and stones. The shed could not have sunk in.' Various investigations are undertaken which seem to rule out any conceivable naturalistic explanation.

Does this not specify the truth-conditions of 'the shed had vanished' quite clearly enough for us to be in no doubt what is meant? Well, let's consider this.

No problem is raised for us by the truth-condition of 'There is a shed in the field on Monday' or by the truth-condition of 'There is no shed in the field on Tuesday'. Furthermore, we *so far* have no reason to doubt that these two statements are perfectly consistent with each other. Of course, in thinking of them as consistent we shall have expectations that there will be some acceptable story which accounts for the removal of the shed between Monday and Tuesday and, very importantly, these expectations will be shaped by our understanding of what sheds, fields, etc., *are*.

There is a point of some importance concealed here and I should like to bring it into the open. As I have said, we should not normally baulk at the conjunction 'The shed existed on Monday and did not exist on Tuesday'. We should suppose the shed to have been, perhaps, burned down in the interim, dismantled, destroyed by an earthquake, bulldozed – or destroyed in some other way *consistent with our understanding of what a shed is*. All right. There are all sorts of ways in which the shed may have disappeared; and our acceptance of the above conjunction as consistent does not depend on any particular one of them having been responsible in the given case. That is, 'The shed existed on Monday' and 'The shed did not exist on Tuesday' are consistent independently of any *particular* story about what happened in the interim.[5]

Now, a *very* simple-minded logician might think: 'O.K., We have here two propositions p and q which are consistent with each other. There are all sorts of propositions $r_1, r_2, r_3, r_4 \ldots r_n$, each of which describes a way in which the shed ceased to exist. The consistency of p and q is quite independent of the truth or falsity of any one of those propositions $r_1 \ldots r_n$. Hence we can assert p and q and not-r_1 and not-r_2 and not-$r_3 \ldots$ and not-r_n.'

The conclusion does not of course follow. From the fact that the conjunction p and q is consistent with the falsity of any one of the propositions $r_1 \ldots r_n$, it does not follow that it is consistent with the falsity of all of them taken collectively.[6] Nor is this in fact true. As I

---

5   Cf. Wittgenstein, *On Certainty*, no. 237

If I say "An hour ago this table didn't exist", I probably mean that it was only made later on.

If I say "This mountain didn't exist then", I presumably mean that it was only formed later on – perhaps by a volcano.

If I say "This mountain didn't exist half an hour ago", that is such a strange statement that it is not clear what I mean. Whether for instance I mean something untrue but scientific. Perhaps you think that the statement that the mountain didn't exist then is quite clear, however one conceives the context. But suppose someone said "This mountain didn't exist a minute ago, but an exactly similar one did instead". Only the accustomed context allows what is meant to come through clearly.

6   I talk as though there were a specifiable, determinate set of propositions $r_1 \ldots r_n$. I do not in fact think this is so, but the point does not affect my argument.

have already said with emphasis, our understanding of the conjunction: 'The shed existed on Monday and did not exist on Tuesday' is such as to presuppose that the shed was destroyed between Monday and Tuesday in *some* intelligible way. And what is an intelligible way is limited by our understanding of what a shed is. That is clear enough if one tries as a substitution for $r_1 \ldots r_n$ a proposition such as 'It died', 'It dissolved in a tumbler of water', 'It went into liquidation' – that is, some report of a mode of ceasing to exist which is conceptually inapplicable to a shed. And this brings out the important point that the sense of an existential assertion is not independent of what it is for something of the kind that is in question 'to cease to exist'. (Something analogous is true if we substitute for 'to cease to exist', 'to come into existence': though I do not wish to suggest that the considerations governing how these two concepts are applied are completely symmetrical.) To use Platonic language to express what is not, perhaps, a Platonic thought: in some respects the nature of Being is dependent on the nature of Becoming.

Still, the most my argument seems to establish so far is that there are some accounts of ceasing to exist which would be inconsistent with the assertion and denial of the existence of a certain x at times t_1 and t_2 respectively because conceptually imcompatible with the kind of x in question. But of course what I am interested in is something different: whether we can consistently conjoin the assertion of the existence of, say, a shed on Monday, the assertion of its non-existence on Tuesday, and the denial that anything of relevance happened to the shed between Monday and Tuesday beyond its barely ceasing to exist at some instant during that interval.

In order to confront this issue I want to go back to something I said earlier. I said that I could understand Singer's story all right, and also understand Zalman's claims about the vanishing peasant and shed as they occur as elements in that story. What I said I should not understand is what someone would be saying who seemed to be seriously trying to convince me that something or someone had vanished in that way. My puzzlement about that, of course, goes along with a puzzlement about what I am supposed to represent to myself as a case of being confronted with such a vanishing object. Being confronted with a story about a vanishing shed is nothing like being confronted with a vanishing shed. From the fact that I understand the former nothing follows about the possibility of my understanding the latter, or about my ability to

envisage what that would be. I have no difficulty in seeing Escher's
famous picture *Ascending, descending*, as depicting a circular staircase
which continually ascends and yet rejoins the point of departure; but
I have no idea what it would be like to encounter an actual staircase
like that. In fact, outside the context of such a picture, I do not know
how to take the expression 'an actual staircase like that'.

The distinction that has to be made here is hard to formulate
satisfactorily. Professor G. .E. M. Anscombe made a similar distinction in discussing the analogous question whether one could attach
sense to the notion of something's beginning to exist without a
cause.[7] She first formulated this as the distinction between 'really
supposing this to happen' and 'just forming a picture of it as
happening'. This approaches what is necessary without quite
reaching it. The trouble is that the phrase 'really supposing it to
happen' sounds too much like contemplating it as a serious quasi-
physical possibility: rather in the way one may, without actually
expecting it, contemplate the bursting of the banks of the Thames
and the catastrophic flooding of London as a serious possibility. But
we are not required to 'really suppose' a bare beginning or cessation
of existence in *that* way – as something, for instance, we might think
it worth taking precautions against. (Indeed, the fact that one has no
idea what such 'precautions' would look like is certainly highly
relevant to the problem of seeing how these controversial expressions
might be seriously applied.)

A little later Professor Anscombe came at the matter in a different
way which, though it may look at first like changing the subject, in
fact seems to me very much more promising. 'But what one ought to
propose to one's imagination', she said, 'is perhaps not the existence
of some object, but oneself seriously judging an object to have come
into existence.' *Mutatis mutandis*, if I am to follow this suggestion I
shall have to consider what it would be for me seriously to judge an
object to have ceased to exist.

Why should this be a superior approach? The point is not, of
course, that the existence, or cessation of existence, of an object is
identical with my, or anybody else's, or a whole lot of people's,
judging it to exist or to have ceased to exist. Rather it is in the
character of the judgement of existence that what we understand by
'existence' reveals itself rather than in anything about the object
judged to exist. But that is *not* to deny that it is indeed the existence

7   G. E. M. Anscombe, 'Times, Beginnings and Causes'.

of the object that is in question. I shall defer to another occasion any discussion of how all this relates to traditional philosophical controversies over whether or not existence is a predicate. But it *is* worth making a remark or two at this point about something Hume says in his famous treatment 'Of the idea of existence and of external existence'.[8] Hume's view is summed up in the sentence: 'To reflect on anything simply, and to reflect on it as existent, are nothing different from each other'. The arguments he gives for this *prima facie* outrageous thesis are tangled and to a large extent dependent on confusions arising out of his general epistemology of 'impressions and ideas'. But he does, in at least two remarks, make a point which stands on its own and in respect of which his position has been rightly compared to that of Kant.[9] The idea of existence, Hume writes, 'when conjoin'd with the idea of any object, makes no addition to it'. And a little later: 'But no object can be presented resembling some object with respect to its existence, and different from others in the same particular; since every object, that is presented, must necessarily be existent.' That last clause, of course, reintroduces the confusions from his general epistemology. He appears to mean by it that to reflect on an object is to have an idea of it and, in so far as someone has an idea, necessarily that idea exists. The confusion comes from his assumption that the *object* of one's reflection is that idea and that is what enables him to think that it is impossible to reflect on a non-existent object.

But let us set that confusion aside. A quite genuine point that seems to be involved in what Hume says could be put like this: the mode of representation involved in picturing an object, either in a mental image or on a canvas, or involved indeed in describing the object ('giving a picture in words') will not convey the difference between the existence and non-existence of the object.

Suppose I am reflecting on the yeti, and wondering whether it exists or not. I represent the yeti to myself perhaps as an animal with a certain-shaped body and head, a certain texture of fur, a certain colour, etc. Perhaps I also represent it in a painting. I am unsure whether its ears are pointed or drooping – travellers' tales conflict – and I imagine or paint it twice, each time with a different type of ear.

8   David Hume, *A Treatise of Human Nature*, Book I, Part II, Section vi.
9   Immanuel Kant, *A Critique of Pure Reason*, Transcendental Dialectic, Book II, Chapter III, Section 4.

Compare that with a representation of the existence and non-existence respectively of the yeti. Would the difference appear in the painting of the yeti itself? Well yes, it might. I might, for instance, represent it as non-existent by painting it in monochrome against a polychrome background; or I might paint it with a broken outline. etc. But whereas I show my correct understanding of the pointed-ear picture, for instance, by looking for a beast with pointed ears, I do not show my understanding of the monochrome or dotted line picture by looking for a monochrome beast, or one with a dotted outline (whatever that would be). I show it rather by, for instance, giving up looking altogether and perhaps discussing how the story of the yeti came to gain currency. I might indeed represent the non-existence of the yeti not by any feature of the yeti-representation itself, but, for instance, by a series of pictures, in the first one of which explorers study a yeti-picture-within-the-picture, while in the second they are shown scouring the mountains and in the third leaving the mountains with disgusted expressions on their faces and tearing up the yeti-picture.

Non-existence is here represented by way of a representation of a *judgement* of non-existence; and that brings us back to the starting point of this excursus: Professor Anscombe's suggestion that, in order to be clear about what coming into existence amounts to, one should propose to one's imagination 'not the existence of some object, but oneself seriously judging an object to have come into existence'. Of course, a heavy accent has to fall on the word '*seriously*' and this places limits on what can be achieved here simply by 'proposing something to one's imagination'. Explorers behaving as depicted in my suggested series of paintings *might* be making a serious negative existential judgement and they might not. Unless we have a clear grasp of the conditions under which we would *count* someone as seriously making such a judgement we can get no further than what Professor Anscombe calls giving 'a mere title' to a picture, without becoming any clearer about what such a title conveys or what makes a picture (or a story) deserving of such a title.

If we look again, more closely, at Singer's story we shall see that we are really offered no more than the title 'the shed vanished' to the story Zalman is depicted as spinning. I want to follow Descartes in focusing attention on the importance of time in this connection though the kind of importance I shall attach to time is far removed from what Descartes had in mind. We are told in the story that one morning (let's call it Tuesday) the shed that had been there previously (let's say on Monday) 'was gone'. In other words the tale is told in a temporally impartial mode. The situations, as they were supposed to hold on Monday and on Tuesday respectively, are given equal status as accepted data. The way things were on Monday is not represented as *inferred* from the way things are on Tuesday, when the judgement is made, but as standing four-square alongside it. What now *is* the situation on Tuesday morning when Zelig is supposed to judge that the shed has vanished? My question is: what in Zelig's situation then, on Tuesday morning, warrants us in saying that he is making a serious judgement that the shed has vanished? (Clearly it is not enough that he utters – or says to himself – the words 'The shed has vanished.')

When Zelig gets up on Tuesday he sees no shed where he expected one to be, where he overwhelmingly seems to remember there to have been one the previous day. There is no sign of a shed's having been removed by natural means. As a matter of fact, interestingly enough, his first reaction in the story is not, 'It has vanished', but 'I must have lost my mind'. His wife and children and neighbours have reactions that agree with his. The whole village first goes berserk and then subsides into bewildered melancholy. The gentile squire rants about 'Jewish tricks' and yells 'If the shed does not stand where it has always stood, and at once, I will whip you all to death'. The doctor says to the druggist 'If a thing like this is possible, what sort of a doctor am I? And what kind of a druggist are you?' The enlightened ones give up playing cards and begin to think there may be a God. Et cetera.

What role does the thought 'The shed has vanished' play in all this psychic pandemonium? It is a thought that is expressed *both* by some of the villagers themselves and by Zalman the storyteller. Or rather, both some of the villagers and Zalman have thoughts which could be expressed in these words. Whether it is, in each case, *the same thought* is precisely the question I am raising. Zalman wants his audience to treat it as a sober objective report of what has caused and explains the pandemonium in the village. But *within* the village the thought that the shed has vanished is the focus, the expression, of the psychic disturbance itself. It is by no means simply accepted as the cause of the upheaval. Indeed, it is the impossibility of simply accepting it, in the face of the overwhelming urge to accept it, that is the immediate cause of the disturbance. The disturbance is not of the kind that would be produced by a very extraordinary and threatening, though intelligible, event such as, say, a totally unexpected pogrom, or an earthquake. Indeed, the loss of the shed is in itself no more than a relatively minor inconvenience and the intrinsic banality of the supposed occurrence is an important feature of the story. It plays its part in the storyteller's dismissal of proposed supernatural explanations: a matter to which I shall return briefly. What is disturbing is that no sense can be made of the situation; 'the shed has vanished' is not accepted by *anyone* (except Zalman) as making sense of it. It is an admission of failure and of a sort of failure which threatens the whole structure of their lives, their entire ability to make sense of anything – as is apparent from the typical examples.

Can we regard it as some sort of hallucination then? Zalman considers, or pretends to consider, this possibility. 'The whole thing must have been an illusion. But how can a whole town be deluded?[10] Needless to say, that is a mere repetition of the storyteller's effrontery, which I noted earlier in connection with the argument over the vanishing ploughman. Why should anyone be more disconcerted by the question 'How can a whole town be deluded?' than by the question 'how can a shed vanish?' In fact the onus lies very much on the other side. That a whole town should be deluded is indeed highly unlikely; but it is a *possible* explanation of events and one that could conceivably itself be investigated and accounted for. We might look for something in the drinking water; or investigate the bread for evidence of ergot poisoning, etc., etc. But it is of absolutely paramount importance to remember that nothing of the sort is possible with the 'hypothesis' that the shed vanished. For to have a naturalistic explanation of the disappearance of the shed would be imcompatible with treating it as a case of the shed's simply ceasing to exist in the sense Zalman (and Descartes, by implication, too) wants us to accept. Even to look for such a naturalistic explanation would be at least to cast doubt on the peculiar metaphysical status that is philosophically interesting.

I have not, as may be thought, lost sight of my promise to focus attention on the importance of time in the putative judgement 'The shed has vanished'. The point I have been trying to make might be put like this: despite appearances, the words 'The shed has vanished' do not express a judgement in which the utterer, as it

10 In Singer's story this is said after the reappearance of the shed some weeks later as though nothing had happened. I omit this complication from my discussion.

were, projects a thought into the past as he might, for example, were he to utter the words 'the shed has had a fresh coat of paint since yesterday'; it does not go beyond expressing present bewilderment at the senseless conflict of one's present impressions.

It is important for me to make my reason for saying this clear. My point is *not* that in the normal case (that of my thought about the shed's new coat of paint, for example), because all my present impressions converge, I am able to move beyond them and base on them a judgement about something that happened in the past. It is not that I have the present *impression* of fresh paint and the present *impression* of remembering that yesterday the paint was old and from that conclude ... etc. No, the correct account seems to me to be simply that I see the shed has been freshly painted since yesterday. Furthermore, it is not just because my present impressions, in the abnormal, vanishing shed case, are in conflict with each other that I find myself unable to go beyond them and make any judgement reaching out to a past event. For there are plenty of quite normal cases of our having conflicting impressions in which our thought ranges beyond our present experience without much difficulty; cases, for instance, in which we seek and find some naturalistic explanation of the conflicting impressions.

I may seem at this point to lay myself open to a charge of inconsistency. Am I not just dogmatically refusing to describe the abnormal case in the same mode as I would describe the normal one? Well, it is perfectly true that in the normal case I do not quarrel with a straightforward report of a temporal sequence in which all the stages of the sequence are given equal epistemic weight. I do not here insist on resting all the weight on my present impressions, sensory and memory. I simply state the sequence as a simple matter of observation: 'The shed has been freshly painted since yesterday'. It's true too that I am refusing to give 'The shed has vanished' the same treatment. Why?

The objection implied in the question is parallel to a claim made by Professor Roy Holland in a paper which I have found very rewarding.[11] Holland tries to isolate one conception of a miraculous event as that of an event which, though 'conceptually impossible' is 'empirically certain'. The notion of conceptual impossibility is explained in terms of laws of nature which have become so entrenched in our thought and language as to be 'stipulative' and to

11   R. F. Holland, 'The Miraculous', p. 169 ff.

constitute 'a framework through which we look at the world and which to a considerable degree dictates our ways of describing phenomena'.[12] Recognizing that this way of looking at things *prima facie* strengthens Hume's argument against miracles, Holland claims nevertheless that there is such a thing as empirical certainty, that is to say, that empirical observation can and does generate more than probability – contrary to what Hume thought; and that such certainty can prevail even in a case where what is observed conflicts with what our concepts stipulate to be possible, that is, we can be empirically certain that something has occurred which is conceptually impossible.

The first part of this counter-claim against Hume seems to me obviously right. What we observe may be, and overwhelmingly often is, absolutely certain. It may be so, moreover, even in the face of very firmly entrenched expectations. It may even be so certain as to force a change in our concepts. That, however, still falls short of what Holland claims, since he wants to recognize the possibility of cases where our observations cannot be accommodated to our existing concepts and where, nevertheless, *both* the reports of what we observe *and* the system of concepts which rules out what is reported are allowed to stand with unabated certainty. The trouble with this position, looking at it from the side of empirical certainty, is that this latter is an intentional notion, requiring an object. One is certain *of* something, or *that* something is so. Certain of what, or that what? The answer has to deploy concepts appropriate to the situation. But in Holland's 'miraculous' situations we do not have the concepts which allow us to formulate an intelligible answer. We are reduced to uttering a form of words to which, in these circumstances, we can attach no sense. So no answer has been given to the question, 'What are we certain of?' As I hope my previous discussion makes clear, I do not at all want to deny that we may be confronted with circumstances which defeat our attempts to describe them coherently. What I am objecting to is the idea that, in such circumstances, the notion of empirical certainty can still be thought of as standing with rock-like firmness.

The only counter-argument to this that I can find in Holland's article is that 'if it were granted that there can be no certainty in regard to the individual case, if there can be no real knowledge that a particular event has occurred in exactly the way that it has, how

12 'The Miraculous', p. 177.

could our system of laws have got established in the first place?'[13] To that I first reiterate that I am very far from thinking that there is no such thing as 'certainty in regard to the individual case' (in regard to *any* individual case, that is); and I remark secondly that the question at the end of the sentence I have quoted, if it is meant to suggest that our frameworks of concepts somehow rest on certain empirical certainties which themselves have *no* conceptual content, must surely itself rest on a quasi-empiricist confusion.

To return, then, to my original question: Why do I not accord parity of treatment, in respect of their relation to the utterer's present experience, to the expressions 'The shed has been freshly painted since yesterday', and 'The shed has vanished since yesterday'? Why, that is, do I not allow the direct connection with the past in the report of the observer's immediate situation in the second case as with the first? After all, it may be said, in making such a report I would equally in each case have to rely at the moment of making it on my memory of how things were previously – yesterday in the case of the shed, a few moments ago in the case of the ploughboy's vanishing father. It's true that normally in making reports such as 'The shed's been repainted' I don't explicitly state what I remember – how the shed was yesterday – I take for granted, as do my hearers, an enormous amount about the immediate (and not so immediate) antecedents to the present situation. And it would not be incorrect to call this taking for granted, in large part at least, a memory phenomenon. So if I am saying that there is something suspect about my memory in the abnormal, metaphysically interesting, case, why can't suspicion be applied equally to the normal cases?

The answer to this is linked with difficulties in the remarks by Descartes with which I started. For Descartes, it will be remembered, what requires explanation is that something *does* continue to exist from one instant to the next, since what is the case at any given instant is not in any way dependent on what is the case at any other instant. In so far as there is continuity of existence, that must be sustained by some external power. So, if a shed suddenly ceases to exist, that, *so far as the nature of the shed itself is concerned, considered as an individual temporal existent*, is no other than we have a right to expect. The focus of my own discussion has been on the conditions under which we can regard certain kinds of utterance,

13   'The Miraculous', p. 177.

ostensibly concerning temporal existents, as expressing significant judgements about such existents. I want to recall now that Descartes's conception of time as a succession of mutually independent atomic instants can be, and in fact is, at an earlier stage in Descartes's overall argument, applied with equal force to the relation between a thought expressed at a given moment and what may or may not be the case at any other moment before or after that given moment. So, whatever it is about my situation at a given moment that makes me certain that there was a shed in front of my window yesterday has no intrinsic connection whatever with what actually was the case yesterday. God is invoked by Descartes not merely to guarantee the shed's continued existence but also to guarantee some connection between my present apparent memory of the shed's existence yesterday and what was the case yesterday.[14] So, if we leave belief in God's sustaining power out of the matter, not merely do I have no reason for expecting the shed to go on existing from one moment to another, I would *also* never have any reason for making the serious judgement that a shed has vanished, since I would have no reason for supposing that my overwhelming present inclination to think there was a shed there yesterday had anything whatever to do with whether there was a shed there yesterday or not. So the same considerations which seem to make possible a shed's vanishing, at the same time make it impossible to see what the serious, justified, judgement that a shed had vanished could look like, or in what conditions there could be such a judgement. The confinement of the thinker to the circle of his own present impressions is thus inextricably linked with the conception of physical things as involving no continuity of existence through time. Indeed, it will be recalled that Descartes himself quite explicitly and emphatically, in the quotation with which I started, grounds his argument on considerations concerning the nature of time *per se*. So the difficulties about continuity which he expresses affect indifferently anything having a temporal existence, be it physical or mental, a shed or a putative memory.

According to this argument, then, I could never have any better reason for saying the shed had vanished than for saying that I was

14 And thus the deductive chain, avowedly involving memory of earlier links in the chain, by which Descartes seeks to establish the existence of a veracious God, is equally undermined. I am unconvinced by any attempt I have read to free Descartes from his Circle.

subject to certain disturbing perceptual and memory impressions.

It may seem, though, that my argument has no relevance to the question whether we could understand Zalman's utterances in Singer's story as expressing straightforward statements of fact. For Zalman after all does not buttress his tale with any such general metaphysical considerations as we find in Descartes; he simply tells a story about the particular case.

However, I believe that the conception which tempts us to think that we could understand Zalman's story as a factual account of something that had happened, is precisely the conception which underlies Descartes's argument. The existence of something or someone at one time, we think, is a totally distinct state of affairs from its existence at another time and is logically consistent with its non-existence at another time. So we can conjoin the judgement of the object's existence on Monday with the judgement of its non-existence on Tuesday with perfect consistency. Any further judgements we may or may not make about what happened between Monday and Tuesday are a completely different matter, having no bearing on the intelligibility of the conjunction under review.

My argument so far has been that such reasoning can have no greater authority than reasoning which calls into question the reliability of my present impressions. And if I were, as of course I might be on some occasion, under the overwhelming impression that a shed had vanished, that would be at least as strong a reason for concluding I was subject to some cognitive disorder as for concluding that the shed had indeed vanished.

At a crucial stage of his philosophical development Wittgenstein wrote as follows:

> The stream of life, or the stream of the world, flows on and our propositions are so to speak verified only at instants.
> Our propositions are only verified by the present. So they must be so constructed that they can be verified by it.[15]

His subsequent enquiries into the nature of following a rule, understanding, meaning something by what one says; and particularly his microscopic examination of the relation between the moment at which one is said to mean something and the temporally extended language-games in the context of which alone this *can* be said of one

15 Wittgenstein, *Philosophical Remarks*, V, no. 48.

– these are attempts to reconcile those two aspects of propositions: their place in 'the stream of life, or the stream of the world', and the sense in which they can be said to be 'only verified by the present'. To regard time in the Cartesian way required by accepting that something like a human being, or like a shed, could just cease to exist from one moment to the next, is to remove both the object in question and oneself contemplating it from that 'stream'. But this removal is a cancellation of the conditions under which anything one says or thinks has sense: *including* the words 'It has ceased to exist'. There is nothing more we can do with these words. This point is dramatized with beautiful comedy in Singer's story: the druggist, replying to the doctor's remarks to him that I quoted earlier, says 'There is some swindle here.' 'He stretched out in the grass and examined the earth. He asked for a spade. He wanted to dig. But Zelig said, "I kept the spade in the shed. It's gone." '[16] In vanishing the shed has, as it were, taken with it the possibility of our making anything of its disappearance, the possibility even of getting clear about what its disappearance amounts to.

I should like to spell out further what is involved in the notion of 'the stream of life, or the stream of the world' in its relation to the main issue I have been concerned with. The main point to elucidate here is the interconnection between my present understanding of the situation I am in at this moment, what I can recollect about the antecedents of this situation, and my understanding of the causal properties of, and relations between, the objects in my environment. I use the word 'causal' in this context very loosely indeed, as a mere abbreviating label to include, for instance, the characteristic ways in which such objects behave, typical shapes of their life-histories, their relatively stable geographical interrelations, etc., etc. Even more loosely, I include under the same label familiar and established functions of such objects in the lives and practices of human beings. For instance, I am writing these words on a piece of paper with a Parker ballpoint pen. Paper and pens (especially Parker pens) come into being in ways characteristic of them. Paper tends to blow about in the wind, a pen not. A pen's main use is writing; paper is used for writing on and for other things, too. . . . My understanding of all this is covered by my use of the expression 'causal understanding' in the present context.

I sit down at my desk writing these words. It is about 9.30 a.m. on

16 'Stories from Behind the Stove', p. 63.

a cold September morning. I am a bit alarmed at how little time I have left to prepare this lecture to deliver to the British Academy, as I have agreed to do. Let that serve as a tiny scrap of what I would offer if asked to describe my present circumstances. It includes, as it were indiscriminately, references to what I can now perceive, to my state of mind, to my expectations for the future, to past circumstances that led to my doing what I am doing. I could expand the description and answer questions arising from it. If asked about the circumstances of my agreeing to give this lecture, for instance, I would say that the Academy's Secretary wrote to me with the invitation, to which I wrote a letter of acceptance. I would give that information quite unselfconsciously and firmly, without a thought as to whether these are things I *remember* or not. If asked about that I would say, yes, I do remember receiving the Secretary's letter, but do not actually remember replying to it. However I certainly did reply to it because I remember receiving a follow-up letter from the Secretary, and anyway, here is a copy of my reply in the file. . . .

What I want to emphasize about all this is the extent to which expressions of recollection, reports of perception, quasi-causal inferences, are indiscriminately mixed up together. It is not merely that they exist side by side; they mutually support each other and it is not even always clear what status a particular report has. For instance, how did this pen come to be in my hand? Well, I picked it up. Do I recollect doing that? To be honest, I am not sure whether I do or not but it does not matter, for there is certainly no other way it could have got there.

My point is not just that when I recollect something I draw psychological support from my causal understanding, though that is certainly true. More importantly, the concepts in terms of which I express what I remember are drawn from the background of that understanding. These concepts should not be thought of in purely verbal terms. This pen is something I reach for in my pocket (thus expressing my memory of where I put it), hold in a certain rather complicated way, and write with (thus expressing my understanding of how a pen behaves and how it is to be used).

This interpenetration of memory and causal understanding is one of the things Kant wanted to emphasize in the 'Second Analogy of Experience', I believe. I have in mind his question about how our idea of an objective temporal sequence is distinct from the sequence of our impressions and his claim that this distinction involves the idea of a necessary *causal* sequence. I do not wish to support everything Kant said about this, but his claim does seem to me particularly important for a proper understanding of what is involved in *remembering* a sequence of events.

The order in which I recollect the events in a sequence need not, of course, follow the order of the sequence itself. I might, for instance, recollect replying to the Academy Secretary's letter before I recollect receiving it. In suitable circumstances, indeed, I may be able to change the order in which I recollect something more or less at will. I should certainly not normally be tempted in such circumstances to identify the order of recollected events with the order in which those events are recollected.

Here is another example. Last week I travelled by air from New York to London. I recall travelling by subway from downtown Manhattan to Kennedy Airport, boarding a plane, and flying for about six-and-a-half hours, then disembarking at Heathrow and travelling by Tube to Earl's Court. I recall making these segments of the journey in that order, although, perhaps, my recollections were triggered off by thoughts of the final stage of the journey and from that point I went back in memory over the earlier stages.

Suppose I were to be under the impression that I had travelled from, let's say, Manhattan to central London by subway, then plane to John F. Kennedy, and thence by Tube to Earl's Court. In that case I would naturally at once correct myself and if, in narrating my recollections of the journey to somebody else, I were to recount the events as having happened in that order, *he* could easily correct me simply on the basis of our mutual knowledge of what is physically and geographically possible. Such a narrative would in fact *make no sense*, considered as a narrative. If a piece of discourse is to count as a narration of a journey from New York to London, a certain order is already imposed on it by the very fact that this is what it is supposed to be. This order cannot be overruled by my impression, however strong, of having travelled in a radically different order. If I do seem to remember it differently that only shows that I am confused or mistaken.

An ability to narrate a remembered sequence of events in their proper temporal order presupposes, then, as this example illustrates, an understanding of how things hang together, their causal interconnections, etc. This is manifest in the very terms, the very concepts in which the narration is expressed: 'travelling by Tube', 'boarding a plane', etc., the reference to geographical localities and the relations between them. The fact that the terms in which a narration is expressed belong to such a background understanding of the way things behave, what can and what cannot happen, what you can and cannot do, is an important part of what makes it possible for memory claims to be accepted or rejected (and hence understood for what they are), for them to be corrected. That is, an account of what *did* happen, what *was* done, depends on an understanding of what *can* and *cannot* happen, be done. 'It can't have been like that', we say, 'because, look, that would have meant such and such and that's impossible.' That kind of discussion and criticism is a characteristic feature of the whole phenomenon of remembering (which it is very misleading to think of, as so often happens in philosophy, as just a matter of issuing certain sorts of report). Someone who could not take part in such discussion would be someone who had, at best, only a very dim understanding of what it is to recount one's recollections. How would such a person distinguish such a narration from a fantasy?

What I want to emphasize most in this part of the discussion is that, within the complex forms of activity that we call 'expressing what we remember', the impression, however overwhelmingly strong, that *this* is what happened by no means has final authority. For the statement 'this is what happened' has to make sense, not merely on its own, but in conjunction with the whole narration to which it belongs. It is easy to be misled on this matter by the fact that, *given* that the requirements of sense and consistency – both internal and contextual – are met, a memory claim may indeed be completely authoritative in a way which is not at all derivative from anything else in the narrative.

Suppose, for instance, that I vividly recall that in the course of a tête-à-tête conversation my interlocutor, out of character and right out of the blue, suddenly said something quite outrageous – perhaps uttered a gratuitous insult. He subsequently steadfastly denies it and there is nothing in the way of evidence to support me. It is my word against his, as we say. Others may or may not believe me when I tell them this. They may think I am lying or that I am subject to some delusion. As to the latter, well, that may be a possibility. My claim is *not* that a vivid memory-experience is self-authenticating in the sense that there is anything about the experience itself which guarantees that it is veridical. I am saying only that this kind of direct, non-inferential memory claim is as such perfectly intelligible to us. We all make such claims constantly without *arrière-pensée* and accept them unquestioningly when they are made by others. Their authority is *sui generis*. Overwhelmingly often, moreover, the claims are substantiated.

But this, obviously, cannot mean that a 'memory-experience' however vivid, and endowed with whatever degree of conviction you like, has any 'authority' to confer narrative intelligibility on a piece of prose which is otherwise unintelligible. However passionately convinced I am that I first travelled by subway from Manhattan to Earl's Court and from there by plane to John F. Kennedy Airport, that will not be treated, by anyone who knows enough geography to assess the coherence of what is being said, as the expression of a possibly genuine recollection. The 'authority' of memory claims and memory-experiences is ascribable only within the limits of what is intelligible as an expression of the objects of those claims or experiences.

Why, then, should the fact that I can imagine myself, as I certainly can, feeling as though I remembered with complete conviction that yesterday a shed stood in a field in which there is now undisturbed ground, be taken to show that there might indeed have *been* a shed there, one that has simply ceased to exist? My question is: why should we treat that any differently from the obviously disordered memory-experience described in my previous paragraph?

It may be important to say in parenthesis that the force of that question is not weakened by the fact that *my* feeling of conviction might be shared by all those round me, as is the case in Singer's story. If that is so, it certainly will make a difference to what account might be given of the whole situation and perhaps make it more difficult to see what account *can* be given. But it will not make any difference to the unintelligibility of what people are claiming to remember. Suppose I have travelled to London with a large party of people, all of whom claimed to recollect the stages of that journey in the distorted way I have sketched. Would that make any difference to the intelligibility of the claim? No.

However, it is true that these two cases are not completely comparable. The difference between them might be put like this. The route I have the impression of having taken between New York and London can be shown to be impossible by reference to generally known geographical facts, the acknowledged powers of human beings along with their limitations, the capabilities of trains and aeroplanes, etc. And the process of showing the impossibility of one route is, at the same time, a step in the direction of showing how others are possible. (Or, of course, there may be cases where *no*

route is possible – but that too is shown in some determinate way.)
But Zalman the storyteller does not describe a route from existence
to non-existence in the cases of the ploughman and the shed, which
we can similarly show to be impossible by reference to our
knowledge of the world. The fact of the matter is that he describes
no route whatever. One moment something is there, the next
moment it is not there; and that is all. The various positive accounts
which are suggested by members of Zalman's audience, or by
Zelig's neighbours, of the mysterious disappearances are quickly
dispatched. But the arguments by which they are dispatched cannot
be said to point in the direction of the storyteller's account since, as
I just said, he gives no account. Indeed, it is not just that he *omits* to
explain how the ploughman and the shed ceased to exist. He is
using the words 'He (It) vanished' in such a way as to preclude there
being any determinate way in which he (it) ceased to exist. That is
the whole point of his tales. His words do not locate any definite
point in the stream of life. So it is not so much that what is said
conflicts with our understanding of things (as with the impossible
route from New York to London). It just *fails to connect* with it.

Perhaps this is more obvious if we take an analogy from the
imperative mood. Suppose I am told to destroy the shed in the field
in front of me by fire. If I have no means of ignition available I shall
not be in a posititon of comply, but I shall understand perfectly *what*
it is that I cannot do. Suppose by contrast that I am told to make the
shed cease to exist – *not* by *any* means. In this case I have not been
told to do something beyond my powers, I have not been told to do
anything at all. What has been said to me merely apes the form of an
order. Similarly, the sentence in the indicative mood merely apes the
form of a factual report.

Finally, I want to disown two interpretations of what I have been
saying which might seem natural, but which would be over-hasty.
First, I have not wanted to say in any absolute sense that purported
reports of some physical thing's ceasing to exist can only have a
sense when it is presupposed that we could, with sufficient
knowledge, give some naturalistic account of what has happened. I
have concentrated on the bewilderment that we – that is, you and I –
are liable to feel at a claim about the bare cessation of existence of
some physical thing where any sort of naturalistic explanation is
ruled out. I have done so simply because the expectation of such
explanations plays such a dominant role within the mode in which
we are brought up to make sense of things. That is the prevailing
direction in which the stream of *our* life goes.

The cultural context of Singer's story, for instance, is rather different from what I imagine most of the people in my audience would be at home in. And Zalman does not merely reject naturalistic explanations; he is equally dismissive of suggestions that demons or the Powers of Darkness were responsible. ('What did they have against the shed?' he asks at the end of his story.) I should not want to deny that people in whose lives thoughts about the Powers of Darkness played a central role could make a sort of sense of accounts of happenings which remained opaque to us. The same goes for miracles. My grounds for criticizing what Holland writes about this concept have to do mainly with his attempt to bring it into usable relation with the habits of naturalistic explanation which are so predominant in our *Weltanschauung*. His failure – as it seems to me – in this attempt is a necessary and not a contingent failure. As such it shows something important. We do not have the same *kind* of difficulty with the concept of a miracle as we do, say, with that of a cause. *Cause* is a notion we are constantly using and it is hard to conceive what our lives would be without it; our puzzlement with it is a purely philosophical puzzlement about giving a satisfactory account of it. *Miracle* is not like that. It is not merely that we find a satisfactory account of it hard to give; we are puzzled – practically puzzled – about how we could ever put it to use. Our lives involve the propensity to ask kinds of questions, and to press those questions in kinds of way, which conflicts with the possibility of untroubled talk about miracles. Our first task in trying to understand what a miracle might be would be the imaginative reconstruction of a mode of life in which there could be such untroubled talk.

To return to my disclaimer: I am far from wanting to deny the possibility of people's making sense of their lives in terms of such a concept as that of a miracle. I certainly do not want to say that all sense must have a basis in a predominantly naturalistic understanding. My objection to the idea of a bare cessation of existence is that it has no basis in *any* general understanding of things, naturalistic or otherwise.

This brings me to my second disclaimer. I have not 'proved impossible' a bare cessation of existence of the kind the idea of which is deployed in Singer's story and required by what Descartes wrote about the dependence of finite things for their continued existence on the operation of some outside conserving cause. I have done no more than raise some doubts about what it would be to understand stories like Singer's as straightforward factual reports. That does not mean that I regard a sentence like 'It has vanished' as meaningless. It obviously is not: it has a perfectly good meaning, for instance, in a story like Singer's. I can even, without great difficulty, imagine myself in circumstances in which I have the overwhelming impression that there was a moment ago and is no longer a shed in front of me with no possibility of explaining what has happened; and I can imagine that I might be driven to say 'It has vanished' in such circumstances, accompanying the utterance with successive mental pictures in which the shed is first there in front of me and then not there. If anyone wants to insist that to imagine this *is* to imagine the shed to have ceased to exist, I can do no more than remind him again how *thin* a context of utterance this is, how many of the connections with other ideas, expectations, possibilities of investigations, etc., are lacking which normally surround our thoughts concerning the coming to be and ceasing to be of things. And the thought can hardly remain unaffected by such a drastic impoverishment of its surroundings.

8

Meaning and Religious Language

I

Contemporary discussions of meaning in connection with religious language commonly take as their starting point certain expressions which seem fundamental in the religious beliefs and theological doctrines of the sophisticated world religions of today and, very naturally, in Anglo-Saxon writings the examples concentrated on tend to be taken from the religions with which the authors are most familiar, roughly the Judaeo-Christian. Furthermore, philosophers are concerned today, as they have always been, with problems about the reference, if any, of the terms under discussion, with problems about the way in which predicates are attributed to these referential, or quasi-referential terms – whether the connection between subject and predicate is necessary or contingent, what kind of necessity or contingency is in question, and so on.

I shall, in the course of this essay, make some comments on aspects of some of these questions, but for the following reasons I shall not take them as my starting point. I am concerned with meaning and *religious language*, not the language characteristically used in this or that particular religion. I want to ask primarily: how do we identify a use of language as a religious use in the first place? If we *start* by asking questions about words like 'God', and expressions like 'God is infinitely good and powerful', we are open to the objections that such expressions do not have analogues in all religions, so that what we say will miss the mark insofar as our aim is to arrive at a characterization of religious language as such; our remarks will be insufficiently general. It is, of course, possible that anything like a general account is after all impossible of achievement, but the approach I have indicated seems likely to *make* it impossible because of the very terms in which the question is raised.

A further reason for adopting a different approach is as follows. The treatment of questions about meaning, reference, predication, necessity, and the like, in Anglo-Saxon philosophy has concentrated very largely on the application of such terms within empirical discourse, scientific theory, and mathematics. But perhaps these provide misleading models. Such logical terminology does, of course, have application to religious discourse, but an application which might be more clearly illuminated by investigating it from a different point of view. There has in fact been a very strong tendency to construe the term 'God' on the analogy of names and descriptive phrases as they occur within empirical discourse and to seek analogies for expressions like 'God is infinitely loving and powerful' in the same area. It may turn out that such analogies are indeed the appropriate ones, but we should not assume at the outset that this is going to be so. I shall in fact suggest some limited analogy between certain aspects of some religious discourse and geometry, but I do not wish to *start* at this point. The helpfulness of such an analogy will depend on a good many prior considerations which I want to develop. There is much more to this question than I shall have space to discuss here. There are deep philosophical disagreements about the proper way to discuss issues concerning reference, sense, truth, etc., quite apart from disagreements specifically concerning religion.

Though it is true of all of us that we first become acquainted with religious uses of language in becoming familiar with a particular religious tradition (or pretty limited range of such traditions), in so doing we acquire some concepts which we feel able to apply outside the context provided by these particular traditions. I am thinking of concepts like *worship, reverence, religious awe, devoutness*. These are concepts which we apply to *human beings* in certain aspects of their lives, demeanour, and practice, and which we think of as characteristic of descriptions of the religious dimensions (or lack of such dimensions) of people's lives. It is a noteworthy fact that, being able to make something of the distinction between a man who is a devout Christian and one who is not, I do not feel at a loss when I hear such a distinction drawn within the context of Buddhism, even though I have very little understanding of Buddhist doctrine.[1]

---

1 I owe this very important observation to a remark made by Rush Rhees in a discussion at King's College, London.

On the other hand, a term like 'Nirvana' will mean absolutely nothing to me until I have learned a good deal about specifically Buddhist doctrine. The fact that, though ignorant of Buddhist doctrine, I can make some sense of the distinction between a devout and a non-devout Buddhist has a great deal to do with my recognition of Buddhism *as a religion*. I do not dispute, of course, that I am unlikely to get very far with recognition of the particular form which devoutness takes for a Buddhist without further understanding of the Buddhist tradition, its types of religious observance, and its doctrines. But if I can apply the concept to a Christian I already know a good deal about the direction in which I should look in applying it to a Buddhist.

It is noteworthy that the concepts of which I have given examples are concepts applicable to the lives and practices of human beings. This raises the important question of the relation between practice and belief in religious contexts.[2] Consider the following remarks by Wittgenstein.

> When he [*sc.* Frazer] explains to us, for example, that the king must be killed in his prime because, according to the notions of the savages, his soul would not be kept fresh otherwise, we can only say: where that practice and these views go together, the practice does not spring from the view, but both of them are there.
>
> It may happen, as it often does today, that someone will give up a practice when he has seen that something on which it depended is an error, but this happens only in cases where you can make a man change his way of doing things simply by calling his attention to his error. This is not how it is in connection with the religious practices of a people and what we have here is *not* an error.[3]

'The practice does not spring from the view, but both of them are there.' Wittgenstein does *not*, of course, here claim any priority for the practice over the view, but I should like to examine *this* possibility further in a way which is suggested by other parts of his writings. My main reason for this springs from questions about

2   The discussion which immediately follows again owes much to Rush Rhees: in this case to three lectures on 'Ritual' given at King's College, London; though I am not at all following the same direction as that taken by Rhees.

3   L. Wittgenstein, *Remarks on Frazer's "The Golden Bough"*.

concept-formation. I want to suggest that what makes a belief a 'religious' belief can best be understood by investigating the roots in religious practice of the concepts at work in religious beliefs. The possibility of doing this seems to depend on our being able to identify a set of practices as 'religious' independently of any beliefs associated with them. This I shall attempt presently.

But first, to explain my remark about concept-formation, let me refer to a suggestion made by Wittgenstein in quite a different area.

> How do words *refer* to sensations? . . . This question is the same as: how does a human being learn the meaning of the names of sensations? – of the word "pain". Here is one possibility: words are connected with the primitive, the natural, expressions of the sensation and used in their place. A child has hurt himself and he cries and then adults talk to him and teach him exclamations and, later, sentences. They teach the child new pain-behaviour.

> "So you are saying that the word 'pain' really means crying?" – On the contrary: the verbal expression of pain replaces crying and does not describe it.[4]

Wittgenstein is here speaking, of course, of a society already possessing a complex language of sensations and of the transmission of this language from adults to children. But we might also think of the possibility that in the dawn of language, a 'language of sensations' gradually grew up and developed out of 'primitive' (nonlinguistic) expressions of sensations. *We* could (and indeed can) recognize people – babies – as well as animals as being in pain even though they have no *concept* of pain, in the sense that they have no 'pain language' and no beliefs *about* pain.

Is this case at all applicable in any analogy with religion? Let us imagine a tribe whose speech includes nothing that we want to identify as the expression of 'religious beliefs'. They have, however, certain striking practices. Let us suppose they live among mountains. When one of their number dies he is buried or burned with a certain ceremoniousness. The ceremony includes perhaps some moment of silent contemplation of the mountains, perhaps

4 *Philosophical Investigations*, Part I, no. 244.

prostration of their bodies before the mountains. Similar things are done at other important moments in the life of the tribe – at a marriage, on the occasion of a birth, when an adolescent is initiated into adult life.

I want to consider something like this as having a certain analogy (in respect of its relation to religious belief) to *primitive* pain behaviour (in respect of its relation to talk about pain). I think that in certain circumstances I should want to say that members of the tribe were expressing something like reverence and even religious awe. And I think I should already be able to recognize differences among individual tribesmen which I should want to call differences in their 'devoutness' in their conduct of these observations. For this reason I want to call such behaviour primitive religious practice.

Of course, there are great differences between this imaginary case and primitive pain behaviour, differences which might make it seem objectionable to use the word 'primitive' of both cases. So it is important to emphasize that in using this word of both cases I am wanting to stress mainly an analogy between the relation of such cases respectively to one in which there is a developed pain language or a developed religious language. One important difference between the cases is that in the case of the rituals which I am wanting to designate 'religious', we are already dealing with an established social practice rather than with the behaviour of individuals considered separately. Other differences are connected with this. For instance, while the form of primitive human responses to pain is, I imagine, pretty well universally the same, there is no reason to suppose that this must be (or is) so of primitive religious rituals. In my example I have supposed a certain gravity and solemnity, but rituals could equally well have a gay, exuberant character. What I think *is* necessary for us to be able to characterize behaviour as ritualistic is that it is in some way set apart from behaviour associated with everyday practical concerns: not in the sense that it has no connection at all with such concerns (on the contrary), but in the sense that it is stylized, ruled by conventional forms and perhaps thought of as stemming from long-standing traditions. I should also expect such rituals to be associated with a sense of wonder and awe at the grandeur and beauty of aspects of the tribe's environment and to be directed toward features of that environment having particular importance in the tribe's life (mountains, the sea, animals – consider the Cro-Magnon cave paintings). This would help to provide connections between the ritualistic performances and other aspects of the tribe's life and would doubtless be associated with differences of attitude expressed on other occasions toward the objects of ritualistic reverence and other familiar objects (consider totems). Last, one would expect differences in the degree of seriousness with which the rituals were regarded as between individual tribesmen: indeed, this would be important in finding an application for expressions like 'devoutness'.

I am suggesting, then, that such a context of behaviour, even in the absence of any recognizably religious talk or belief, may *already* force the description 'religious' on us. Suppose, however, that we do now add such talk to the original picture; that we think of such talk as growing out of the primitive ritualistic observations. There might for instance be talk of the 'gods' who inhabit the mountains – all sorts of elaborations of different kinds are imaginable. And now the rituals are explicitly regarded as showing reverence toward the mountain gods, concerning whom other stories come to be told and handed down between generations.

It is important to the case I am trying to make that we should not take for granted the introduction of a term such as that we perhaps translate by our word 'gods'. I am suggesting that what would make such a translation appropriate would be precisely the connection of the talk in which it occurs with the rituals. The term acquires its sense from its connection with the rituals (which does not preclude the possibility of further elaborations of the talk of a kind in which the connection with the rituals is not explicit or obvious).

We should be wary at this point of supposing that the role of such talk is to 'explain' why the rituals are performed. The analogy with pain may help to make my point clearer. We may say of an individual, 'He is limping because he has a pain in his leg': this *does* give an explanation of this individual's limping. But if we say, 'People tend to limp when they have pains in their legs' the situation is different. Here we have something much more like a conceptual, or 'grammatical' observation pointing to the connection between phenomena like limping and the application of the term 'pain'. It is hard to imagine someone who understood the term 'pain' who would not already recognize that pains in the leg tend to go with limping; and, of course, if he did *not* already understand the term 'pain', the remark 'People tend to limp when they have leg pains' could not explain anything.

Similarly, I am suggesting that to say of my tribesmen, 'They look to the mountains in order to show reverence to their gods', is not to *explain* why they look to the mountains, but to point to a conceptual connection between what they understand by their gods and their ritualistic practice. (*Of course*, this does not mean that what they understand by their gods will have no other conceptual connections.) We use the term 'gods' here because of its connection with their rituals. The case is quite different with, 'They look toward the mountains to seek animals to hunt'. This is explanatory and can be so because the term 'animals' can be given a sense quite independently of this habit of the tribesmen of looking toward the mountains.

What is the status of what I have been saying?[5] I do not, of course, want it to be taken as a sort of *a priori* history of the origin of religious belief. It is intended instead to suggest certain conceptual connections, rather in the manner of certain social contract accounts of the state. It may be asked (as it was by Sydney Shoemaker) why the talk and the stories should not come first and only subsequently come to be associated with rituals of reverence and worship. My answer is that this could, of course, happen, but that *before* the connection of such talk with worship and the like, we should have no reason to attach any religious significance to it, and hence we should have no reason to say that such talk concerned 'gods'. This would not preclude such talk becoming associated with worship; but then, so I contend, its sense (its grammar) would have undergone a fundamental change.

At this point I am touching on issues concerning the nature of the 'reference' of certain religious expressions of the kind I mentioned at the beginning of this section as being of particular interest to philosophers; and associated issues concerning the possibility of attributing 'existence' to what such expressions refer, or seem to refer to. Here I only want to remark that how a term refers has to be understood in the light of its *actual* application within its surrounding context in the lives of its users. I italicize '*actual*' by way of contrasting what I am talking about with some ideal 'application' imagined by philosophers and also with what users of the term may be inclined to *say* about their application of it if asked. (Compare how people actually do use the verb 'to think' and what both philosophers and non-philosophers may say about 'what thinking is'.) Notice that I am *not* saying the 'existence' of what is spoken of

5 The immediately following remarks are a response to a question put by Sydney Shoemaker, for which I am grateful.

simply consists in the fact that people talk in a certain way; I am saying that what the 'existence' of whatever it is amounts to is expressed (shows itself) in the way people apply the language they speak.[6]

II

Against the background of the foregoing discussion, let me now address myself more directly to some of the issues constantly raised in the contemporary literature of philosophy of religion. Much is made in this literature of the distinction between questions about truth and questions about meaning. Unfortunately, this by no means always reflects an adequate grasp of the relations between such questions. Commonly, questions about the meaning of religious language are conflated with questions about the possibility of verifying or falsifying theological claims, and questions about the rationality of religious belief are thought of as depending on the verifiability or falsifiability of the theological claims associated with particular forms of religious belief.

So we are presented with something like the following picture. The use of religious language is seen, by virtue of the meanings of the terms used, as committing the believer to certain 'existential' claims; these claims are articulated in theologies. Unless those theologies are verifiable or at least falsifiable, there is in principle no way of telling whether those existential presuppositions are warranted. Thus the believer's language has no clear meaning and his belief fails of rationality.

My aim is to undermine this position.

A man may be a very devout believer and have little understanding of, or interest in, the sophisticated arguments and doctrines of theologians. Perhaps he prays to the Lord Jesus Christ to intercede for him with God the Father; or he prays for the grace of the Holy Spirit. But perhaps too he is lost when it comes to learned discussions of the Trinity and of the sense in which Father, Son and Holy Spirit are One God. Does this make his belief, religiously speaking, inferior to that of the theologian? The difference between them is not like that between a laboratory technician who sets up an

6 Most of the qualifications in this paragraph are designed to meet comments made by John Hick.

experiment without having a clear idea of what he is doing and the scientist who directs him. That is to say, in respect of its scientific significance, the technician's activities differ from those of the scientist. There is no reason why the unsophisticate's belief should not be religiously deeper than that of the theologian.

Of course, the discussions of theologians affect the teachings of a church; and believers are brought up on those teachings which, in their turn, influence the forms of worship offered to the church's adherents. Thus the doctrine of Cathar theology that the world of matter is the work of the Devil was connected with the rejection of sacraments in the worship of the Cathar church.[7] The traffic, however, is not one way. Theological doctrines are not developed independently of their possibilities of application in the worship and religious lives of believers; and these latter have a certain, though not a complete, autonomy. I mean that if a doctrine were felt by believers to be hostile to their practices of prayer and worship, that would create a difficulty for the theological doctrine itself. I emphasize that the traffic goes in both directions and there is give and take. Believers' attitudes toward worship may be modified under the pressure of priests, for example, who in their turn are influenced by the theological doctrines in which they are trained in their church. But the attitudes of priests toward theological doctrines may also be affected by the resistances they encounter in the attitudes toward worship among their flocks. Of course, not all believers (or priests) will react in the same way, and thus arise possibilities of schism and heresy.

These jejune remarks are not absurdly intended as a contribution to ecclesiastical history or to the sociology of religion. They are meant to point to some of the complicated conceptual issues involved in the relation between theology and the language and practices of religion. In particular they are intended to raise questions about a pervasive view of such a relation: that the practices of believers are, at the most fundamental level, to be explained by the believers' 'belief in the truth' of certain theological doctrines. I have already suggested that worship (which may naturally take many forms) is a primitive human response to certain characteristic human situations and predicaments, that it is, to use a phrase of Wittgenstein's, part of the natural history of mankind. These practices will involve certain characteristic uses of language (again

7   See Fernand Niel, *Albigeois et Cathares*.

taking many different forms between which, however, analogies will be discernible). Given the existence of these practices and uses of language, theological doctrines will be elaborated which in their turn will react back on the practices and language of believers. In order to understand the sense of these doctrines (their 'relation to reality') we need to understand their application. This application takes place in contexts such as those of prayer and worship within which language is used according to a certain grammar. This grammar itself imposes limits on what will count as an acceptable theological doctrine, even though, as I have said, a doctrine may itself lead to modifications in the grammar of the language in which belief is expressed in worship.

The temptation to which we are subject in philosophizing about religion and theology is similar to temptations familiar enough in other areas of philosophy: that of seeming to see a quite different (and apparently more direct) kind of relation between language and reality which is a result of disregarding the complexities of the *actual* application of that language. In succumbing to this temptation we are led to the view that, if someone uses religious language, he is committed to a theory about the nature of the world which this language somehow enshrines. To deny, as I wish to do, that this is so is not to deny that one whose thoughts are couched in the language of religion has in a sense a very different view of the world from one who does not think thus. It is to deny that the difference is one between men who accept opposing theories.

I have spoken of the uses of religious language in the lives of believers, and fairly clearly the context of belief is fundamental to the sense which such language has. But the distinction I have just drawn – between a man whose thoughts are, and one whose thoughts are not, couched in the language of religion – is not the same as the distinction between one who has religious faith and one who does not. A difficulty here is that this last phrase may mark various distinctions. Tolstoy's Father Sergius, at the climax of the story, has lost his religious faith. But this loss can only be expressed by him – or by Tolstoy or by us – in the language of religion. The case is very different from that, say, of a Kai Nielsen, or of the 'sceptical young professor' who has a discussion with Sergius and who 'had agreed with him in everything as with someone who was mentally inferior. Father Sergius saw that the young man did not believe but yet was satisfied, tranquil and at ease, and the memory of that conversation now disquieted him.'[8] The difference is in some ways like that between the case of two music lovers who disagree on the relative merits of, say, Brahms and Wagner and the case of a music lover and one to whom music (and also what the music lover says (as we say, 'means nothing'. There are many to whom the language of religion means nothing. In trying to describe how they view life one would not need to use the language of religion. This is certainly *not* true of all those who 'do not believe' or who have 'lost their faith'.

The distinction between language and theory is obviously important to the way we approach the question of meaning in religion. It may be an important criticism of a theory that it has been made immune to falsification by the sandbagging of subsidiary hypothesis ('death by a thousand qualifications'). Sometimes a theory of which this is thought to be true may be said to have become 'meaningless'.

A theory requires a language in which it may be expressed. One theory may be opposed by another. Sometimes the opposition between the theories may be stated in a language which both share. In cases of very radical opposition this may not be possible in that the differences between the theories involve quite fundamental differences between some of the concepts expressed by shared verbal expressions, between the 'grammar', the mode of application, of those expressions. In such cases the opposition between the theories may not be satisfactorily stateable, but will make itself manifest in the differences in modes of application.[9]

Philosophers often assume that the very use of certain forms of linguistic expression itself commits the speaker to something like a theory about the nature of things.[10] And it will certainly be objected to what I have been saying that religious practices and beliefs can be made no sense of without the thought that their adherents make certain theoretical, theological presuppositions. 'Praying to God presupposes that there is a God to pray to.' This treats the phrase 'praying to God' as if it were analogous in a certain way to, say, 'writing to the Yugoslav ambassador at the Court of St James'. If I

8 Leo Tolstoy, *The Kreutzer Sonata and Other Stories*, p. 339.
9 The formulation of this point owes much to some trenchant criticisms of an earlier version for which I am greatly indebted to Cora Diamond.
10 This assumption is one of the targets constantly under attack in Wittgenstein's writings. It is discussed more fully in the final chapter of the present volume.

learn that Yugoslavia has broken off diplomatic relations with the United Kingdom, then obviously it would be mad of me to address letters to the Yugoslav ambassador, because I know that no such person exists.

Compare this with the following: 'What if someone were to say to me, "I am expecting three knocks at the door", and I were to reply: "How do you know that *there are three knocks?*" Wouldn't that be entirely analogous to the question, "How do you know that there are six feet?", if someone had said, perhaps, he believed that A is six feet tall?'[11] Before asking which of these cases is the better analogue for 'praying to God', let us consider the nature of the differences between the cases. The first and obvious difference is that while there is a clear sense to 'Does x exist?' where x = the Yugoslav ambassador, this is not so where x = three knocks or six feet. At least, it seems obvious to me, though some philosophers of mathematics talk as if they thought there were sense in questions about the existence or nonexistence of six feet. But I cannot go into such aberrations here.

A second and connected difference is this. If someone were to question the existence of a Yugoslav ambassador he would be questioning the point of my sending letters addressed in this particular way. My sending letters to other people – my wife, say, or the US ambassador – would not be in question. If it *were* to be called in question it would have to be done so separately and new arguments would be needed. That is, the rationality of the *practice* of sending letters to people would not be in question. On the contrary, that would be presupposed by the arguments against my sending a letter in this particular case; it is precisely because we in general understand the point of sending letters to people that we are able to see the senselessness of addressing a letter to a nonexistent person. In the first of Wittgenstein's examples a case completely parallel to this would be one in which my expectation of three knocks at the door is criticized on the grounds that the person I am expecting to knock does not exist or is not in the vicinity; again, such a criticism does not question, but presupposes, the point of knocking at doors. But that is not the case that Wittgenstein considers, or that is interesting. Insofar as we try to make sense of the question, 'How do you know that there are three knocks?' at all, I suppose we should have to construe it as a suggestion that the practice of knocking at doors (or knocking as much as three

11 *Philosophical Remarks*, III, no. 36.

times at doors) has fallen into desuetude or has for some reason lost its point. This latter kind of suggestion would be easier to imagine in the case of the second example – perhaps the country has gone metric and nobody understands talk about 'feet' anymore.

Philosophers who say that praying to God makes sense only if it is presupposed that God exists seem to be offering the following account. There is the practice of talking to people and making requests of them and the rationality of this practice is not in question. Particular instantiations of the practice may be criticized on the ground, for example, that the person addressed does not exist, is in no position to hear what is said, or in no position to fulfil the request. Praying is a particular instantiation of this practice and can, therefore, be treated in a similar way. Perhaps the method of establishing God's existence or nonexistence, or his capabilities, is peculiar; but that is thought of as a distinct issue.

Against this I want to argue that there is a difference in grammar between 'asking something of God' and 'asking something of the Yugoslav ambassador'. I mean that there is not merely a difference in the method it is appropriate to use in the two cases or in the nature of the requests it is appropriate to make, though both these things are true. I mean that what constitutes asking (and also answering) is different; or that the point of prayer (presupposed in any discussion of the rationality of particular cases of prayer) can only be elucidated to considering it in its religious context; that it cannot be elucidated by starting simply with the function 'making requests to x', substituting 'God' for 'x', and and then asking what difference is made by the fact that God has different characteristics from other xs. 'Making requests of x', that is, is not a function which retains the same sense whether 'God' or some name or description of a human being is substituted for 'x'.

It would certainly be wrong to say that the existence of the addressee is presupposed in the one case and not in the other. But this does not mean that the existence of the addressee *is* presupposed in both cases. It would be better to say that this question of 'existence' cannot arise in the one case in the way it can in the other, as the existence of six feet cannot arise in the case of someone wondering how tall a certain person is (which does not, of course, mean that the existence of six feet is 'presupposed' here). It is true that there would be something wrong with a man who claimed to be praying to God while saying he did not believe in God's existence. But would the same kind of thing be amiss as with a man who claimed to be writing to the Yugoslav ambassador while saying that he did not believe in the existence of such a person?

I feel inclined to say that, in the latter case, ceasing to see any point in writing is a *consequence* of ceasing to believe in the ambassador's existence, whereas ceasing to see any point in praying is an *aspect* of ceasing to believe in God.[12] In other words there are internal connections between ceasing to believe in God's existence and ceasing to see any point in prayer of a sort which do not hold between ceasing to believe in the ambassador's existence and ceasing to see any point in addressing letters to him. This is not to say that seeing a point in praying is identical with believing in God's existence. For one thing, believing in God has many other aspects: thinking of one's life in terms of obedience to God's will, for instance, or regarding all men as God's creatures. And, on the other hand, a man may cease to see any point in (at least *his*) praying without ceasing to believe in God's existence (as in the case of Claudius in *Hamlet*.) But ceasing to see any point in prayer is *one* form which ceasing to believe in God may take. A man who has had a religious upbringing and has prayed regularly as he was taught to do in childhood may someday realize that he is doing so quite mechanically and that it really 'means nothing to him'. He may express his realization in the thought; 'I don't believe that God exists'. But this will not necessarily mean that his attitude toward prayer is the *result* of his lack of belief.

But, it may be said, a man's belief in the nonexistence of the ambassador may also express itself, *inter alia*, in his no longer addressing letters to him; so can we not equally say that his attitude toward addressing letters thus is an 'aspect' of his not believing in the ambassador's existence? Yes, we can say this: there are internal connections *of a certain sort* here too. But in this case there is something that we can call 'discovering that the ambassador does not exist' which does not itself depend on any changed attitudes toward letter writing and the like. Here the changed attitudes are a consequence of the discovery, though we may also say that they express the fact that the discovery has been taken to heart. In

12   It is noteworthy that *this* is the phrase which comes naturally to mind here, rather than 'belief in the existence of God'. But the expression and discussion of religious doubts can and sometimes does involve 'questioning God's existence'. However, what such questioning amounts to is quite different from what is involved in questioning the existence of a man and can only be understood as an aspect of what, in general, is involved in 'religious doubts'.

religion, on the other hand, while there may be reflection on God's existence which may sometimes result in a cessation of belief, this reflection cannot itself be separated from reflection on prayer, worship, and the like. That is the form which reflection on God's existence takes.

When Michelangelo represented the creation of Adam, did he presuppose, or surmise, that there had been some event looking rather like this? And when we respond to his painting in a way which respects the religious ideas which it expresses, what sort of consideration is relevant? Well, one might speak here of how the power of God the Father and Adam's dependence are, on both sides, inseparably linked with love. God's power is not simply combined with his love; it *is* his love. And likewise with Adam's dependence on and love for his Creator: they are one. The point of this representation has to be seen in relation to the way in which worship and love are connected in the life of a believer. It is here that the picture is 'confronted with reality'. The form of representation, the sort of connection with reality, involved are totally different from that in a diagram of an accident presented with a claim on an insurance company. That is shown by the difference between the question it is appropriate to ask in the one case as contrasted with the other.

The kind of philosopher I am arguing against rightly makes much of the importance of being able to confront religious beliefs with reality if we are not to end up with a set of practices and beliefs hermetically sealed off from any relation to life or to our understanding of the world. The position is sometimes made to look by philosophers on both sides of the fence (and perhaps I have not always been careful enough about this myself) as though religion is something people engage in part of the time, taking care not to let it be confronted with what they are doing and thinking the rest of the week: sealing the door between the chapel and the laboratory to make sure there is no intermingling of the incense and the hydrogen sulphide. Of course, this is a travesty; and if it does characterize the lives of some believers, that is an important criticism of them: a criticism as much of the depth and sincerity of their religious beliefs as of their general intellectual honesty.

My point, however, is not that there cannot or should not be any confrontation between a man's religious convictions and the understanding of the world which he has in other contexts. But the form which 'confrontation with reality' takes is very misleadingly represented in terms of 'evidence for God's existence and non-existence'. The point is quite analogous to that made by Wittgenstein in his treatment of the attempt to explain the lack of an application for the expression 'reddish-green' in terms of the assertion that 'there is no such colour'. ('How do you know?', he asks.) ' "Yes, but has nature nothing to say here?" Indeed she has – but she makes herself audible in another way. "You'll surely run up against existence and non-existence somewhere." But that means against *facts*, not concepts.'[13] 'Nature' makes herself heard, both in the case discussed by Wittgenstein and in the case of religious language, by way of factual circumstances in which language is applied. These are of different sorts, including both general facts of human existence – such as the complex conditions of dependence of men on the rest of nature and on each other described so well by Spinoza; and also the more 'internal' facts of human nature, such as the rich and varied responses (exemplified, for example, in Simone Weil's writings) which may be elicited when religious language is used in, say, encounter with affliction. This is not to say that the expression 'God' really *refers* to such facts; it is to say that the reality which it expresses is to be found in the conditions of its application. Simone Weil makes a similar point in a different way: 'The Gospel contains a conception of human life, not a theology.' And, astonishingly: 'Earthly things are the criterion of spiritual things. . . . Only spiritual things are of value, but only physical things have a verifiable existence. Therefore, the value of the former can only be verified as an illumination projected on to the latter.'[14]

To say 'Earthly things are the criterion of spiritual things' is not to say they are *identical* any more than Wittgenstein was saying that 'inner processes' are identical with their 'outer criteria'. To think otherwise is to miss the crucial importance of the grammatical difference between the way we speak of the criteria and of that of which they are the criteria.

To say that expressions are used in accordance with different grammars is to say, among other things, that the kind of consideration which would count for or against one use would not do so in the case of the other; it is not to say that there are no relations between the two cases or even that the one is conceivable apart from the other. (Compare 'Then I murdered her', (a) in a

13   *Zettel*, no. 364.
14   *First and Last Notebooks*, p. 147.

report of what I did and (b) in a report of my dream.) Thus the grammar of the function 'x loves his children' is altered when 'my brother' or 'God' respectively is substituted for 'x'. What would go into an explanation of the sense of the one is of a different kind from what would go into an explanation of the sense of the other. And what, for example, would be relevant to the genesis of a doubt about the one is different from what would support a doubt about the other. This is so even though the two uses of 'loves' are connected: one would hardly be able to speak of God's love for his children if one could not also speak of the love of human fathers for their children; and conversely, the way in which we think about human love will be different if the notion of God as a loving father occupies a central place in our thought.

One might compare this situation with the relation between the way we use expressions like 'triangle', 'circle', etc., in our descriptions in geometry. A man would hardly be in a position to grasp the proof of Pythagoras's Theorem if he were not able to recognize triangular and square figures when he saw them. But, having grasped the proof, we will be able to think about such figures differently. I shall return to this comparison. But let me first consider some remarks by Michael Durrant[15] which seem to me to betray confusions – by no means peculiar to Durrant – about what is involved in speaking of 'differences in grammar' between the uses of expressions in religious and other contexts.

Durrant objects to the claim that sentences of the form 'God is F' (for example, 'God is infinitely good') 'have the function of determining what is possible within such a [for example, Christian] system of discourse'. In particular Durrant discusses the claim that to say 'God is infinitely good' is to insist on the senselessness of saying that God's goodness might sometimes 'fail to operate' and thus to point to a contrast between the grammar of 'good' as predicated of God and as predicated of some human agent. He develops an argument of A G. N. Flew's (part of Flew's polemic against 'death by a thousand qualifications') which relies on the assertion that if, in a given context, it makes no sense to speak of x's goodness 'failing to operate', then it can make no sense, in that context, to speak of x's goodness 'operating' either. Such a conclusion, Durrant says, no doubt rightly, must be unacceptable to a believer who wishes to speak of God's goodness.

15 *The Logical Status of 'God'*, Ch. 4.

The argument is presented as a general logical thesis which must be accepted independently of any individual peculiarities of context in which the expressions in question are being used. The thesis is that expressions like 'operating' and 'failing to operate' are 'necessarily correlatives, irrespective of context' and that this can be denied only

> at the cost of ignoring an important point. Granted, it is possible that in various "universes of discourse" (language games) what constitutes X operating or failing to operate will be different as between those language games, but this concession does not mitigate against [*sic*] the above argument – rather it supposes that in such areas of discourse the distinction between "operating" and "failing to operate" is itself in operation, which has to be denied on the construction of "God is infinitely F" as remarks of grammar concerning God.[16]

Durrant here commits an error similar to one of which the philosophers he is criticizing are often accused: that of treating the uses of expressions in religious contexts as if they are independent of their uses elsewhere. This leads him to overlook the possibility that when a believer speaks of God's goodness operating in the world, a contrast is indeed presupposed with cases in which goodness fails to operate in the world (cases, for instance, in which a human agent falls short of his usually high standards). But the contrast in this case is *itself a grammatical contrast*. The contrast *shows itself* in the different *applications* of the term 'goodness' by someone who talks of man's goodness and a believer who talks of God's goodness. If it is said that my account treats 'God is infinitely good' as saying nothing about the world, my reply is that this is so only if one takes as one's model an expression like 'Saint Francis was a good man'. Does 'red is darker than pink' say anything about the world? Not in the way that 'this material is darker than that' does (said of two pieces of material one of which is red and the other pink). 'Red is darker than pink' draws our attention to relations between the ways in which we use the 'red/pink' and the 'dark/light' distinctions respectively. 'God is infinitely good' draws attention to the difference in the way we use 'good' of God and the way we use it of human beings. This

16   *The Logical Status of 'God'*, p. 83.

difference, as I shall try to illustrate in part III of this chapter, affects the way we speak about things, people, and events in the world. So 'God is infinitely good' does reflect important things about the way we regard the world. To call it a 'grammatical' observation is not to cut it off from any relation with the real world.[17]

A believer who says that God's goodness cannot fail to operate is not in the position of being unable to attach any sense to talk of 'goodness failing to operate'. Indeed, the force of talking of God's infinite goodness does depend on an understanding that (in the case of man) goodness may, and frequently does, fail to operate. Such talk is largely a response to such an understanding – a response which in its turn provides a point of view from which the frequent failure of human goodness may be understood and treated differently than would otherwise be possible. In a similar way the force of speaking of the interior angles of a Euclidean triangle as necessarily equal to two right angles lies in the way such talk enters into our treatment of empirical triangles whose interior angles are found not to be equal to two right angles.

The following is an adaptation of a sentence on page 82 of Durrant's book, in which I have substituted geometrical expressions for the original references to God and his goodness.

> If it is part of the "grammar" of the interior angles of the triangle, or follows from that "grammar" that nothing can possibly constitute the triangle's interior angles failing to be equal to two right angles, then it must also follow from that "grammar" that nothing can constitute those interior angles being equal to two right angles either and if nothing can possibly constitute this then the notion of the triangle's interior angles being equal to two right angles is itself a nonsensical one, for the sense of "being equal to two right angles" is dependent upon the sense of "failing to be equal to two right angles"; they are correlatives.

As far as I can see, Durrant has given no reason for thinking that his argument, if good against the grammatical construction of 'God is infinitely good' is not equally valid against such a construction of 'the interior angles of the triangle are equal to two right angles'. Of

---

17 I have amplified my original presentation of this point as a result of discussion with Michael Durrant.

course, he might want to reject such a construction of geometry too
– and I cannot defend it here. But what seems initially clear is that
his own mode of argument is going to face him with the formidable
task of showing that sense *can* be attached to the idea that the
Euclidean triangle might fail to have interior angles equal to two
right angles.

III

I have already noted that while geometry does not describe the
properties of empirical structures, it does have an application in
such descriptions and makes possible ways of thinking and
techniques (for example, of measurement) in dealing with them
which would not otherwise be possible. *This* is its 'relation to reality',
which does not lie in its being a description of some other 'realm of
reality' distinct from that to which empirical structures belong. (This
expression, 'realm of reality', is a sticky one to which I shall come
back later.) Religious uses of language equally, I want to say, are not
descriptions of an 'order of reality' distinct from the earthly life with
which we are familiar. (Compare the passage from Simone Weil
which I cited in Section II.) These uses of language do, however,
have an application in what religious people say and do in the course
of their life of earth; and this is where their 'relation to reality' is to
be sought.

Earlier I discussed Michelangelo's representation of the creation
of Adam and remarked that, in it, God's power and love are
combined into a single whole: God's power here *is* his love. And
similarly for Adam's dependence on, and love for, his Creator. In
Plato's *Symposium* Agathon says, 'Whatever Love may suffer, it
cannot be by violence – which, indeed, cannot so much as touch
him; nor does he need to go to work by force, for the world asks no
compulsion, but is glad to serve him.' The model for God's power
in Michelangelo's representation (which corresponds to and enriches
an important strand in Christian – and not only Christian – religious
belief) is the love that moves the human heart by *consent*. What it
elicits in those who have a sense of it is not mere external
compliance but gladly willing compliance.

Without any explicit reference to religious ideas we do sometimes
speak of the limits of the kind of power which operates through
forces. We may perhaps say that there is something in a man which

force cannot reach. If we speak thus, we are making the kind of remark Wittgenstein might have called 'grammatical'. *Consent* (and especially loving consent) has to be *given*. If it seems to be exacted by force this is an illusion; what is so exacted is something different.

A test case for the application of this grammatical observation might be the position of Winston Smith at the end of George Orwell's *1984*, where the final triumph of the Party is expressed by saying that Winston 'loved' Big Brother. And this is, of course, presented as the ultimate outrage: a violation, as it were, of that which of all things we had believed cannot be violated. People may react in different ways to this part of the story and these differences may correspond to acceptance or rejection of the grammar of 'love' and 'consent', suggested in my remarks in the previous paragraph. I express no opinion on who would be 'right' in the case of such a disagreement. I am not sure that there *is* any answer to such a question, though it may certainly give rise to searching inquiries into the 'nature of the human condition' – as the works of Simone Weil, among those of many other writers, testify. This is characteristic of the kind of grammatical question which goes deep: the kind which interests philosophers.

It is possible to speak as Orwell seems, despairingly, to be speaking. But it is also possible (which does not mean easy) to maintain our conceptual limit. We may want to say that Winston's is not 'true' consent. And I think there are few who would want to say, or who would not at least feel a twinge about saying, that what Winston felt for Big Brother was genuine love. 'Love isn't *like* that', we want to protest. And we may go on to say that Big Brother is deluding himself if he thinks that his power is at last able to breach this conceptual barrier.

To think that 'God is Love' and at the same time to think of him as 'all-powerful' is not to *conjoin* the thoughts of someone as both loving and powerful, as we might in thinking of some benevolent human despot, and then to raise the qualities of love and power to the nth degree ($n = $ infinity). It is not so, any more than to think (geometrically) of the perfect sphere is to think of ball bearings manufactured with such perfect precision that no margin of error at all is presupposed in our thought of their sphericity. We have no clear idea of what this could mean in either case. We are making a conceptual, or grammatical, move in speaking of the power and love of God in the way we do; just as we are making a conceptual, or grammatical, move when we treat the idea of sphericity (which we may indeed have originally formed in connection with our observation of things like ball bearings) in a system such as Euclidean geometry. These moves will have their repercussions on what we say, and the ways in which we act in connection with the power of men or the sphericity of ball bearings, but they are not mere extrapolations from these cases. The way in which notions like infinity and perfection are here introduced makes the idea of any mere extrapolation unintelligible.

I can do no more than sketchily illustrate the kind of repercussion which the conceptual amalgamation of love and power as predicated of God may have on what we say and do in the course of our lives. The conception of God as all-powerful and all-good carries with it the idea that we owe him absolute obedience – 'absolute' not merely as regards external compliance, but, much more important, as regards the spirit in which one obeys, that is, with reciprocal love as expressed on the face of Michelangelo's Adam. When we are dealing with a benevolent despot – let us call him the Duke of Omnium – we can raise questions like: 'Is he really as powerful as we think?', 'Or as good?'. Connectedly we can raise the further question: 'Do we really owe him such absolute obedience?'; perhaps he is not as good as we thought and is demanding actions of us which we have no right to commit; or perhaps, though very powerful, there is the chance that he will sometimes be unable to detect or punish acts of disobedience. Such doubts will be relevant to our decision whether or not to obey him. In this case too, the doubts about the duke's power or about his goodness may well be quite independent of each other.

On the other hand, because God *is* Love and because here Love cannot be distinguished from Power, the situation is quite different. We cannot ask whether his love may not sometimes fail. (How can Love's power of love fail?) Or, if we *do* find ourselves forced to a question expressible in some such terms, it will not be the same kind of question as we ask of the Duke of Omnium; we shall be wondering rather whether we can continue to think in such terms at all; and I should think it could be only a rather shallow believer, or one whose life had been *extremely* sheltered, who never had to face such a doubt. Equally, because of the way power and love are conceptually linked in the case of God, we cannot ask whether our lapses of obedience might sometimes escape his notice or whether it is always true that vengeance is his and he will repay. This is because, if we are thinking in these terms at all, we are judging ourselves and our lives against a certain conception of the power of love. (Here I am touching on issues aspects of which receive fuller treatment in my essay 'Ethical Reward and Punishment'.)[18] Once again, if we find ourselves led, forced, to frame questions in these words, they will not be the questions we wanted to ask about the Duke of Omnium, but questions about whether we can find it in us to continue to think in such terms.

How are these ways of thinking to be applied to earthly situations? If we think that absolute obedience is due only to absolute love, we shall have a standard against which we can judge the extent of the obedience due to earthly authorities. (I am not suggesting that this is the *only* source of such a standard, but it will be connected in different ways with our thinking and acting in other aspects of our lives from standards which do not involve the idea of such a God.) We may say, for instance, 'I owe obedience to the Duke of Omnium's will only insofar as it is God's will that I obey him'; and this is a way, one way, of measuring the Duke of Omnium's will against some higher standard.

But the notion of obedience to God's will goes far beyond questions about the attitude to be taken toward the will of earthly authorities. (It also *connects* such questions with these further issues in characteristic ways.) Religious people will talk of 'obedience to God's will' when the question of obeying or not obeying temporal authorities is not an issue at all. To think in such a way is to approach moral questions from an entirely different point of view from that expressed, for example, in a utilitarian outlook, where actions are judged against the standard of what the agent achieves, or at least intends to achieve. Where an act has the character of 'obedience' on the other hand, care for the good rests with the will of the one who commands, not with the will of the one who obeys. And while this would sound like an abdication of moral responsibility of an objectionable sort where the will of a temporal authority is in question, the case is not so obvious where obedience is to love itself. The sense of such an attitude toward moral questions lies in its connection with very many different aspects of human existence. For instance, a man often will not be in a position to know whether he will have the strength or the favourable circumstances to carry his action through to the achievement of the good he aims at; and he will, arguably, *never* be in a position to know with certainty that what his action results in will be good in the way he had hoped, or to know that, even if it is, this good will not be outweighed by other future circumstances which he will be in no position to foresee or evaluate. Such consider-

18 *Ethics and Action*, p. 210 ff.

ations are familiar enough in criticisms of utilitarian morality. The point about action which has the character of 'obedience' is that it may be thought of as retaining its sense and value nevertheless.

Consider a stock case from the literature on utilitarianism. A man is threatened by a horrible death which I have the power to prevent. I know him perhaps to be an evil man whose continued existence is far more likely to result in more evil in the world than would his death, however horrible. (Though: how far can a man judge such things?) I may feel, however, that I cannot, that it is impossible for me, simply to leave him to his fate; and, if I am a religious man, this impossibility may present itself in the form that it is God's will that I should save him. Against this, I may feel that balancing the probabilities of good and evil involved in the alternatives open to me count for nothing. 'These are in the hands of God.'

I am not, of course, claiming that no objections can be mounted against such a way of thinking, that the arguments are all in favour of the believer and against, in this case, the utilitarian. I am not advocating the attitude of the believer, but trying to understand what it is. And my purpose in doing this is to suggest that it is in the discussion of questions like this, about the *application* of notions like the infinite power and goodness of God, that the character of 'necessity' with which such notions are predicated of God lies. We have to see the *point* of regarding such predications as necessary and that can only be done by seeing what their application looks like, not by trying to press them into prefabricated logicians' pigeonholes.

Finally I return, as I promised earlier, to the notion of 'different realms of reality'. My line of argument throughout has been that, if we want to understand the way in which a system of ideas is related to reality, we had best proceed by examining the actual application in life of those ideas rather than, as it were, fastening our attention on the peculiar nature of the 'entities referred to' by them. Philosophers who speak either for or against the notion of 'different realities' often give the impression that they conceive the matter as if they were discussing the differences between various planets. But when talk of 'different realities' is introduced *into philosophical discussion*, the issue is nearly always one involving the differences in grammar and the differences in application of different ways of speaking. And we only land ourselves in confusion if we treat it as one about the differences in the nature or properties of things referred to.

I italicized the phrase 'into philosophical discussion' just now. My reason for doing this was that it seems to me that expressions like 'a different reality', 'a higher order', may perfectly well be used by a religious believer, as part of the expression of his belief, without confusion. Similarly, I do not think any confusion is involved when someone, say, who cannot understand what is the attitude toward him of a woman he loves, says: 'I wonder what is going on in her head'; whereas someone who, in the course of philosophizing about the nature of thought, speaks about it as 'something which goes on in the head' (or anywhere else for that matter), *is* confused. The problem for the philosopher in all such cases is to understand the grammar, the proper application, of such expressions within the sort of discourse to which they belong.

There are features of religious belief and practice which seem to me to make it very natural, and not at all objectionable, for believers – and I do not mean only Christian believers – to find a use for expressions like 'not of this world'. This is connected with what I said about the importance of ritualistic practices for our understanding of what religious belief is. A feature of such practices is that they characteristically involve a demeanour which *sets them apart* from everyday, practical ways of behaving. I hope that my discussion has made it clear that I do not at all mean by this that such ritualistic practices (and the 'beliefs' which may be associated with them) *have no connection* with what the practitioners do, say, and think at other times in the course of their lives. On the contrary, were this the case, I should be inclined to think the rituals could only with very great difficulty be interpreted as having religious significance. Nevertheless, I think that such rituals do have the sense of expressing a contrast with the order (or the lack of order) in the lives of human beings. And I think too that this is connected with the ways in which expressions used in religious contexts differ importantly in their grammar and application from the same or similar expressions used in contexts where religious belief is not being explicitly emphasized. It is connected with the ways in which expressions used with a religious emphasis may serve to articulate a standard from the point of view of which the disorder and wretchedness which so largely characterize human life in its fundamental aspects may be assessed and come to terms with. Though what sort of 'coming to terms with' this is, I have neither the space nor the comprehension to say more about.[19]

19 I am very grateful to Stuart Brown for his comments on the original version of this essay, comments which helped me to say much better what I wanted to say.

9

Darwin, *Genesis* and Contradiction

A sympathetic reading of what Wittgenstein says about 'language games' in the treatment of particular philosophical issues may help to clear a lot of fog. We often get into difficulties through supposing that some of our most deeply rooted ways of speaking and thinking – for instance, about the thoughts and feelings of others, or of ourselves, about intention, expectation, remembering, meaning and understanding – stand in need of a kind of justification which, on reflection, we see as impossible to provide. Wittgenstein's often repeated remark: 'This language game is played', cuts the Gordian Knot by persuading us that the source of our difficulties lies further back than we had imagined: in confusions involved in the very asking of the question which generated the difficulties.

But in philosophy we constantly find that we achieve the removal of one set of puzzles only by embroiling ourselves in another, just as intractable as the first and bearing a strong family resemblance to it. That applies here. The activities, webs of human relationships and ways of speaking that go with these, which Wittgenstein calls 'language games', are not sealed off from one another. They are untidily tangled together, they react on each other, and, what is more, they may seem sometimes to come into conflict. Wittgenstein gives many examples. There is a striking one in *On Certainty*, section 239, where he refers to the belief of Catholics in the Virgin Birth and in the transformation of wine into blood in the Eucharist: beliefs which seem to fly in the face of what is normally accepted as evidence, not merely by non-Catholics, but by Catholics themselves in other contexts. If, in the face of such examples, we simply say: 'This language game is played', are we not abdicating our prime philosophical responsibility – the responsibility of seeking clarity and consistency? Aren't we giving hostages to irrationalism? So many have thought. If two beliefs contradict each other, both cannot be right. Shouldn't we investigate which, if either, *is* right? – But then we are faced again with the question we thought we had banished: the question about the *justification* of our language-games.

But before the fog descends on us again, let's try to be clear whether what we have here *is* a matter of two beliefs which 'contradict' each other in a sense which commits us to saying one of them must be 'wrong'.

It's extremely important to remember that Wittgenstein's use of the expression 'language game' is meant to focus our attention on systems of *action* rather than of ideas. It's not, for instance, to be confused with what logicians sometimes call a 'universe of discourse'.[1] We are to think of human beings responding systematically in action to real situations. This is important if we're to understand what he wants to say about 'contradiction'. In a conversation with Friedrich Waismann, Wittgenstein insisted that the idea of a '*hidden*' contradiction is confused. 'A contradiction is only a contradiction *when it arises*', he said; we shouldn't think of it as of a germ concealed in an organism, so that 'a man doesn't suspect anything and then one day he's dead'. He was thinking of the widespread idea that Russell's paradoxes showed there were hidden contradictions in the so-called logical foundations of mathematics; and that therefore there was a danger that mathematical reasoning would prove to be invalid.

Consider the following comment from Wittgenstein's 1939 *Lectures on the Foundations of Mathematics* on the "Liar Paradox", which is closely related to Russell's.

How do we get convinced of the law of contradiction? – In this way: We learn a certain practice, a technique of language; and then we are all inclined to do away with this form – on which we do not naturally act in any way, unless this particular form is explained afresh to us.

This has a queer consequence: that contradictions puzzle us. Think of the case of the Liar. It is very queer in a way that this should have puzzled anyone – much more extraordinary than you might think: that this should be the thing to puzzle human beings. Because the thing works like this: if a man says "I am

1   See the quotation from Michael Durrant, p. 124 above.

lying" we say that it follows that he is not lying, from which it follows that he is lying and so on. Well, so what? You can go on like that until you are black in the face. Why not? It doesn't matter.

Let me develop Wittgenstein's point in the following way: Suppose someone were to say that the contradiction in the Liar Paradox lay hidden in the verb 'to lie' from the start: so that, perhaps, without noticing it, we have been using a verb which is actually incoherent and all our talk about lying has been somehow 'invalid'. Clearly this would be absurd. What's happened is that we've discovered a new application of 'to lie', which looks analogous to other familiar uses, but which we find we don't know what to do with. But this doesn't undermine the old applications. All we need do is just *avoid* saying 'I am lying', except perhaps when playing party games or wanting to puzzle someone.

A contradiction is objectionable because we do not know what to *do* with it, how to go on. If we find that a certain way of speaking leads us to a situation where we don't know how to go on, we can either just avoid that way of speaking or, if for some reason we are attached to it (and we may have *important* reasons for being attached to a way of speaking), we can look for a way of reacting to it which we will find natural, and which will help to lead us further.

I want now to apply these ideas to difficulties people have felt in the juxtaposition of the *Genesis* story of Creation and Darwin's theory of evolution. I shall treat these difficulties as arising out of the uncomfortable coming together of two language-games. That's to say, I want to look beyond what appear to be contradictions in certain formulations of the two accounts of the origin of living things, towards the systems of practices and attitudes to which those accounts belong. Perhaps the nature of the conflict will look clearer from this point of view.

Genesis tells how God created heaven and earth and all living things in six days. This story has been fundamental to Judaeo-Christian religious belief. In the nineteenth century Darwin published *On the Origin of Species*, in which he claimed to show that living organisms belonged to an enormously long period of evolution, the mechanism of which was a combination of random variations in congenital characteristics and the 'survival of the fittest'. In this process some species became extinct and entirely new ones gradually came into existence.

The juxtaposition of these two accounts troubled many believers, who saw a conflict between them. Different people dealt with the conflict in different ways. Some thought they saw a straightforward contradiction between the two accounts and found it necessary to abandon one or the other. For some of these again this was a factor in a loss of religious faith, while others rejected Darwin's account of evolution as blasphemous and tried, sometimes successfully, to have the teaching of it in schools forbidden. Others again denied that there was any real contradiction and offered accounts of *Genesis* which would make it look compatible with evolutionary theory.

At this point I do *not* want to ask what may seem to be the natural question: namely, what would have been the "right" reaction? This is not, I hope, because I am being evasive, but because the very asking of such a question may already be a symptom of confusion. The idea behind the question is something like this: men have an interest in the origin of themselves and of the world in which they live. Genesis was an expression of that interest and constituted an attempt to satisfy it. The growth of natural science is another expression of the very same interest – so we might think; Darwinism is an outcome of that development and constitutes a different and rival answer to the questions raised in *Genesis*.

To think in this way is to suppose that the system of thinking that went with the acceptance of *Genesis* somehow contained, hidden within itself, a determinate relation to a yet unformulated Darwinism. This is a case of what Wittgenstein called the temptation to think of a possibility as a sort of 'shadowy reality', which is somehow 'there' before it has manifested itself. But, as he said to Waismann: 'A contradiction is a contradiction *only when it arises*'. And, he wrote in *Philosophical Grammar*: 'In logic there is no such thing as a hidden connection. You can't get behind the rules because there isn't any behind'.[2]

How are we to apply these remarks in the present context?

Let me say first that our understanding of such a phrase as 'an account of the origin of things' depends on the context in which we put it to use. Imagine a man who, before the scientific developments which made it possible for Darwin to raise *his* questions about the origin of species, had been brought up on the Bible. I mean, of course, not merely that he had been familiarized with the *text* of the Bible, but that he had been taught to connect that text with

2 Wittgenstein, *Philosophical Grammar*, II, I, 1.

characteristically religious attitudes and practices, such as worship and prayer. If asked where living creatures came from, such a man would have answered in terms taken from *Genesis*. Those would have been the terms in which he understood the question and that understanding would be connected with, for instance, worship of the Creator from whom no secrets are hid, rather than with the kind of patient observation and scientific reasoning which Darwin undertook in his expedition as naturalist aboard HMS *Beagle*.

On the other hand what Darwin and his scientifically minded readers understood by 'an account of the origin of species' presupposed those methods of scientific investigation. It's important to remember this. We may be so mesmerized by the idea (which I'm not saying is 'wrong') that Darwin was simply trying to describe a natural order which was 'there', independently of what he or anybody else thought belonged to it, that we forget that the very idea of such a 'natural order' was dependent on these *practices* of science in terms of which questions as to what did or did not belong to it could be thought as receiving an answer. This is part of what Wittgenstein is getting at in *On Certainty* section 167, when he notes that Lavoisier, observing the results of an experiment in his laboratory, does not say that perhaps it might turn out differently another time, but thinks in terms of a particular 'world picture' which he didn't invent but learnt as a child. This is not of course to say that Lavoisier does not make genuine discoveries of facts which obtain independently of what he thinks. It is to comment on what *counts* as a 'fact' in the context of such investigations.

The difference between the backgrounds of practice and belief which respectively underlie *Genesis* and *On the Origin of Species* are mirrored in striking differences in the forms of language used in the two books. 'And the Spirit of God moved upon the face of the waters.' What would Darwin's scientifically minded readers have made of it if *he* had said – *or denied, and I emphasize this* – any such thing? And we can ask the same question about the *Genesis* talk of God's finding his creation 'good' and 'blessing' his creatures. It's not that Darwin's account denies these things: such a denial would be as much out of place there as the contradictory assertion. It would be something like asking whether a piece belonging to a jigsaw of the *Mona Lisa* does or does not go in a certain position in a jigsaw of Picasso's *Les Demoiselles d'Avignon*.

Here I want to be very careful how I express what I intend in reminding you of all these things. I want to *weaken* the idea that the

Genesis account of the creation of living creatures in two days by God *must* be seen as coming into headlong collision with Darwin's insistence that complex species gradually evolved over an enormously long time-span. That's to say, I am suggesting that this is not the *only* possible way open to us of viewing the situation. My suggestion has been that it is not obvious that we have a single, unambiguous notion of 'an account of the origin of things', such that we can say that *Genesis* and Darwin offer two mutually contradictory versions of such an account. On the other hand I *don't* want to say that we are merely punning if we say that both are 'accounts of the origin of things'; or that the two stories have absolutely nothing to do with each other. I want to say that, looked at from one point of view, they seem to contradict each other, and looked at from another point of view, they seem not to. But I don't want to say that either point of view is '*the* right' one. We must not lose sight of either.

In *Philosophical Remarks* Wittgenstein wrote: 'Show me *how* you are searching and I will tell you *what* you are looking for'.[3] In so far as we see *Genesis* and *On the Origin of Species* as the outcome of different kinds of search, we shall see the respective objects of those searches as equally diverse. This alters the terms in which we see the relation between the two books, but it does not of course answer the question: What *is* the relation between them?

I want to say now that there is no universally valid, definitive answer to this question. It's a question individuals have to answer for themselves by considering what significance religious worship and scientific investigation have in their lives; and by meditating on whether, and if so how, they can live with both of them.

People have different kinds and degrees of commitment to the activities they take part in and to the traditions and institutions which touch their lives. This is obviously true both of religion and of science. A scientist, for instance, may see his work as a way of making a comfortable living, as a vehicle of his ambition for prestige; it may satisfy a fascination with solving puzzles; and it may express his wonder at the glory of the universe. (There's a hint of both these last two attitudes in Darwin's characterization of his problem as 'that mystery of mysteries' in the Introduction to *On the Origin of Species*.) Of course the possibilities I have mentioned aren't exhaustive; neither are they, for a given individual, mutually exclusive, though their juxtaposition may create internal tensions. A man's reaction to

3 *Philosophical Grammar*, III, no. 27.

the confrontation between *Genesis* and Darwin will be very much influenced by the kind of relation, in this sense, that he has to scientific inquiry; and also of course to religious worship.

I spoke just now of scientific inquiry as sometimes expressing a man's sense of wonder at the world; and the same can be said of some expressions of religious worship – think of some of the Psalms for instance. In what I said earlier I emphasized the diversity of, respectively, scientific and religious attitudes and practices. However, I don't think it's any accident that we can sometimes use this same expression – 'a sense of wonder' – of both. We may feel like saying that the two sets of attitudes can express a common tendency. The different expressions of this tendency have grown far apart and they sometimes come into collision. But in spite of the potential conflict the analogies which we can see between them betray their common root in a tendency which in a sense unites mankind. Their conflicts may also divide mankind – and divide a man from himself. But what divides men most bitterly is usually not far distant from something which unites them. Otherwise, why should these be *conflicts* rather than simply *differences*?

It's worth reflecting here on something Wittgenstein says of his own work in his foreword to *Philosophical Remarks*. That book looks about as far removed as it could well be in style and content from, say, the Psalms; and yet he was able to write: 'I would like to say: "This book is written to the glory of God", but nowadays that would be chicanery, that is, it would not be rightly understood.'

I have been suggesting that an examination of apparent contradictions like those between *Genesis* and Darwinism may sometimes take the form of an examination of certain kinds of conflict *in oneself*, where what is important is to clarify the nature of one's commitments. Wittgenstein leads us in the direction of this view of the matter through his emphasis on the role of our language in our practices and in the lives we lead. In doing so, he at once forges a link between contemporary philosophy and the tradition exemplified by Socrates' response to the Delphic injunction: 'Know thyself', and gives an exciting new twist to that tradition. What a man finds it possible or impossible to say, the difficulty or ease with which he can combine diverse ideas, are important indications of the kind of man he is. And in clarifying his own mind about what he can and can't accept, a man is making important discoveries about himself: discoveries that may be barely distinguishable from decisions about what manner of man he wants to be. All these issues are involved in the examination of what seem to be deep contradictions in one's thought. It is not just a mechanical exercise in which the work has, as it were, already been done in a hidden realm by logic and simply needs to be revealed to view.

10

"Eine Einstellung zur Seele"

The focus of my remarks will be *Philosophical Investigations*, Part II, Section iv, from which the phrase that gives me my title is taken. Let me remind you of the opening paragraphs of that section.

"I believe that he is suffering" – Do I also *believe* that he isn't an automaton?

It would go against the grain to use the word in both connexions.

(Or is it like this: I believe that he is suffering, but am certain that he is not an automaton? Nonsense!)

Suppose I say of a friend: "He isn't an automaton". What information is conveyed by this, and to whom would it be informative? To a *human being* who meets him in ordinary circumstances? What information *could* it give him? (At the very most that this man always behaves like a human being, and not occasionally like a machine.)

"I believe that he is not an automaton", just like that, so far makes no sense.

My attitude towards him is an attitude towards a soul [*eine Einstellung zur Seele*]. I am not of the *opinion* that he has a soul.

For those who want a philosophical pigeon-hole into which Wittgenstein can be neatly popped, there is a good deal that will be disconcerting in these few sentences. Those who still, despite Wittgenstein's own many hints about the mistakes involved in this, harbour the suspicion that Wittgenstein was a behaviourist at heart, may think they find encouragement in the remark that the most that 'He isn't an automaton' could convey to anyone is that he always behaves like a human being. But then they may well feel themselves brought up short by Wittgenstein's use of the word 'soul' ['*Seele*'], feeling that it has an almost provocatively 'dualist' flavour about it. And that's by no means the end of the matter. Both behaviourists and dualists do at least think that to regard another man as a conscious being with thoughts, feelings, emotions, hopes, intentions, etc. is to have certain beliefs about him – though they differ of course about the nature of those beliefs. But Wittgenstein seems to be denying this. It's not a matter of holding a belief or opinion at all, he seems to say, but a matter of having a certain sort of 'attitude' to him.

The contrast between 'belief' and 'attitude' will stimulate yet another salivary gland through a reflex carefully conditioned in C. L. Stevenson's work on ethics. Doesn't Wittgenstein think, then, that the distinction between an automaton and a conscious human being is a genuine objective, factual distinction at all, grounded in a real difference in the nature of things? Is it just a matter of the attitude we take up? So it's all arbitrary and subjective and we can *deny* the difference without fearing that we're saying anything contrary to the way things are in reality!

It will help us to consider first another passage in which Wittgenstein uses the word '*Einstellung*' in a different, though closely connected, context.

> I tell someone I am in pain. His attitude to me will then be that of belief; disbelief; suspicion; and so on.
>
> Let us assume he says: "It's not so bad". – Doesn't that prove that he believes in something behind the outward expression of pain? – His attitude is a proof of his attitude. Imagine not merely the words "I am in pain" but also the answer "It's not so bad" replaced by instinctive noises and gestures.[1]

Whereas in my earlier quotation from II, iv Wittgenstein was concerned with a *contrast* between believing that someone is in pain on a particular occasion and reacting to him as to something other than an automaton, here in I, section 310 he *is* discussing the belief that he is in pain in particular circumstances. And what he writes must dispel any idea that II, iv involves a quasi-technical distinction between 'attitude' and 'belief' analogous to that introduced by C. L.

1 *Philosophical Investigations*, I, no. 310.

Stevenson. For here he is quite willing to characterize belief and disbelief themselves as 'attitudes'.

His point, I take it, is to urge that if we want to be clear what a belief (for instance) that someone is in pain comes to, we should not allow ourselves to be hypnotized by its verbal expression ('He is in pain'), but should look at the whole range of behaviour, demeanour, facial expression, etc. in which such verbal expressions are embedded, and with which they are continuous, which give the words their particular sense and by some of which indeed the words may often be replaced. The purpose of such an enquiry is not to show that what we are dealing with here is not 'really' a case of belief at all, but something else. That would quite misleadingly imply that we have a secure paradigm of what it is to believe something which does *not* draw its sustenance from the expressive behaviour in which it is embedded.

The sentence 'His attitude is a proof of his attitude' is not a rejection of the claim that he really believes something. It is a rejection of a particular characterization of what he believes – namely that 'he believes in something behind the outward expression of pain'. But Wittgenstein's rejection of this does not take the form of insisting that all he believes is that the other person is behaving in a certain way. His belief concerns someone to whom he has '*eine Einstellung zur Seele*' and this helps to make his belief what it is.

We might say that what Wittgenstein is really protesting against in section 310 is a sort of *impatience*. We are so familiar with the sort of behaviour and expressive demeanours that go with typical human feelings and emotions and with the expressive *responses* to such behaviour on the part of others, that we think we have a firm grasp of it and do not stop to look properly at it. 'His attitude is a proof of his attitude' means 'Just stop and look at what his attitude does actually consist in, perhaps you will be surprised at the subtleties and complexities involved; and when you have noticed them perhaps you will be less inclined to suppose that their significance must depend on something below the surface of which they are merely symptoms.'

Here is an example.

Portia, when Anna looked straight at her, immediately looked away. This was, as a matter of fact, the first moment since they came in that there had been any question of looking straight at each other. But during the conversation about Pidgeon [Anna's former lover], Anna had felt those dark eyes with a determined innocence steal back again and again to her face. Anna, on the sofa in a Récamier attitude, had acted, among all she had had to act, a hardy imperviousness to this. Had the agitation she felt throughout her body sent out an aura with a quivering edge, Portia's eyes might be said to explore this line of quiver, round and along Anna's reclining form. Anna felt bound up with her fear, with her secret, by that enwrapping look of Portia's: she felt mummified. So she raised her voice when she said what time it was.[2]

This is unquestionably a description of an emotional, even spiritual, encounter; a description, however, couched largely in 'physical' terms.[3] It would be a fine scene for an illustrator to draw! Of course, the significance of what is described here depends on the whole context in which the encounter takes place, on the history in which Anna's slyness, her past relations with her lost lover Pidgeon, her equivocal relations with her husband and with her husband's orphaned half-sister Portia, have been displayed to the novel's readers. Actually, I feel that what I have just said is too weak. It's not just that the *significance* of what's said about the bodily interaction between Anna and Portia depends on that background; that is, it's not a matter of our seeing the bodily situation and interpreting it. Rather, I feel inclined to say, the physical interaction between the two itself is what it is and is revealed as what it is only within such a web of human relationships. I think that could be denied only by someone who insisted on ascribing a misleadingly narrow sense to the word 'physical'. (This might, incidentally, be said to be one of the main troubles about 'physicalism' as a philosophical theory.)

But the stage my discussion has reached takes me back to the passage from *Investigations*, II, iv, with which I started and which is my main concern. I said just now that the physical interaction between Anna and Portia is, and is regarded as, what it is only

---

2 Elizabeth Bowen, *The Death of the Heart*, end of Chapter 3.

3 Cf. *Philosophical Investigations*, II, v (p. 179): ' "I noticed that he was out of humour." Is this a report about his behaviour or his state of mind? ("The sky looks threatening": is this about the present or the future?) Both; not side by side, however, but about the one *via* the other.'

within a complex web of human relationships. It is a feature of such relationships that those who are involved in them have to each other *eine Einstellung zur Seele*. What we have to consider next is the relation between *this* notion and the particular beliefs people may have about each others' thoughts and feelings on particular occasions. And this is precisely at the centre of Wittgenstein's attention in the passage before us.

Human beings normally treat each other and react to each other differently from the ways in which they treat automata (and also other living beings). It seems natural to ask why this is, as David Wiggins for instance does (amongst other things) in the final chapter of his *Sameness and Substance*.[4] And if one does ask it, it is natural to answer by ascribing to human beings certain beliefs about each other (as Wiggins also does). Wittgenstein is rejecting this whole way of treating the matter.

As we have already seen, he has no objection to speaking of 'belief' in connection with the ascription of *particular* states of thought and feeling to people. His point here is that we cannot characterize the *general* view, or conception, we have of other people in the same way. To start with, Wittgenstein notes that 'it would go against the grain' to use the same word 'believe' in 'I believe that he is suffering' and 'I believe that he isn't an automaton'. The suggestion here is that to do so would be to mask how fundamental are the differences between what I am trying to say in the two cases. There is no suggestion that we cannot appropriately be said to 'believe' that another person is suffering. It is rather that this case is fundamentally different from that of acknowledging a man *as* a man rather than an automaton. The difference cannot, for instance, be measured on a single scale of 'degrees of belief'. Nor is it the case, as we shall see, that 'to believe him not to be an automaton' is, as it were, simply a summation or amalgam of lots of particular beliefs about how he is thinking and feeling on this or that occasion.

Before showing this, however, I want to note that Wittgenstein's objections to the use of the word 'believe' here do not rest *merely* on the too close parallel it suggests with 'I believe that he is suffering'. ' "I believe that he is not an automaton", just like that, so far makes no sense.' Here, Wittgenstein's point is that it is not clear what information I would be given if someone were to say to me of a man 'He isn't an automaton'. '(At the very most that this man always

4 Ch. 6, no. 9.

behaves like a human being and not occasionally like a machine.)'
And of course, if the remark *were* made in circumstances which gave
it the sense expressed in that parenthesis of Wittgenstein's, it would
lose its connection with the philosophical problem that interests us
here: how, namely, not being an automaton is connected with
behaving in a normal human way. What Wittgenstein is saying is
that we find no application for 'He isn't an automaton' to a human
being concerning whom no question has arisen whether he *behaves*
normally. If I know of a man that he behaves like a perfectly normal
human being, I am not given any further information about him in
being 'told' that he is not an automaton. But this is not to say that
we can settle philosophers' worries about the nature of the
distinction between human beings and automata just by pointing to
their characteristically different ways of behaving. There is
something else: but not a further piece of information about the
human beings whose behaviour we observe.

How is my regarding someone as other than an automaton related
to my having some particular belief about how he is feeling or
thinking? The most obvious thing to say, first of all, is that it is a
much more *general* view of a person. My belief that someone is
suffering is confined to a particular (though possibly extended)
occasion, whereas my view of him as not being an automaton is a
view of the kind of being he in general is. But it takes only a little
reflection to see that such a view of the kind of being he in general
is cannot be simply a generalization of my particular beliefs about
how he feels and thinks at different times during his life (of which
my belief that he is suffering now would be an example). If that *were*
so there would be no reason why I shouldn't think that, though for
most of the time he is an automaton, he experiences something
(suffering, for instance) on just *one* occasion. Of course I can *say* I
believe this. The difficulty is to see in what circumstances my saying
it would be taken as a serious expression of belief.

Again, if my view of someone as a conscious human being were
simply a general summation of my beliefs about his states of
consciousness on this or that occasion, it looks as though it would
have to be very much more liable to doubt (because so much more
ambitious) than any such particular beliefs. But if anything, things
are the other way round: though not (as Wittgenstein remarks)
because the fact that he is not an automaton is something of which I
am certain. Rather, because doubt and certainty – at least as
modifications of belief – don't come into the matter.

In this connection it's important to notice the obvious enough fact that it's no more relevant to my view of a man as other than an automaton that he should *be*, than that he should *not* be, suffering. And the difference between the way I regard a man and the way I regard an automaton is not that I think the one conscious and the other unconscious, since we can no more intelligibly say of an automaton that it is unconscious than that it is conscious. I can say of a man whose brain has been damaged in an accident, say, that he has been unconscious for several months – I could say this even though he had showed signs of bodily movement, but I could not say anything like this of an automaton. And this, I think, supports my contention that his not being an automaton is not a generalization *from* his states of consciousness at particular times, so much as a *condition* of his having (*or not having*) any states of consciousness at particular times.

But this still leaves it quite unclear how this 'condition' should be understood, what it amounts to, and how it is related to particular attributions of specific states of consciousness. Concerning this last point, what I have so far said does not commit me to denying – and I am far from wanting to deny – that typically, when we ascribe a state of consciousness to someone on one occasion, we take it for granted (it goes without saying) that he has had other states of consciousness on other occasions. And this 'taking for granted' is *part* of what Wittgenstein would have included in '*eine Einstellung zur Seele*'. But it is not a hypothesis, or series of hypotheses, about any particular modes of his consciousness on specific occasions. An attitude towards a soul is not something I have only to someone I know fairly well and about whose life I am in a position to know very much. It is directed also towards strangers whom I meet, or even pass, in the street.

> The human beings around us exert just by their presence a power which belongs uniquely to themselves to stop, to diminish, or modify, each movement which our bodies design. A person who crosses our path does not turn aside our steps in the same manner as a street sign, no one stands up, or moves about, or sits down again in quite the same fashion when he is alone in a room as when he has a visitor.[5]

5   Simone Weil, 'The *Iliad*, Poem of Might', *A Simone Weil Anthology*.

The important phrase in that passage from Simone Weil is 'just by their presence'. Our characteristic reactions towards other people are not based on any theory we have about them, whether it is a theory about their states of consciousness, their likely future behaviour, or their inner constitution. We may well, of course, have our ideas about all these matters. We may for instance notice at once that someone in the street is joyful or distressed; and we have our expectations concerning their likely behaviour, at least to the extent that many things would astonish us. We should be aghast if someone were deliberately to approach a stranger and gouge out his eye.[6] But such recognitions and expectations, together with our own reactions to other people, are on the same level, equally primitive. That is not to deny that often our reactions *are* based on reflections about others' states of mind, or probable future behaviour. The point is, first, that it is not always so; and second, that our *un*reflective reactions are part of the primitive material out of which our concept of a human person is formed and which makes such more sophisticated reflections possible.

Let me expand this point by way of some remarks about the actual German *phrase* Wittgenstein uses in *Investigations*, II, iv – '*eine Einstellung zur Seele*'. I cannot think of a better English rendering than Professor Anscombe's 'an attitude towards a soul', but there is, all the same, a subtle shift of emphasis in the translation. Firstly, the use of the definite article in the German ('*zur*' = '*zu der*') suggests more strongly than does the English 'towards a' an internal relation between the *Einstellung* and its object. In other words, – we need the concept of *Seele* in order to characterize the *Einstellung* for what it is: even, as I think the Elizabeth Bowen example brings out, to characterize certain of the physical features of the *Einstellung*.

If this sounds wild, consider the analogy of laughing at something seen as funny. Imagine someone laughing at one of the more extravagant scenes in Act II of Rossini's *Barber of Seville*. And now imagine laughing in just the same way at the portrayal of Peter's grief after his denial of Jesus in Bach's *St Matthew Passion*. I think everybody ought to feel uneasy at my phrase 'in just the same way'. It isn't merely that there's an incoherence in the idea of someone's finding the scenes 'funny' in the same way (though of course that's one important aspect of the matter). It's also that, in the sense in which to describe someone as 'laughing at' something he finds funny

6   Simone Weil, 'Human Personality', *A Simone Weil Anthology*.

is to describe his physical response (and will anyone deny that it is?), we cannot fit a conception of 'the same physical response' into a description of someone confronting first *The Barber of Seville* and then the *Matthew Passion*. The *New Yorker* cartoon by Charles Addams, discussed above in chapter 3 exploited this conceptual point. It depicted rows and rows of grossly guffawing faces as seen from a music hall stage with, in an inconspicuous position near the back, the face of Leonardo's *Mona Lisa*: in that context it would have been impossible to describe her as *La Gioconda*. As Wittgenstein remarks in quite another context: 'the purely corporeal can be uncanny'.[7]

I have mentioned above an 'internal relation' between an *Einstellung* and its object. The point can also be put another way. Instead of saying that '*eine Einstellung zur Seele*' is an attitude towards a particular object, characterized by the fact that that *is* its object, let me say that the concept of the soul serves to highlight certain features of my attitude (which, however, it can only be intelligibly said to have in certain kinds of context). Similarly, if my reaction to what someone says is described as 'laughing at a witticism', that is to see my reaction in the light of the concept of the witty. Consider another analogy from Wittgenstein's writings. 'The miracle of nature. One might say: art shows us the miracles of nature. It is based on the concept of the miracles of nature. (The blossom, just opening out. What is *marvellous* about it?) We say: "Just look at it opening out!" '[8]

Someone who responds like that to the opening blossom is seeing it as a miracle of nature. We can say that, of course, only because it is an instance of countless analogous human responses to natural events; in that respect it has a generality that enables us to speak of it as exemplifying a certain concept. That concept ('the miracles of nature') explicitly characterizes the *objects* of such responses rather than the responses themselves, and it is extremely important that such responses are typically made to some objects rather than others. If someone were to make a similar gesture, use similar words with a similar expression, towards a mound of rotting flesh, for example, we should be puzzled. Indeed, there are some difficulties about my use of the word 'similar' there. This demeanour, in such a context, would certainly strike us very differently from that of

7 *Culture and Value*, p. 50.
8 *Culture and Value*, p. 56.

someone confronted by a blossom opening out. (This is not to deny that even a heap of rotting flesh might, in suitable circumstances, be seen as a miracle of nature; as Wittgenstein's remark also suggests, an artist might succeed in displaying it in that light.)

Most of these remarks apply, *mutatis mutandis*, to the idea that 'my attitude towards him is an attitude towards a soul'. Particularly important is the point about the typicality of such responses as a condition for the applicability of a certain concept (in the present instance the concept of the soul). This is relevant, for instance, to the uneasy feeling many may have that Wittgenstein's position is in a certain way 'subjectivist'. I shall return to it later.

I want next to make a few observations about the word '*Einstellung*', which seems to me to have certain connexions in German which are lacking, or at least less well marked, with 'attitude' in English.

Many of you will remember a song made famous by Marlene Dietrich, called 'Falling in Love Again'. In the original German version it contains the line: '*Ich bin von Kopf zu Fuss auf Liebe eingestellt*'. I don't know how that is rendered in the English version of the song, but I would translate it roughly as 'I am all set for love from head to foot'. The participle '*eingestellt*' is of course from the same root as the noun '*Einstellung*'.

Now it is perfectly true that in its actual use the English word 'attitude' is not *only* applied in situations where one speaks of attitudes either deliberately adopted or at any rate more or less subject to the will and controlled by a deliberative intelligence. Nevertheless, I think it is true to say that such ideas *have* been prominent in what fairly recent philosophers, who have made extensive use of the concept of an attitude, have said or implied about that concept. And I have already suggested that one source of resistance to Wittgenstein's treatment of our present subject may well be the feeling that an attitude, after all, may be taken up or abandoned almost at will. On the other hand, the suggestion in the line I have quoted from Marlene Dietrich's song is quite different. To be '*von Kopf zu Fuss auf Liebe eingestellt*' is to be in a certain condition whether one likes it or not. And I think this is the suggestion in Wittgenstein's '*Meine Einstellung zu ihm ist eine Einstellung zur Seele*'. There is no question here of an attitude which I can adopt or abandon at will. My *Einstellung* may no doubt be strengthened, weakened or modified by circumstances[9] and to some

---

9 Cf. Simone Weil, 'The *Iliad*, Poem of Might', *passim*.

extent by thought too, but usually, in given circumstances, it is a condition I am in vis-à-vis other human beings without choosing to be so. This aspect is strongly brought out by the passage from Simone Weil I quoted earlier describing some of the ways in which our own behaviour is affected, quite unconsciously, by the mere presence of other human beings. This, to use a phrase that Wittgenstein himself applied in various contexts to his description of aspects of human life, is 'part of the natural history of mankind'.

I want to end this chapter with some remarks about what Wittgenstein is doing when he uses *this* expression – and other analogous things. In the first place he is obviously emphasizing the *instinctive* character of the phenomena he is interested in and the analogy between a description of them and the sort of description of the habits of a species one might find in a biological study.

Wittgenstein might be compared from this point of view with David Wiggins, another philospher who has recently emphasized the biological dimension of those features of human beings that go with our conception of what he calls 'personhood'. Though the point of the comparison will be to emphasize the strong *contrast* between their approaches, I should like to say first of all that they are both interested in elucidating certain striking facts: that, as Wiggins puts it, 'presented with the human form we entertain immediately a multitude of however tentative expectations'.[10] We also of course respond to other human beings in characteristic ways and apply concepts to them, many of which we would not apply or, if at all, would apply differently to other kinds of being.

What sort of question do these striking facts raise and what sort of elucidation do they require? Connectedly, what kind of description is appropriate to these facts? For Wiggins, entertaining such expectations, applying such concepts, etc. is *classifying* the being with which we are confronted as belonging to a certain 'natural kind', namely as being a *person*. And that means regarding it as

> a persisting material entity essentially endowed with the biological potentiality for the exercise of all the faculties and capacities conceptually constitutive of personhood – sentience, desire, belief, motion, memory and the various other elements which are involved in the particular mode of activity that marks the extension of the concept of a person.[11]

10 *Sameness and Substance*, p. 222.
11 *Sameness and Substance*, p. 160.

On this view, then, reacting to someone as a person is in the first instance classifying him as belonging to a certain natural kind and this in its turn involves having certain quasi-theoretical beliefs about him. Anything that is peculiar to our attitudes towards and treatment of persons flows from and is justified by the beliefs we hold about what properties persons essentially possess; and what justifies these beliefs is ultimately scientific investigation. That is why Wiggins attaches so much importance to holding that *person* is a natural kind concept: 'Persons are a class of organisms, and they are identified under concepts that are nomologically conditioned.' Moreover, 'the values recognized by persons ... (are) ... the outcome of the impinging of the external world upon persons constituted as persons are constituted.'[12] Biological science will give an account of how the external world impinges on persons, thereby giving an explanation of the values they recognize. Whether Wiggins would also want to speak of 'justification' at this point I am not clear. But a desire for justification is certainly present in the argument as a whole. For instance, as we shall see, Wiggins certainly thinks that our expectations of, and immediate responses to, human beings need a justificatory underpinning in the form of a theory of human nature.

The important fact that underlies this idea is that my reaction to a particular human being on a specific occasion is typical of my reaction to *any* human being. It has a certain generality about it and the important question is where we are to locate this generality and how we are to characterize it. It is temptingly easy to think it must lie in certain general beliefs I hold about human beings.

Suppose you and I are present when a man is being given some terrible news – the death of someone he loves perhaps. I say 'poor man! How he will suffer' and you ask, 'What makes you think he will suffer?' That would be a strange question and I should most naturally assume at first that you had not grasped the situation, did not realize what was going on, what he was being told, etc. Of course, if the question is being asked in a philosophical way, that will not be the point. It will be an invitation to reflect that my supposition that this man will suffer is rooted in my general experience of human life. The outcome of that general experience is that I should expect *any* man to suffer in such circumstances.

At this point I am perilously close to formulating a syllogism: 'All men suffer at such news. This is a man hearing such news.

12 *Sameness and Substance*, p. 187.

Therefore. . . .' Why do I say 'perilously'? After all the inference is valid and I don't dissent from the premises. The trouble is that, as an account of how I came to fear that this man would suffer, the syllogism is a completely mythological construction. Yes, the life I have lived with other human beings is responsible for my reaction, but not by way of any general theoretical beliefs it has led me to hold – though it may of course be that I do hold such beliefs. Making the same point in a different connection, Wittgenstein remarks, 'the real generality lies elsewhere'.[13]

The real generality in the present instance is that my reaction to the man I see receiving bad news is a typical, characteristic, constantly repeated feature of the human life in which I share. I may of course observe that life and theorize about it, but I am also part of it and that relation of participation in a life with other human beings (which is an aspect of our 'natural history') itself introduces a generality into my particular reaction to a man on a specific occasion. I said a moment ago that I should expect any man to suffer in such circumstances. But that should not be construed as: 'I believe that any man would suffer in such circumstances and I believe that therefore this man will suffer in these circumstances.' The correct expression of my belief is simply 'I believe that this man will suffer in these circumstances'; and the belief thus expressed is one which I should hold concerning any other man in like circumstances; moreover so would anyone else who understood the situation.

This is not of course a generality which could play the same role as that in the major premiss of a syllogism or, for that matter, as that in a theory about what kind of thing a person essentially is. But then my belief does not require any such justification; nor is it based on any reason (over and above the knowledge that he is receiving bad news). In these circumstances I just do expect that he will suffer, and most people would accept that as a reasonable expectation; that's the sort of thing almost everybody calls 'a reasonable expectation' in such circumstances. It is in the context of a shared life involving such a consensus that our *Einstellungen* towards each other can be understood in the way they are. That does not *justify*

13 Wittgenstein, *Remarks on the Foundations of Mathematics*, V, no. 50. See Rush Rhees, 'Questions of Logical Inference', for discussion of Wittgenstein's point. I also owe much to Rhees's contributions to discussions on causality at King's College, London in 1980.

them, but it does provide the conditions under which they can be called *intelligible*. One feature of that intelligibility is our ability to apply certain concepts in the expression of our attitudes. 'Poor man! How he will suffer'. Those of course are the accents of pity. It is in the context of relationships involving such expressions (amongst numberless others of course) that we understand what suffering is. That does not mean that it is impossible for anyone to know that someone else is suffering without pitying him; but it does mean that one cannot (unless a very special context is supplied) ask why the fact that someone is suffering should be a reason for pitying him.

David Wiggins remarks that if we did not believe in such a thing as human nature we could not 'regard the human form as a clue to so much. We ought to check ourselves in a way that we do not and cannot check ourselves'.[14] His use of the word 'cannot' at this point seems to me exactly right, but I think he diagnoses our inability wrongly. It's not that we cannot check ourselves because our beliefs in human nature are so well entrenched, but rather because our reactions are at least as primitive as any such beliefs we may have themselves are (and probably more so).

14 *Sameness and Substance*, p. 223.

11

Who is my Neighbour?

Philosophical discussion needs well-formulated examples; and I
want to introduce my subject with a very well known example from
the New Testament: the parable of the Good Samaritan. I will give
myself the pleasure of quoting from the King James Version:

> And, behold, a certain lawyer stood up, and tempted him,
> saying, Master, what shall I do to inherit eternal life?
>
> He said unto him, what is written in the law? How readest
> thou?
>
> And he answering said, Thou shalt love the Lord thy God
> with all thy heart, and with all thy soul, and with all thy
> strength, and with all thy mind; and thy neighbour as thyself.
>
> And he said unto him, Thou hast answered right: this do,
> and thou shalt live.
>
> But he, willing to justify himself, said unto Jesus, And who is
> my neighbour?
>
> And Jesus answering said, A certain man went down from
> Jerusalem to Jericho, and fell among thieves, which stripped
> him of his raiment, and wounded him, and departed, leaving
> him half dead.
>
> And by chance there came down a certain priest that way:
> and when he saw him, he passed by on the other side.
>
> And likewise a Levite, when he was at the place, came and
> looked on him, and passed by on the other side.
>
> But a certain Samaritan, as he journeyed, came where he
> was: and when he saw him, he had compassion on him.
>
> And went to him, and bound up his wounds, pouring in oil
> and wine, and set him on his own beast, and brought him to an
> inn, and took care of him.

And on the morrow when he departed, he took out two pence, and gave them to the host, and said unto him, Take care of him; and whatsoever thou spendest more, when I come again, I will repay thee.

Which now of these three, thinkest thou, was neighbour unto him that fell among the thieves?

And he said, He that shewed mercy on him. Then said Jesus unto him, Go and do thou likewise. (Luke, 10: 25–37)

The structure of this parable is remarkable. It starts with a request for practical advice. ('What shall I do to inherit eternal life?') The law is appealed to and supplies an answer in the form of a prescription. And this is met with a theoretical, perhaps even linguistic, question concerning the meaning of one of the terms in the prescription ('my neighbour'). So far there is nothing to cause us to raise our eyebrows. But look what happens next. Instead of answering with a definition or a set of criteria, Jesus *tells a story*. Nor does he extract a definition or a criterion from the story but instead confronts his interlocutor with a further counter-question concerning the story itself. When this is answered, he simply *gives an injunction* ('Go and do thou likewise'). End of episode. What is going on here?

In preparation for answering this I want to notice some further interesting features of the parable: features of a linguistic nature.

The lawyer's question contains an indexical – I mean the first person possessive pronoun 'my'; and, correspondingly, the word 'neighbour' is *relational*. 'Neighbour' in this context might be rendered as '*fellow* human being'. The question is not the impersonal 'What is a fellow human being?', but something like: 'How do I recognize someone else as my fellow?'. This corresponds to the fact that the law which gives rise to the question ('thou shalt love thy neighbour as thyself') although it is clearly to be taken as applicable to all human beings, is couched in the second person singular: it is addressed, that is, to the particular individual who hears it. Hence the importance of the indexical in the ensuing discussion of the law's interpretation. Any one familiar with Kierkegaard's writings on the relation between religion and philosophy will recognize one of his central themes here. The lawyer, like the philosophers whom Kierkegaard so witheringly attacked, obviously expected an answer in terms of some general defining characteristics of the sorts of beings who constitute fellow human beings. Jesus, in responding to him with a story about the relations between two individuals, obliquely conveys to him that his question is not one that can be answered in that way. And the context of the story emphasizes the same point. It is narrated in the process of answering a question apparently concerning the criteria by which I should recognize my neighbour; one might, therefore, expect it to contain some account of the Samaritan's criteria. But it is very pointedly silent about that: 'and when he saw him he had compassion on him, and went to him, and bound up his wounds, pouring in oil and wine, and set him on his own beast, and brought him to an inn, and took care of him.' Nothing intervenes between the Samaritan's taking in the situation and his compassionate reaction; nor can we ignore the contrast in this respect with the priest and the Levite, especially the latter, who went over and looked at him in a calculating way before passing by on the other side. The contrast is all the more striking, of course, given that the encounter is between a Samaritan and a Jew (as it were a Palestinian Arab and an Israeli): that is, just the sort of situation in which one might expect questions and hesitations.

What is more, once the story is over Jesus does not invite the lawyer himself to extract from the incident the criteria which might be presumed to have implicitly informed the Samaritan's recognition of the traveller as his neighbour. His question is at first sight a curious one: 'Which now of these three, thinkest thou, was neighbour unto him that fell among the thieves?' I call it curious because the *original* question seemed to be about who was the *Samaritan's* neighbour (and perhaps how the Samaritan recognized him as such, though I have now eliminated that interpretation). But now the question is who was neighbour to the man who fell among thieves. Has the subject been changed? No, of course not. The point, first of all, is that the relation is a reciprocal one. Thus, *recognizing another as fellow human being* is in a certain way inseparable from *behaving towards him as a fellow human being*. What the connection precisely is between these notions is the real subject of this chapter. But it is in virtue of the connection that it is possible for Jesus to answer the lawyer's theoretical-sounding question with a practical injunction.

I want to make another point about the conclusion of the incident as recounted by Luke. Jesus does not *tell* the lawyer which of those who encountered the wounded traveller was his neighbour; he *asks* him. I believe that this is more than just an effective rhetorical device; just as when, in Plato's dialogue *Meno*, Socrates introduced

the slave boy to Pythagoras' Theorem not by *telling* him the answer
to the problem but by *eliciting* the answer from him, *that* is not just a
rhetorical device either. The suggestion in both cases is that each of
us has within him or herself the resources for answering the
question: a point which Plato expressed picturesquely in terms of
'recollection'. The further suggestion is that, in both cases, no one
truly *has* the answer who has not arrived at it for him or herself. If
the lawyer has needed to be *told* the answer to Jesus's last question
he would have been in no position to understand it.

Answering the question 'Who is my neighbour?', or: 'Who was
neighbour to the wounded man?', has to take the form of a practical
response. It 'has to be' because anything arrived at in another way
would not be an answer to the question. In fact I should say that the
lawyer – and also those of us who feel that his answer to Jesus's final
question is the only possible one – are making a response analogous
to that of the Samaritan himself. It is tempting to say that we are all
responding to the same thing: to whatever it is that falls under the
concept 'fellow human being'; but this, though it is not wrong,
misleadingly suggests that we have some access to this otherwise
than through such responses. Whereas what we have to do, I think,
is to describe the character of the response itself more helpfully.

The Samaritan responds to what he sees as a *necessity* generated
by the presence of the injured man. What I mean by introducing this
word can be brought out by considering what someone in the
Samaritan's position, and responding as he did, might say if urged
by a companion to hurry on so as not to miss his important
appointment. 'But I *can't* just leave him here to die'. The word
'can't', as used in such a context, expresses the kind of necessity – in
this case an impossibility – I have in mind.

I know that some will be inclined at this point to say that the
words I have put into the Samaritan's mouth cannot be 'literally'
true, since there is no relevant difference between him and the
priest and the Levite who, after all, did not even find it difficult, let
alone impossible, to pass by on the other side. How then can what is
possible for them be impossible for him? The objection would be
misconceived, however, since there *is* a relevant difference: the
Samaritan *sees* an impossibility here and the others do not. *That* is
the difference.

Of course, that was not what the objector meant by a 'relevant'
difference. He was thinking perhaps of something like a broken leg,
or paralysis, of a sort which would prevent the Samaritan from

moving away. But it is clear enough on reflection that this would, on
the contrary, be an *irr*elevant difference. This can be brought out if
we imagine a bit more conversation. When he says: 'I can't just leave
him here to die', his companion retorts 'Of course you can, you
don't have a broken leg, do you?' He would not be meeting the
Samaritan's point, so much as making a black, tasteless joke. And
the 'joke' such as it is, would derive precisely from the *irrelevance* of
that notion of impossibility in this context.

But our reflection on the point has not been uninstructive. It has
brought out an important peculiarity of the concept of impossibility
or necessity we are dealing with here: it demonstrates a difficulty,
and perhaps suggests the impossibility, of giving any account of it in
'naturalistic' terms.

An example of what I mean when I speak of 'an account in
naturalistic terms' would be the following. Suppose that *this* time
France and Britain really do build a tunnel under the English
Channel. (Outlandish examples are a convention in philosophy.)
Engineers might determine that, at a certain point, it is *necessary* to
excavate at a greater depth than originally planned because of what
they have discovered about the rock and soil composition of the sea-
bed at that point. That is to say, the necessity of a course of action is
here derived from an independent determination of the properties of
something. An example from human relations would be the
following. In George Eliot's great novel *Middlemarch* Dr Lydgate
finds it impossible to oppose the banker Bulstrode's policies for the
community hospital because of the control Bulstrode exercises over
Lydgate's financial affairs. In both these examples the necessity or
impossibility of a certain course of action is supported by reference
to probable *consequences*. This is characteristic of such cases; but
more central to my present concerns is the fact that in these cases
necessities and impossibilities are supported by reference to
characteristics of the elements affected by the proposed action:
characteristics which can be determined independently of reference
to these and similar necessities. A proposed action, or range of
actions, is no longer a possible choice for a prospective agent
because environmental conditions make the desired end impossible
of attainment or generate further consequences which are unacceptable.

A naturalistic account of moral necessities, then, would be one
which treated them as limits on the possibilities of an agent's
achieving ends which, either as a particular individual or, at the

other extreme, as a member of the human race, he is presumed to
have. Roughly speaking, this is to treat such modalities as imposing
limits not on what someone may *will*, but on what the will is capable
of *carrying into effect*, given its presumed fundamental motivation.
Such a way of thinking is characteristic of a trend in moral
philosophy which has certainly been extremely influential, and
perhaps dominant, in the latter part of this century. One proponent
of it was Professor Elizabeth Anscombe in a seminal article entitled
'modern Moral Philosophy', first published in 1958,[1] the reverberations of which have continued through the influential writings of
Philippa Foot and broken forth with a considerable augmentation of
decibels in Alasdair MacIntyre's recent book *After Virtue*, the whole
structure of which is provided by the main point in Miss
Anscombe's article. It is the idea, as Miss Anscombe expressed it in
1958, that moral philosophy must wait on 'an adequate philosophy
of psychology': by which she certainly meant a psychology which
would account for practical human rationality in terms of the
adaptation of means to human ends. Behind this, I think, was the
thought that human ends are derivative from human needs; and
behind this again the thought that human needs flow from the kind
of being a human being is. In other words the conception as a whole
is that morality is somehow based on and perhaps derivable from (an
independently graspable) human nature.

That phrase 'independently graspable' marks where the difficulty
lies.

Let me return to the parable. I emphasized that the Samaritan is
depicted as reacting with compassion without asking any questions
(beyond those involved in ascertaining the need for help and the
nature of the help needed, of course). He does not ask whether the
wounded traveller is a proper object of his compassion. This indeed
is essential to the *purity* of the compassion which the parable
depicts. It is a reaction expressing the Samaritan's conviction that it
was *necessary* to help the traveller, that *nothing else was possible* in the
circumstances. Now if I put the matter that way, someone may
object that I am representing the so-called 'necessity' of helping as
completely *arbitrary* and therefore no genuine necessity at all.
Indeed this is, I think, pretty much the same thought as Miss
Anscombe expressed in 1958 when she claimed that a so-called
unconditional moral 'ought' (of the sort which Kant discussed) is

1   G. E. M. Anscombe, *Collected Philosophical Papers*, Vol. III.

really unintelligible. And Alasdair MacIntyre feels the same about contemporary morality as a whole: its demands are arbitrary and therefore unintelligible.

Miss Anscombe's argument rested on the claim that such a use derives from the notion of being 'obliged', 'required', 'bound' etc. *by law*. According to her the historical explanation for this state of affairs was that a Judaeo-Christian 'law conception of ethics' had originally made it intelligible (the intelligibility deriving presumably from a human need – however understood – to fulfil the will of such a law-giver). But, she continued, the usage had lagged behind the disappearance of any general acceptance of ethics as required by a divine law-giver. The situation, she claimed, 'was the interesting one of the survival of a concept outside the framework of thought that made it a really intelligible one'.

I am not competent to discuss this bold (and unsubstantiated) historical thesis. Let us accept it for the sake of argument. But I do want to question her philosophical conclusion about the alleged unintelligibility of this use of moral modalities in present-day circumstances.

A preliminary point: It clearly does not *follow* from the alleged disappearance of circumstances which once gave a certain intelligibility to a linguistic usage that such a usage now has *no* intelligibility. The most we can conclude is that it now has to be understood rather *differently*. Whether it means anything, and if so what, can only be determined by an examination of its present use – something we do not find in that early Anscombe article.

As a step in the direction of supplying this deficiency let us examine the Samaritan's use of the word 'cannot' in my slight addition to the parable. Now it might be thought that this use would fit peculiarly well Miss Anscombe's conjecture about the dependence of such absolute modalities on a law conception of ethics. After all, Jesus tells the parable precisely in a discussion about 'what is written in the law' and we may suppose his auditors to have had a conception of God as law-giver. But his parable did not appeal to the conception: it *challenged* it. Or at least it commented on the conception in a way which presupposed that the moral modality to which the Samaritan responded would have a force for the parable's hearers *independently* of their commitment to any particular theological belief. It is the lawyer's own response to that modality which enables him to answer Jesus's final question and thus to expand his comprehension of the law. So his understanding of and response to the modality cannot itself be thought of as dependent on his conception of the law. And I might add that it is perfectly possible for *us* to understand and respond to that modality whether or not we have a conception of God as the author of a moral law. Otherwise the parable would mean nothing to someone who did not share that conception – something which is not only untrue, but which would radically thwart one of Jesus's apparent intentions in teaching in this way, by parable.

I should like to go a bit further: in a direction that will anticipate my subsequent argument. According to Miss Anscombe, the intelligibility of the obligation to help the injured traveller to which the Samaritan responded depends on accepting that it is a divine law that one should act thus. I think on the contrary that the concept of a divine law can itself only develop on the basis of our response to such modalities. What I mean can be elucidated by noticing first that in another New Testament context[2] Jesus says of the Commandment which the Samaritan parable elucidates that it is 'like unto' another which precedes it: 'Thou shalt love the Lord thy God with all thy heart, with all thy mind and with all thy soul'. The second Commandment might indeed be regarded as an application, or even a particularly central case, of the first. That is supported by remarks like St John's: 'If a man say, I love God, and hateth his brother, he is a liar: for he that loveth not his brother whom he hath seen, how can he love God whom he hath not seen?'[3] The suggestion here, as it seems to me, is that we do not first have a conception of God on the basis of which we form our conception of the Commandment to love our neighbour. On the contrary the conceptual development goes the other way. The responses to moral modalities that we share with the Samaritan (however much they are modified or stifled by circumstance) are amongst the seeds from which, in some people, grows the conception of divinity and its laws. Of course, our understanding need not develop in this direction at all; and if it does not, I do not see why this should stand in the way of someone's grasping the force of such a modal expression in its original context.

I do not want to spend too long talking about Professor Anscombe, partly because this is not the right occasion for that and partly because what I have to say about this is being published

2   Matthew, 22: 39.
3   1 John, 4: 20.

elsewhere. But I do need to refer to a remarkable fact about the direction taken by some of her later work: remarkable because it seems to me to undermine her earlier views about the moral 'ought' but without explicit recognition on her part that this is so. In two papers published twenty years after 'Modern Moral Philosophy' Miss Anscombe discusses certain problems about the use of modal concepts like *must, cannot, ought*, identifying Hume as the philosopher who first brought these problems to light.[4] Hume, in a famous section of his *Treatise of Human Nature*, had worried over the source of the obligation to keep a promise. How, he asked, can the mere utterance of the words 'I promise' create an obligation, or a necessity, which did not exist before, of conducting oneself in a certain way in the future. There is no 'act of mind' corresponding to these words which could do the trick, and to suppose that the words could achieve it all by themselves seems a magical conception.

Miss Anscombe's suggestion is that this case belongs to a class of modal expressions which she colourfully labels 'stopping modals'. Children, while learning the language, are actually prevented by adults from doing certain things and are at the same time told 'You can't do that' and perhaps given a reason, such as 'It belongs to someone else', or 'It's her private room', or 'You promised not to', or 'It's none of your business'. Children trained like this subsequently come to respond to the words themselves without the physical prevention which was part of the learning process; and they come themselves to use such words, both in what they say to others and also in their own deliberations about what to do. The reason which is offered in support of such a 'stopping modal' is called by Miss Anscombe its 'logos' and it has the peculiarity of being intelligible only to someone who has already acquired the appropriate response to the cluster of modals which the logos is used to 'justify'. Professor Anscombe further makes an observation, important both in itself and more particularly in relation to what I am discussing here, that similar considerations spread right through human life, and are involved in the learning of any sort of language involved in the idea for instance that there are certain things you 'can't' say and certain things you are committed to (that you 'must' acknowledge) given that you have accepted certain other things. A particularly striking example is the grasp of simple arithmetical

4 'Rules, Rights and Promises' and 'On the Source of the Authority of the State', *Collected Philosophical Papers*, Vol. III.

concepts of number, addition, subtraction etc. When a child learns to count, it has to be trained, first of all, in a very strict, rigid drill; it has to learn the series of numerals, the *ordering* of which of course is all-important and is, moreover, at least from the point of view of the learner, entirely arbitrary. Again, the disciplines involved in counting objects of various kinds – what sort of 'correlation' is required between numeral and object, etc. have a similarly strict and arbitrary character. Unless a child responds appropriately to such training and goes along unquestioningly with it, concepts of number will never be properly learnt. As I said, that is a particularly striking example, but it is an example of something that runs right through language learning, which involves rote training in procedures to a far greater extent than we may at first appreciate.

It would be wrong, however, to dwell too exclusively on the fact that such procedures have to be *learned*: wrong, anyway, if it distracts our attention from the indispensable role of quite spontaneous reactions on our part in circumstances of different sorts. Indeed, if such characteristic reactions were not the norm, the sort of learning I have referred to would be impossible, since training in procedures relies for its success on the predictability of responses to such training. Not all those responses can themselves be products of training; to suppose so would be to involve oneself in an infinite regress. It seems to me that failure to take account of this spontaneity is a gap in Miss Anscombe's account of 'stopping modals' and one which perhaps hinders her from pushing her argument as far as it will go.

I want to concentrate on the application of these ideas to our understanding of each other. Miss Anscombe, as I have said, emphasizes the importance of the fact that in our acquisition of concepts which form what she calls the '*logoi*' of the modals we respect in our dealings with each other, we are actually prevented by our teachers from doing certain things in various kinds of circumstances. I want to add that it is an important fact about us that our reactions to each other are in all sorts of ways quite different from our reactions to anything else. In the present context its importance lies in its connection with our understanding of the kinds of creature we are having commerce with. If for instance I see another person accidentally strike his thumb a heavy blow with a hammer, *I* will wince, cry out and clutch my own thumb. I have not learned to do this; neither do I do it as a result of reflection on the pain my companion is in. It is itself *an expression* of my recognition of the pain he is in.

And consider the following (wonderful, I think) passage from Wittgenstein's discussion of the relation between mind and body:

> But isn't it absurd to say of a *body* that it has pain? – And why does one feel an absurdity in that? In what sense is it true that my hand does not feel pain, but I in my hand?
>
> What sort of issue is: Is it the *body* that feels pain? – How is it to be decided? What makes it plausible to say that it is *not* the body? – Well, something like this: if someone has a pain in his hand, then the hand does not say so (unless it writes it) and one does not comfort the hand, but the sufferer: one looks into his face. How am I filled with pity *for this man*? How does it come out what the object of my pity is? (Pity, one may say, is a form of conviction that someone else is in pain.)[5]

Wittgenstein characterizes such observations as this as 'remarks on the natural history of mankind'. His point is that thought and understanding have to be looked at in a 'natural historical way': as concepts characterizing the kinds of life lived by human beings. If one looks at things in that way it will seem more than natural that the understanding human beings have *of each other* should be a function of the lives they lead.

Jonathan Swift was a writer whose peculiar sensitivities reflect very well what is involved in this thought. I am thinking both of the chilling 'A Modest Proposal' and the (in a way equally chilling) 'Voyage to the Houyhnhnms' in *Gulliver's Travels*. Out of respect for the squeamish I will refrain from discussing the former at length. I will simply note that the effectiveness of Swift's savage satire on the bureaucratic mind is almost entirely due to the way in which his proposal, and his way of presenting it, completely short-circuit our shared humanity with the wretched Irish peasantry and their offspring. This could serve as a starting point for reflection on the nature of the bafflement and incomprehension, as well as horror, we feel in the face of such a phenomenon as the Holocaust in Nazi Germany. I feel like saying that it is important to recognize that here there is something which in a certain sense is not to be 'understood', if we are to retain our sense of what human life is. What I mean is that retention of this sense requires a quite different sort of response from that which seeks an explanation, but I shall not pursue that difficult point further here.

5 *Philosophical Investigations*, Part I, nos 286–7.

As for 'The Voyage to the Houyhnhnms' I am thinking especially of Gulliver's relation to the Yahoos. He was, very naturally, anxious to distance himself from these repulsive, and disconcertingly humanoid, creatures. There is a telling incident, late in his stay in the country, in which he is pursued with lustful intent by a female Yahoo while he is swimming naked in the river. At that point, he says, he could no longer conceal from himself that he was one of them. His hysterically horrified flight registers the conflict between the *necessity* and the *impossibility* of acknowledging his own common humanity with one of these depraved creatures.

The counterpart to this is the difficulty *we*, Swift's readers, have (I do not believe I am idiosyncratic in feeling this) in taking seriously – except as an intellectual *jeu d'esprit* – the completely rational Houyhnhnms. I hope I shall not be accused of 'specism' if I say that we cannot relate to *horses* in the way we would have to relate to them in order to be able to recognize such qualities in them. The reason I say this is not so-called 'specism' is that it has nothing whatever to do with regarding human beings as *superior* to horses. It could just as well signal the opposite of this.

We should remember that the upshot of the combined influence of Yahoos and Houyhnhnms on Gulliver was years of madness after he left their country. I think Swift knew what he was doing when he ended the story like that.

In all these cases, the situation is not that I first recognize my common humanity with others and that this recognition then provides the intellectual justification for my response to certain modalities in my dealings with them. On the contrary it is a recognition which is itself a function of those responses. In this respect it something like Miss Anscombe's *logos* to a stopping modal. It is the point Wittgenstein is succinctly making in his remark: 'My attitude towards him is an attitude towards a soul. I am not of the *opinion* that he has a soul.'[6]

I want now to try to draw the threads together and see what conclusion they point to. I will express this conclusion by saying that the practical modalities to which we respond in our dealings with each other – responses which may of course be modified, blunted or intensified in particular circumstances – are akin to what Wittgenstein called "rules of grammar": perhaps even a special case of these. He spoke of the "arbitrariness" of such rules:

6 *Philosophical Investigations*, Part II, iv.

Why don't I call cookery rules arbitrary, and why am I tempted
to call the rules of grammar arbitrary? Because "cookery" is
defined by its end, whereas "speaking" is not. That is why the
use of language is in a certain sense autonomous, as cooking
and washing are not. You cook badly if you are guided in your
cooking by rules other than the right ones; but if you follow
other rules than those of chess you are *playing another game*;
and if you follow grammatical rules other than such and such
ones, that does not mean that you say something wrong, no,
you are speaking of something else.[7]

Analogously, we might say, the priest and the Levite saw
something different from what the Samaritan saw when they came
upon the injured man in the roadway. We might say: they did not
see a neighbour in him. Perhaps it would sound odd to say that they
did not recognize him as a fellow human being. Of course, in many
contexts we would not say this. But in some contexts we *do* speak
like this. Consider the attitudes of Europeans and white Americans
to slaves in the seventeenth and eighteenth centuries. It was
sometimes said of them – indeed, they sometimes said of themselves
– that they did not regard slaves as human.[8] To say that is not to
make a point about their competence at biological classification,
though no doubt such matters were confusedly mixed up with what
was really at issue, namely the nature of their moral sensibility. My
central point is that in questions concerning our understanding of
each other our *moral* sensibility is indeed an aspect of our *sensibility*,
of the way we see things, of what we make of the world we are living
in.

7 *Zettel*, no. 320.
8 See Stanley Cavell, *The Claim of Reason*, for an interesting discussion of this.

12

Particularity and Morals

I will start with an example. It is taken from a play called *Rabbit Pie Day* by Tim Rose Price which was shown on BBC Television some years ago. The theme of the play was the forced repatriation of a group of Russian prisoners of war in British hands in consequence of a political deal between the British and Soviet Governments. The prisoners could expect little good from their home-coming. The play is set in a transit camp in England. The commandant is a middle-class English intellectual whose mildly left-wing political sympathies incline him to sympathize with the purpose of the agreement from which the imminent repatriation of the prisoners results. His senior NCO is a working-class chauvinist with little interest in politics, contemptuous of all foreigners and particularly outraged by the anarchic foreign strangeness of the prisoners in his charge. In the course of the play the transit camp staff become gradually aware of the grimness of the fate awaiting the prisoners on arrival 'home'. The commandant protests ineffectually to his superiors; but there is nothing he can do to stop the transfer. Were he to decline to carry out his orders he would probably make things worse for the prisoners – to say nothing of the consequences to himself. In the meantime the prisoners begin to emerge in his and his NCO's consciousness as very real, vivid – though anything but saintly – human beings whose lives willy-nilly become entwined with those of their British guards. The play concludes with the prisoners being loaded on to trucks, unaware of their destination, leaving their guards with a sense of utter disgust: pre-eminently in the case of the commandant and, perhaps even more interestingly, in that of his senior NCO too.

The commandant's disgust might be expressed in the judgement that he has done something squalid in betraying these human beings who trusted him. I assume this to exemplify a certain sort of moral judgement; and I assume the disgust experienced by the commandant to be characterized as 'moral' disgust. It is the connection of the judgement and of the disgust with notions like *betrayal, breach of trust* and the like that I take to provide the warrant for this label: 'moral'.

I am concerned with the question: what sort of logical constraint do the facts of the situation in a case like this exert on what moral response or responses to facts are admissible. To explain my question a little further here is an analogy – A man who wants to say what time it is is constrained by certain features of his environment: the position of the sun, readings of clocks, etc., etc. Such features determine a certain answer to the question 'What time is it?' as the correct one; and it is a feature of the meaning of words like 'determine' and 'correct' in this context that the *same* answer would be determined as correct by those features of the environment for anyone else who asked the question. Indeed, anyone who did not observe these constraints on what he said would hardly be *counted* as 'asking the same question'. By contrast two men (whose tastes are identical) may ask the question 'Where should I like to spend my holiday?' and, even though their circumstances are identical in all relevant respects they need not come up with the same answer. The phrase 'need not' here means something like: if they came up with different answers that would be no reason to think that one of them must be wrong. Indeed, it is not altogether clear what 'wrong' would mean in these circumstances. So, if we return to our original question and take these last two examples as paradigms, what are we to say of the commandant's judgement that he has been involved in a squalid betrayal of men who trusted him? If someone else in the same situation were to judge himself morally clean (on the grounds, perhaps, that he was only doing his job and obeying lawful orders) must it be the case that either he or the commandant is mistaken?

I think it is important to phrase this question in such a way as not to prejudice the form of answer that is going to be acceptable to it. This sort of prejudice has been created, for instance, by the very widespread formulation of the question in some such terms as: 'Does the judgement that my behaviour towards these people was a squalid breach of trust itself express a *fact* about the situation or perhaps rather an *attitude* towards the facts of the situation?'

We cannot get far with questions of that form. For one thing, the considerations inclining us in contrary directions are too evenly balanced. We cannot deny the admissibility of such locutions as: 'It's a fact that my behaviour was squalid'. We cannot deny that someone may, with perfect linguistic propriety, endorse my remark by saying: 'That's true', or contest it with: 'That's not true'. And how can we contest the applicability of the Tarskian formula: ' "My behaviour was squalid" is true if and only if my behaviour was squalid'? Yet, on the other hand, it would be absurd to deny that if the commandant judges his behaviour to have been squalid, what he thinks is quite differently related to what happened in the camp from his judgement, say, that the prisoners left the camp on 14 January. This difference is one that it seems quite natural to express by saying that the one judgement states a fact about the situation while the other expresses an attitude towards the facts of the situation.

Philosophers have not all reacted towards this general situation in the same way. On the one hand they have sometimes spoken of a 'moral reality' which exercises the requisite constraint on moral judgement. There is nothing wrong with that phrase as such and it has all kinds of perfectly good uses *within* moral discourse. But in the present context, used in the service of a general characterization of 'the relation of moral discourse to reality', it represents a lapse into mythology. We do not have much more here than a sort of metaphysical counterpart of the Tarskian formula about truth: something which is simply used to buttress the claim that there is indeed a logical constraint on moral judgement without providing an actual account of what that constraint is. On the other hand, philosophers who are impressed (or perhaps depressed) at the suspiciously mythological appearance of the moral reality thus introduced, have sometimes denied that the facts of the situation exert *any* genuine logical constraint on what moral judgements are admissible.

The trouble here arises partly from the fact that the grammatical form in which the judgement is expressed is, in itself, no reliable guide to the way in which the judgement is in fact applied. Formulae of the form ' "p" is true if and only if s' may contain any instantiation of 'p' of which it is grammatically permissible to say that it is true; but for all that, different instantiations of 'p' may be applied in totally different ways. The metaphysical interpretation of the Tarskian formula encourages the idea that the differences lie in the 'different kinds of fact' expressed by the values of 's' occurring in the second half. On this interpretation the fundamental relation to the facts is always the same and is what is expressed in the part of the formula which reads 'is true if and only if'. We then take as our paradigm value of 'p' a sort of sentence of which the application to the facts seems particularly simple and perspicuous ('Snow is white'); we compare with this paradigm sentences of a type the application of which to the facts strikes us as philosophically problematic ('My behaviour was squalid'). Now the way is clear for us to suppose that the (metaphysically interpreted) Tarskian formula for 'is true' gives us the relation to the facts in the problematic case too: it will be a relation in principle identical to that which holds in the simple case. The difference will lie in the complexity of the facts stated by 's'.

This whole way of thinking is an example of what Wittgenstein was attacking in what he wrote concerning the distinction between what can be said and what can only be shown. We take the Tarskian formula to give us the relation between the expression in quotation marks and the world. But of course all we have on the right-hand side of the formula are more words. The presence or absence of quotation marks does make a difference to the way the words are supposed to be taken, but such notational devices cannot transform words into something else. The sentence gets its relation to something other than words (what we are calling 'the world') only through its use, its application. That application can be described. But the words to the right of the Tarskian formula are *not* a description of the way the words to the left, in quotation marks, are applied; they are *supposed* to express the facts to which the words in quotation marks apply (their truth-conditions). But we do not get out of language by the notational device of using quotation marks on the left-hand side of the formula and omitting them on the right-hand side. We make contact with the world only through the *application* of language.

This point is sometimes only half appreciated, which gives rise to new confusions. For instance, philosophers will sometimes say – a recent example is Alasdair MacIntyre in his book *After Virtue* – that the meaning of moral judgements conflicts with their use. The idea here is that the subject–predicate grammatical form in which such judgements are expressed gives their *meaning*: which is, perhaps, to ascribe a property to an action, a person, a situation or whatever. But their actual *application* is said to be quite at odds with this meaning: it has to be, since there are in fact no such properties to be ascribed. The use of such sentences is rather to express and/or influence attitudes. But the supposed mistake about their meaning thought to be engendered by their misleading grammatical form is claimed itself to play a role – and an illegitimate one – in furthering their influence on attitudes. Hearers (and perhaps speakers too) of such sentences are bamboozled into taking up attitudes to situations because they think of these attitudes as somehow required of them by those essentially mythological properties of the situations. They think they are being told something of a certain kind when in fact nowhere in the world does there exist anything of that kind to be told.

In my opinion the confusion here lies with the philosophers who make such a diagnosis. The mode of application of a judgement is in *no* case directly expressed in the grammatical form of its expression. This is just as true of the grammatical form of those utterances which are taken as the paradigms for the ascription of properties as it is of that of those utterances subjected to the sort of criticism I adumbrated in the previous paragraph. ' "Snow is white" is true if and only if snow is white' says nothing about the proper mode of application of the expression 'Snow is white'. (Indeed, what *is* its proper mode of application? Has anyone ever seriously inquired? The answer is by no means as obvious as seems commonly supposed, since it is not at all clear when it might be said; except, perhaps, as part of an explanation of the word 'white' or of what snow is, to someone who has heard of it for the first time.)

The notion of 'ascribing a property' as it enters into this line of thought, is really only a metaphysical shadow cast by a certain syntactical form. And philosophers who say that the application of such an expression 'to the world' consists in its 'stating a fact' do little more than make a gesture – a gesture, as it were, to the whiteness of the snow. They do not inquire very closely into what surrounding circumstances would be necessary for the gesture to achieve what they want. And then when they say of expressions that they find more problematic, such as those belonging to ethics, that they too 'state facts' (*or* when they deny this) they merely repeat the gesture, thinking they have done enough to make the gesture intelligible in the right sort of way if they say that the facts in question are in this case facts belonging to 'moral reality'. But this only serves to disguise the emptiness of the gesture by surrounding it with mythological elaborations.

But we remain subject to essentially the same confusion if we conclude that reality therefore places no logical constraints at all on the applicability of ethical expressions. The point is that as long as we continue to move about along the syntactical paths connecting superficial grammatical forms, we shall not even have started to investigate the actual relations to people, situations and things that we express through our ethical concepts.

With these thoughts in mind I return to the example with which I started: to the camp commandant reacting to the part he has played in the forcible repatriation of the prisoners of war in his charge. How are the moral concepts that inform his reaction related to the facts of the situation towards which he is reacting?

I remarked earlier that what warrants us in saying that what he experiences is *moral* disgust is its connection with notions such as betrayal, breach of faith, etc., etc. His disgust, however, is not merely disgust at an *instance* of betrayal, breach of faith, etc. That is to say, his disgust is not to be explicated by any commitment on his part to general principles – he may or may not have such a commitment – however such principles may be conceived. It is not that he applies a set of such principles to the facts before him and thereby sees that he is committed to a certain view of those facts. Of course, there *are* situations that are characterizable in that way; only this is not one of them. The example, moreover, apart from its highly dramatic character, is not, I believe, at all untypical of a wide range of cases in which moral concepts are applied to particular situations.

What stimulates the moral sensitivity of the commandant (who, as far as general principles go, is inclined to favour the policy under which the repatriation is being carried out and to suspect its critics) is his involvement with these particular human beings and his realization of what he is doing to them. And this is certainly not on account of any special liking he has for them; on the whole he finds them tiresome and incomprehensible. The situation is even clearer in the case of his senior NCO, who positively dislikes the prisoners and whose principles certainly do not include any injunctions to bother with the interests of foreigners. But his involvement with them as individuals makes him unaccustomedly ill-at-ease with himself over what he is doing. And, I contend, the nature of this involvement and the nature of his discomfort cannot be expressed without the use of moral concepts.

The general point has been made very clearly by Grete Hermann[1] in the course of an argument against the neo-Kantian conception of morality held by her former teacher, Leonard Nelson.

1 Grete Henry-Hermann, 'Die Überwindung des Zufalls', p. 49 (my translation).

If someone is indignant about a lie, then it's about the particular lie that he heard or that was told to him. He is not indignant about the class of all possible lies. The mere value judgement: "Telling that lie is wrong!" may be based on the general conviction that all lying is wrong. But the indignation I feel at this lie is certainly not derived from an indignation with regard to all lying.

This of course runs deeply counter to Kant's moral philosophy according to which reason of itself (as manifested in universal law) must provide the motivating force for any action or reaction which merits designation as moral. Otherwise, so Kant thought, the agent could be motivated only by how he happened to feel about the circumstances of his particular situation; and this would mean that there was no objective consideration by which his will would be *bound*.

Opponents of Kant since Schopenhauer have retorted that a rational principle could not of itself dispose of the force necessary to make a man act counter to his own strong interests. That force could come only from some strong practical engagement of the agent in the situation in which he has to act. It is the same point as that made by Spinoza: 'An emotion can only be controlled or destroyed by another emotion contrary thereto, and with more power for controlling emotion.' And: 'A true knowledge of good and evil cannot check any emotion by virtue of being true, but only in so far as it is considered as an emotion.'[2] In fact Spinoza maintained (in my opinion with some justice) that 'knowledge of good and evil', expressed in a purely general way, is a confused form of awareness. In his view I can attain clarity only through a sharpening of my perception of the particular circumstances which characterize my individual presence in the world, a sharpening of perception which is at the same time a purification of my practical involvement. Since the most important aspect of this practical involvement is involvement with other human beings, what is required is an account of our knowledge and understanding of other human beings which will make it possible to see how such knowledge and understanding can of itself impose moral bounds on our will. An account that would achieve this is one which makes recognition of such moral bounds on the will a criterion for the knowledge and understanding of human beings that is in question.

2 Spinoza, *Ethics*, Part IV, Propositions VII and XIV.

That the commandant in our example is disgusted at his role in the betrayal of his charges in the way he is, is itself a mark of how he has come to understand the individual human reality of those charges. It is *this* way in which the application of moral concepts is connected with our awareness of the reality of human beings that I want to emphasize.

Kant himself comes close to this conception in what he says about respecting human beings as ends in themselves. But though he does say something of great importance here, he seems to me nevertheless just to miss the essence of the matter. On his account it sounds as though respect is due to another in virtue of, and because of, some feature he possesses (his 'rationality'). But consider the parable of the Good Samaritan, which offers us a paradigm of respect for another: this says nothing of any reasons which justify the Samaritan's reaction to the wounded traveller. That reaction is simply described and contrasted with the behaviour of the priest and the Levite; and we are admonished to go and do likewise. It would be a great mistake in my opinion to suppose that the parable is elliptical and in need of supplement on Kantian (or any other) lines. Its point and its force spring precisely from the fact that *no* justificatory supplementation is offered. That this is so shows what is wrong with Alan Donagan's attempt to reconstruct Judaeo-Christian morality on a neo-Kantian foundation.[3] The force of the parable comes from the sight I am asked to contemplate in imagination of this wounded man lying here in my path. That it is a man with whom I am confronted is of course essential. But though he is indeed – like any other man – an instance of humanity, he does not confront me under this aspect, but rather as a particular individual with his own nature and history. And it is important that the help I offer him should indeed take account of that individual nature and history; otherwise I can be charged with not really attending to *him*.

Of course, the parable does *also* insist that help is due to any man who is afflicted solely by reason that that is what he is. That is the importance of the fact that the helper is a *Samaritan* and hence a traditional foe of the man he helps. But my point is that what is going to count as genuine 'help' will be discerned only by one who attends carefully to the nature and circumstances of the particular individual who is afflicted.

It is difficult to get the balance and emphasis right in stating this

3   Alan Donagan, *The Theory of Morality*.

point, and understanding the nature of the difficulty will be a help in understanding the point itself. Consider the following remark by Wittgenstein: the first remark printed in *Culture and Value*:

> Wenn wir einen Chinesen hören, so sind wir geneigt, sein Sprechen für unartikuliertes Gurgeln zu halten. Einer, der chinesisch versteht, wird darin die *Sprache* erkennen. So kann ich oft nicht den *Menschen* im Menschen erkennen.

> We tend to take the speech of a Chinese for inarticulate gurgling. Someone who understands Chinese will recognize *language* in what he hears. Similarly I often cannot discern the *humanity* in a man.[4]

I have given the German as well as my English translation, because a certain difficulty about the translation is integrally connected with the point under discussion. Wittgenstein's very concrete phrase 'den *Menschen* im Menschen erkennen' is very much better than my abstract 'discern the *humanity* in a man' (but I could find no idiomatic English expression which would really do justice to the original). Wittgenstein's formulation catches the particularity that is in question. It is noteworthy that the same issue could not arise if what were in question were, say, recognizing the animal in front of me as a chipmunk. That there is an issue is, one might say – using another much later phrase of Wittgenstein's – part of the grammar of the word 'man'. The analogy with speech in Wittgenstein's remark brings this out beautifully. By 'recognizing language in what one hears' we should understand, I think, not just recognizing that we are hearing a piece of language but understanding what is being said, that is, the particular thing that is being said. And 'den *Menschen* im Menschen erkennen' means recognizing *this* man for what (who) he is, though of course in doing so we deploy the general category 'man'.

There are objections to Kant's way of treating this issue in terms of an imperative to treat men not merely as means, but as ends in themselves. On the one hand the terminology of 'ends in themselves' is misleading. It suggests too strongly the contrast between climbing a mountain as Hannibal did the Alps, so as to get to the other side, and climbing it, as is said, 'because it is there',

4   *Culture and Value*, p. 1.

where you might call the activity of climbing an 'end in itself'. That could be misleading here since, although of course one has the idea of the mountain as an external challenge that elicits the mountaineer's desire to climb it, that is nevertheless only the case in the context of a given man's fascination with mountain-climbing. As we know, some are subject to this fascination, others not; and while a mountaineer may think those in the latter category are missing something, it would be absurd for him to condemn them for this. But the respect due to another man is not like that – certainly not on Kant's view. If someone does not exhibit it, the appropriate response is neither to shrug one's shoulders nor to say that he is 'missing something'. Again, the way the word 'due' as used in this connection is important. We do not speak of anything being 'due' to a mountain. Or rather, though we *do* speak of the respect due to a mountain, that has more to do with concern for the climber's safety than with concern for the mountain. But to say of someone that he fails to accord a fellow human being the respect that is due to him is a condemnation, or at least a criticism. And so the parable of the Good Samaritan ends with the injunction: 'Go and do thou likewise'. One could not tell a story of a man who, on seeing a mountain, goes and climbs it and end it with the moral 'Do likewise'. Or, if one did, the injunction would certainly not have the same relation to the story as has Christ's injunction to the parable he has just told.

My second misgiving about Kant's way of putting things is his attempt to give a reason, to provide a foundation, for the respect which is due to a fellow human being. Sometimes he almost makes it sound – though it must be added in fairness that this can hardly be his intention – as though respect is due to the rationality a person instantiated rather than to the person himself. It is not very easy to get straight about this, since as a matter of fact something one might want to call 'rationality' is indeed closely bound up with what we understand by the respect due to a person. But one must avoid the suggestion that one owes a person respect *in virtue of* his rationality. What is true is that the kind of respect that is in question here can be intelligibly accorded only to a being who is in a certain sense rational. This is because the form of respect for another person is, as Simone Weil puts it, the recognition of his power of consent and refusal. And this power can be attributed only to a being who is capable of distinguishing between alternatives and of judging the relevance of those alternatives to what he himself values. I do not want to deny that in some attenuated sense one could speak of allowing a dumb animal to choose and of 'respecting' its choice; but I *do* want to insist that the sense would be attenuated.

I mentioned Simone Weil just now and had in mind what she writes on this general theme in essays like 'L'Iliade, poème de la force', 'La personne et le sacré' and 'Luttons-nous pour la justice?'. But instead of discussing what she says further, I want to note a remarkable similarity between what she says and the main argument of the brilliant middle section of Stanley Cavell's monstrously uneven book, *The Claim of Reason*.

The focus of Cavell's discussion is a difficulty involved in the description of human action: how an action is to be described when it is up for moral consideration is itself necessarily a matter for discussion. In such a discussion a central, though not perhaps a finally authoritative, place belongs to what the agent himself says about the description of his action. This will be connected with the stand he takes about his commitments, intentions, relations with others, etc. The concept of respect for another person will then be importantly connected with that of taking seriously his own conception of himself, his actions and his relations with others. 'Taking seriously' itself is of course something that will take extremely diverse forms according to the particular circumstances of the situation.

Like Simone Weil, Cavell links respect understood in these terms to the concept of *justice*. Treating a person justly involves treating with seriousness his own conception of himself, his own commitments and cares, his own understanding of his situation and of what the situation demands of him. This means that it cannot be spelled out, after the manner of Kant, in terms of imperatives having a specific content. Kant, although insisting that moral imperatives are *self-legislated*, also thinks that the rationality involved in such legislating requires *universality* of content and thus gives rise to a sort of calculus which shows what in particular must be legislated. But these last two requirements are, it seems to me, mutually inconsistent. Unpalatable as it may be to the theorizing moral philosopher, he has to accept in the end that men of moral good will may indeed occupy or arrive at different and even opposed moral positions – and on the basis of circumstances which cannot be differentiated from each other so as to justify one of those positions against the other in a way that would have to be accepted by any rational being. That may sound like anarchy and the ultimate denial of reason, but I believe that if we look at the way it works in practice we shall see that this is not so.

The main role of reason in such matters is not to arrive at a position the acceptance of which will be, as it were, definitive of a rational man of moral good will. In saying this I do not mean to commit myself on the question whether there are *ever* any circumstances in which arriving at such a position is a possibility; I mean only that such circumstances, if they exist, constitute a very special case. One way in which a man may exhibit reason in the context of moral disputes is through understanding the moral positions of others opposed to his own, seeing the difficulties in them to be sure, but equally allowing them to highlight difficulties in his own position. There is absolutely no ground *a priori* for expecting that it will be possible to arrive at some position free of difficulties which everyone will be able to accept. Choice, will and responsibility come into the matter because in taking up a position one *ipso facto* assumes responsibility for the difficulties in which that may involve one – and here I include amongst the difficulties dangers of a moral sort. In other words, problems of this sort do not necessarily have what we would want to call a 'solution'; but that does not imply that anything goes or that what any one person may say must be as worthy of notice as what anyone else may say. Though, it must be said, what is said with good will deserves a response – even if adverse – of at least equal good will.

The direction in which the argument has led shows that what is at issue is not just a local question about what is involved in one sort of application of moral concepts. It concerns our understanding of the concept of a human being and its relation to concepts like those of rationality and action. This is hardly surprising. For it seems obvious enough that, in the example with which I started, the peculiar involvement of the commandant with his charges is possible only for a creature with the complexities of a human being. The explication of the involvement must require the unravelling of at least some of those complexities.

I have resisted the Kantian, or neo-Kantian, suggestion that what commands moral respect in a human being is some characteristic – such as rationality – which he exemplifies in common with other normal human beings. I have claimed rather that the sort of respect that is in question takes the individual in his or her particularity as its object. That is not to *deny* that rationality is a common characteristic of normal human beings. Indeed it is; and the use of the word 'normal' in this context signals that what is in question is a conceptual determination. One may perhaps even say that the manner in which rationality characterizes the normal human being helps to give the notion of 'particularity' its special sense here.

What I am struggling to say is beautifully expressed in a passage from Pico della Mirandola's *Oratio de hominis dignitate* which M. O'C. Drury reports as having greatly impressed Wittgenstein. I append Drury's own translation of the passage.

> Nec certam sedem nec propriam faciem, nec munus ullum peculiare tibi dedimus, O Adam: ut quam sedem, quam faciem, quae numere tute optaveris, ea pro voto, pro tua sententia, habeas et possideas. Definita caeteris natura intra praescriptas a nobis leges coercitur: tu nullis angustiis coercitus, pro tuo arbitrio in cuius manu te posui, tibi illum praefinis.

> To you, Adam, we have assigned no fixed place in the scale of created beings; no one determined facial expression will characterise your race; you have no special service to perform. Thus it will be that whatever rank you select, what you want to express, what function you want to perform, by your decision, by your own wish, that you shall both have and keep. All other created beings are bound fast by the laws and ordinances we have laid down for them; but you are not hedged around with any restrictions, in order that by the free choice which is placed in your hands you may determine your own destiny.[5]

The passage brings out the connection between taking a human being seriously and subjecting what he says or does to critical scrutiny. The connection is not an arbitrary or trivial one. Pico says: 'by the free choice which is placed in your hands you may determine your own destiny'. But there would be no question of one's decision's 'determining a destiny' unless it took place within a space in which it had consequences and were capable of incurring risks. Indeed, outside such a context there would be little content in the notions of taking a decision, making up one's mind on an issue, and so on. How would doing these things differ from sticking a pin in a piece of paper?

5   M. O'C. Drury, 'Some Notes on Conversations with Wittgenstein', pp. 106–07 and p. 111.

What is equally important is the way one person may impinge on another in such a way as to call in question for him his own conception of himself and of his place in the world. *Things* too impinge on a person of course, but not in the same way. The difference can be put by saying that human beings are essentially potential critics of each other. I mean this not just in the narrow sense in which one person may explicitly criticize what another says and does, important though that is. I want to say too that the prisoners in my example, each in his own way by virtue of his own character and of the particular history of his relations with the commandant and his NCO, constituted an implicit criticism of them, of their views of life and of their own roles in life. These people learn from each other something which only they, in this situation, can teach. There may be some sense in which what they teach can be expressed in some explicit statement which has a more general application. But being convinced, however rationally, of the truth of such a statement is not the same as being taught what these individuals teach each other. This is obviously closely bound up with the importance for morality of learning by example rather than by precept.

13

Ethical Relativism

I

The word 'relativism' is used, probably more often than not, as a term of abuse; and discussions of the issues involved are apt to be bad-tempered. Part of the reason for this is, no doubt, that certain extreme forms of relativistic position seem, and perhaps even seem designed, to undermine the very possibility of honest argument. But not all those who have been attracted by relativistic positions have been dishonest; and there are perfectly genuine and important difficulties to which they have been trying to draw attention. If we wish to be clear about these difficulties, it seems to me important that we should not treat the word "relativism" as a slogan, or as the introduction to a manifesto we are going to feel obliged either to attack or to defend.

I am sure that most teachers of philosophy are periodically infuriated, usually by freshmen in the first semester of an academic year, by a very general and radical form of relativistic position, which seems to blight any possibility of serious intellectual enquiry. But it has serious intellectual antecedents, often being associated – rightly or wrongly – with the name of the great Sophist Protagoras, on the strength of his alleged aphorism: 'Man is the measure of all things: of things that are, that they are, and of things that are not, that they are not.' The argument might be formulated schematically as follows.

If somebody A thinks something p true then, as far as he is concerned, it *is* true; in other words it is true for him. If somebody else B disagrees with A, then something precisely parallel may be said of him: p is false for B, or not-p is true for him. As a result of discussion, either *A* or *B*, or both, may change their opinions, but the upshot will be of the same form: namely *p* will be true for *A* and/or *B* respectively. If they agree, then the situation is simply that *p* is true or false for *A* *and* true or false for *B*. Thus truth and falsity will still be relative to the person whose belief we are speaking of. We shall have come no closer to a notion of truth which transcends this sort of relativity. And if I, an outside observer of the dispute, decide that one or other of the parties is in the right and that *p* is (say) true, then, correctly stated, the situation is simply that *p* is now true for me. In fact, the argument concludes, we should do better not to speak, misleadingly, about truth and falsity *simpliciter*, but to use hyphenated expressions like 'true-for-*A*', 'false-for-*B*' etc. For a claim that *p* is true is, of its nature, a claim that *p* is true in the opinion of the one who makes the claim. Thus his claim can only be that it is true for him; and we shall avoid the misleading separation of 'true' and 'for *X*' if we hyphenate the whole expression.

The apparent strength of this argument is at the same time its real weakness. It insists, I think rightly, that there is no such thing as a judgement about the truth of some matter which is not, at some point, *somebody's* judgement. And, it might be added, the most anyone can do is to state the truth as he or she sees it with as much care and skill as is at his or her disposal. It remains a possibility that somebody else, using just as much care and skill, may disagree. Let us concede that for the sake of argument (though in fact I do think that it needs qualification). What the argument does not do is pay due attention to the *content* of such a judgement. If my judgement is that the Earth is flat then, in my judgement, it is true that the Earth is flat. But my judgement is not that in my judgement it is true that the Earth is flat; my opinion is not that it is true in my opinion that the Earth is flat, but simply that it is true that the Earth is flat.

The verb 'to believe' plays tricks on us here. It conjugates in the first, second and third persons like other verbs. But its force in the first person singular conjugation is not what it is in, say, its third person singular conjugation. If I say 'He believes that the Earth is flat' I may add, with perfect propriety, 'but he is wrong'. But I cannot say 'I believe that the Earth is flat but I am wrong'. Of course I am not here denying that I may as a matter of fact *be* wrong in my belief. I am only remarking that when someone says 'I believe that *p*' he is endorsing the truth of *p*; but not when he says of someone else 'He believes that *p*'.

The general relativistic argument I have so far been considering exploits (or perhaps is exploited by) this complexity in the notion of belief and in the relations between this notion and that of truth. It is just because of this complexity that we cannot advance from

    1   'A believes that p' = 'p is true for A'

to

    2   'I believe that p = 'p is true for me'.

Whereas in 1 'true for A' does not become part of the expression of A's judgement, 'true for me' *does* become part of *my* judgement in 2, simply because the 'I believe' is part of my judgement and 'A believes' is not part of A's judgement.

As a matter of fact, I should much prefer not to make the initial move from 'A believes that p is true' to 'p is true for A'. Then we shall not be tempted illegitimately to hyphenate 'true-for-A'. To say that there is at no point any room for the judgement that something is, quite simply, true is in the end to say that there is no room anywhere for the notion of judgement. And that is why arguments of this type were so well adapted to the ends of the Sophists who wished to exalt rhetorical persuasion over informed discussion – as long, that is to say, as it was not noticed that they also undermined the intelligibility of rhetorical persuasion itself, by undermining the intelligibility of any judgement of which someone might be persuaded. (This I take to be one of the points involved in Socrates' complex argument in the first part of Plato's *Gorgias*.)

II

Many people who are not much attracted by such a general relativism about truth may nevertheless be drawn to a relativistic view of moral values. I now turn to this. It is argued for on a variety of grounds: sometimes indeed by way of relativistic arguments concerning truth without its being realised that such arguments apply more generally than merely to moral judgements. But more usually the argument will involve a *distinction* between moral judgements (or, more comprehensively, 'judgements of value') and other sorts of judgement (which may be gestured towards rather vaguely in such phrases as 'judgements of fact and of mathematics and logic'). This distinction is made precisely because it is thought that the notions of truth and falsity (in a non-relativistic sense) apply to the latter but not to the former. Very often this claim will be justified with such observations as that there are no 'facts in the world' for moral judgements to 'correspond' to. Now while I do think that there is an important distinction, or range of distinctions, to be made under headings of 'fact' and 'value' (though I am not going to discuss that large issue here), when the distinction is made in association with a correspondence theory of truth, I believe that nothing but confusion results.

People who speak of the truth of factual judgements as consisting in correspondence with the facts usually have in mind, at least in the first instance, certain very simply paradigms: such as that old favourite of children's reading books and textbooks of philosophy, 'The cat is on the mat'. On the one hand here is the sentence (Listen, you can hear it; or, Look, you can see it); and on the other hand there is the mat, with the cat either on it or not on it (You can see that too). Even in this apparently simple case it is not at all easy in practice to say satisfactorily and precisely how the notion of correspondence is supposed to be applied; and the attempt to do so reveals countless complexities about reference, identity, spatio-temporal location and the like. But let us allow that these complexities may be unravelled and a satisfactory account of correspondence given – for this sort of case. We do not have to look far beyond the simple paradigm before we are struck by the difficulty of applying the paradigm in the case of other judgements which are undoubtedly 'factual'.

Suppose, for instance, that we simply transform the paradigm into the past tense. The formal 'correspondence' formula surely still applies; my statement, 'the cat was on the mat yesterday' is true if and only if the cat was on the mat yesterday. But the *application* of the formula is no longer as obvious as was the case with the present tense case. The cat is not on the mat now. And even if it were, that would have no very direct bearing on whether it was there yesterday. Of course, if I know that it is a creature of regular habits, I may be able to infer from its presence on the mat today that it was probably there yesterday as well. But now I am already drawing on considerations which take us pretty far afield from anything suggested in the simple correspondence formula. And if I really want to establish the truth of my statement I have to appeal to all kinds of indirect evidence – such as the testimony of people who may have seen the mat yesterday, or of others who may claim to have seen the cat somewhere else at the appropriate time (and what convinces me of the veracity and/or reliability of all these witnesses?). My point is not that the truth of my statement *consists* in my getting appropriate answers to all these questions – to suppose this is the mistake of verificationism – no, it consists in the cat's having been on the mat yesterday. My point is rather that this formula throws little light on the ways in which we actually *apply* the terms 'true' and 'false', on how we determine, in actual cases, that one or other of these terms is applicable. And the gulf between the simplicity of the formula and the complexity of the conditions of its application becomes even more daunting if we bethink ourselves of what goes into, say, determining the truth of the Darwinian Theory of Evolution or of a theory of the origin of the solar system (something about which popularizing expositions of such theories are usually conspicuously silent).

With considerations of this sort in mind, I want now to consider briefly the question whether moral judgements can be genuinely true and false. But I first want to make the proviso that it is actually highly misleading to raise the issue in this very general way, since what we call 'moral judgements' constitute a heterogeneous bunch and we have absolutely no business to assume that we can give an account that will fit all of them. So while I shall continue to speak expansively of 'moral judgements' I wish to imply no claim about the possibility of extending what I say about the examples discussed to other sorts of example as well.

The first thing I must say is that it seems to me absolutely undeniable that we do actually use words like 'true' and 'false' and 'fact' of many judgements that it seems appropriate to call 'moral'. If, for instance, I were to hear someone say that the British government sordidly betrayed a sacred trust when after the Second World War it agreed with Stalin to repatriate the Russian prisoners of war who had been found in German hands, knowing full well that they were going to almost certain death, I might respond by saying 'That's absolutely true', or 'That's an undoubted fact'. And whether you agreed with me or not (which is not of course the issue here), I do not think you would suppose that I was misusing language. Nor do I see any plausible way of denying that the 'correspondence' formula which was used in the case of 'The cat is on the mat' applies equally well here: 'The British government sordidly betrayed a sacred trust . . .' is true if and only if the British government sordidly betrayed a sacred trust. . . .

But, it may be objected, we cannot validate the opinion that the

British government behaved sordidly, etc, through a simple examination of the facts. No: but the sting has been drawn from that retort once we have noticed how very limited is the usefulness of this idea of 'examining the facts' in an account of how we use the words 'true' and 'false' even in connection with judgements that are uncontroversially factual.

In making these points I do not want to deny that there is any important difference between factual and moral judgements of a sort to which these considerations about truth and falsity are designed to point. I want merely to suggest that the difference cannot be brought out in that way. The idea that it can be derives, I think, not so much from the peculiarities of moral judgements themselves as from obscurities surrounding the notion of truth in general. But it would take me too far afield to discuss these obscurities further here.

I return to ethics. The fact of ethical disagreement is always prominent in discussions of relativism here; and no doubt radical disagreement about certain fundamental issues is characteristic of many ethical arguments, though it is not at all easy to be clear exactly what its significance is. For one thing it is obviously not true that there are no disagreements in other areas of human interest, nor that such disagreements elsewhere can never be resolved. Nor is it true that disagreements over ethical issues can always be resolved. We may feel convinced that disagreement is more widespread and intractable in ethics than elsewhere, but this, though interesting in itself if true, hardly seems even to point to any relativistic conclusion. It could be that such issues are so difficult and tangled that it is often merely *difficult*, or even *practically* impossible, to arrive at a solution of them; or that they are issues peculiarly apt to excite passions which cloud the judgement necessary to reach a resolution. We need something stronger than this, and perhaps something of a different kind altogether, to justify the conclusion that talk about 'agreed solutions' is conceptually altogether out of place here.

At this point it is necessary for me to take more seriously than I have hitherto done the thought that what we call 'ethical issues' do not all have the same conceptual character and cannot all, therefore, be fitted without distortion into a uniform account. One important distinction is that between the case in which we consider conflicts between judgements made by people who share a common culture and that in which we are comparing moral judgements characteristic of very different cultures. I do not pretend that this is a clear-cut

distinction or that we shall always be able to decide in particular
cases how to classify in this respect the sort of questions we are
raising. But the distinction is no less important for that.

I will take an example that I have also discussed on another
occasion.[1] George Orwell was fascinated by the figure of Gandhi, by
what Gandhi stood for. (That last phrase points, I think, to
something important: the extent to which understanding a moral
position depends on seeing how it can actually be embodied in the
lives of human beings. This aspect of the matter is too frequently
overlooked in discussions of morality in terms of abstractly stated
principles and judgements.) Orwell recognized the moral power of
Gandhi's asceticism and of his turning away from types of human
relationship which involve emotional entanglements with other
individuals – or even the risk of such entanglements. Orwell did not
deny the truth or the relevance of the kinds of reason with which
Gandhi supported his advocacy of renouncing such relationships.
He agreed for instance that such entanglements may lead one into
wrong-doing. But he thought that the willingness to accept such
dangers – and I mean *moral* dangers – is required if we are to accept
our human nature; that to live in such a way as to protect ourselves
from such risks by avoiding emotional entanglements is a sort of
rejection of life in favour of an inhuman conception of purity. The
outcome of such a rejection may be a petrification of one's own
humanity, and I think Orwell felt that something of the sort had
happened with Gandhi: something which he found deeply repugnant.
(It is not my purpose to consider here the justice of Orwell's
judgement about Gandhi.)

Did Orwell and Gandhi share a common culture? Obviously there
can be no simple answer to that. Their backgrounds were indeed
enormously different, no doubt sometimes engendering a certain
mutual incomprehension. But one can press that too far: Orwell
understood very well much of what Gandhi was saying. Not merely
were the cultures of India and Britain deeply intertwined, but there
are ascetic paradigms in the moral traditions of Europe as there are
in Hinduism. They certainly had enough in common to engage with
each other on certain matters, if not on all. But one can go further
than that. It is not just that Gandhi's and Orwell's conceptions of

1   See Peter Winch, 'Apel's Transcendental Pragmatics'. Orwell articulates his
attitude to Gandhi in 'Reflections on Gandhi'. I am grateful to Cora Diamond for
first drawing my attention to Orwell's essay.

morality *may* engage with each other; in a sense they necessarily do
so: they *require* each other. They are internally related to each other
in the sense that standing in a certain relation to each other helps to
constitute what each is. Gandhi's ascetic morality can hardly be
formulated except by specifying a relation in which it stands to a
conception of morality like Orwell's, and *vice versa*.

It is natural and correct to characterize this relation by saying that
the two moral conceptions are not merely different and mutually
exclusive, but that they are *opposed* to each other: the one involves a
rejection of the other. But at this point I believe we have to proceed
with extreme care. It is tempting, but I think mistaken, to continue
along the following lines: *If the two views are opposed to each other in
some sense of the word 'opposed' that has logical significance, then to accept
the one view is to think it true and hence to think the other false. It isn't
like accepting a proposal to spend one's vacation in Italy rather than in
Greece, where one's decision might equally well have gone the other way
and there would be no question, except in special circumstances, of
regarding the one proposal as having any more 'validity' than the other.
But if the ethical case is not like that, we must be able to characterize one
or other position as being true and the other, opposed to it, as false.
Conversely, if we find that we cannot characterize the positions in that
way, such issues do in the end reduce to personal preference and one
person's view will have as much, logically, to be said for it as anyone else's.*

There is a very widespread mistake in this argument: that of
thinking there can be a genuine logical opposition between two
views only in so far as those views are characterizable as 'true' or
'false' in some use of those terms that implies that we know what it
would be to find considerations which would settle the issue
between any persons of good will who understood what the issue
was. I mean by this: considerations pointing to a conclusion in such
a way that the fact that someone did not accept the conclusion on
their basis would thereby show that he did not understand the
considerations in question or that he was not addressing the issue in
good faith. But the issue between Orwell and Gandhi is not like
that. There is no reason to suppose that two such men would ever
reach agreement on what divides them, whatever arguments were
adduced. (I do not mean to say that such agreement is 'in principle'
impossible – partly because I do not understand what 'in principle'
means in this context.) But equally there is no reason to think that
failure to agree must be a sign of deficient understanding or of bad
faith in either one of the disputants.

If that is thought to be a relativistic conclusion, then I do indeed think there is at least that much truth in relativism. But it would be very surprising if a position which has shown such strength over such a long period of history had nothing to be said for it whatever. Just as the opposition to relativism, given *its* historical strength may also be expected to have powerful arguments in its favour. The difficulty lies in formulating the strengths and weaknesses in a way which does not topple over into exaggeration on one side or the other.

It would for instance be a relativistic exaggeration to conclude from the above reasoning that there is no genuine logical opposition at all between Gandhi's and Orwell's views. I remarked a while ago that their views stand in internal relation to each other. That internal relation, I now want to add, is mediated by the context of argument and controversy in which each is formulated. These formulations *consist* in large part in pointing out the dangers involved in the opposing view. Those dangers are real enough. Gandhian asceticism may indeed (though it need not in all cases) lead to a sort of inhuman detachment from life from the point of view of which individuals are hardly seen as real except as instantiations of some abstract ideal of humanity. And Orwellian humanism may indeed (though it need not in all cases) lead to insufficient regard for considerations of justice which conflict with personal commitments.

In matters of this sort – and I am not suggesting that all issues of morality are like this – the role of reason is not to arrive at a position the acceptance of which will be, as it were, definitive of a rational man of good will. One way in which a man exercises his reason in such disputes is precisely in understanding the moral positions of others opposed to his own, along with the difficulties in them, but equally in allowing them to highlight the difficulties in his own position. There is no ground whatsoever *a priori* for expecting the emergence of some position free of difficulties which everyone would be able to accept. But that does not mean at all that there is no difference between someone who accepts and lives by a position with clear understanding of its strengths and weaknesses, of where it may lead him, of what the alternatives are, and someone who does not understand these things.

Some way back I suggested we make a broad distinction between conflicts within a common culture and conflicts between cultures. Though it may seem perverse, I have treated the conflict between Gandhi and Orwell as occurring within a common culture, though I also used the example to illustrate the impossibility of drawing a hard and fast line between cases of the two sorts. I turn now to the other sort of case: that of conflicts between cultures. And here we are dealing with an issue that has helped to define a sub-discipline within cultural anthropology: that of 'cultural relativism'.[2]

The leading thought of ethical relativism as it occurs in this context might be expressed as follows: that the moral values and principles which spring from one culture (and perhaps historical epoch) are not applicable to the life of another. I use the cautious phrase 'might be expressed' here, because it is not at all clear to me exactly what the thought actually comes to. That is what I now want to consider.

Relativistic anthropologists will support their position by appealing to manifest differences between the kinds of moral judgement made within different cultures. It has often enough been remarked that it is difficult to determine when such differences really do mark genuine conflicts of moral outlook and when they express the application of a similar moral outlook to different factual conditions of human life. (What has not so often been remarked is that this difficulty arises in good measure because of the vagueness in the concepts used in stating the contrast.) I shall not consider that question any further, not at least directly. It has also been remarked that the mere fact that judgements differ is in itself no reason for thinking that we cannot distinguish between truth and falsity in relation to them. After all it is perfectly possible for people to be just wrong.

As a sheer matter of history there seems no doubt that, amongst social anthropologists, a wider and closer acquaintance with the facts concerning moral outlooks in different cultures has gone along with a greater degree of moral tolerance towards values differing from those to which the anthropologists were accustomed in the lives of their own societies. But it is certain too that other historical factors were at work as well.[3] In any case I am more concerned here with the logic than with the history of the matter and it seems to me clear that *reason* places no premium on tolerance as the appropriate reaction to moral diversity rather than, say, on righteous indignation at the obscene blasphemies of the heathen, or on mocking laughter. In saying this I do not mean that I should not, in particular

2   There is a useful short discussion in Elvin Hatch, *Culture and Morality*.
3   Hatch's *Culture and Morality* contains a good discussion of these factors.

circumstances, approve of some reactions and disapprove of others. I mean that quite contrasting reactions *may* manifest equal understanding of what those facts amount to. (Again, I do not want to *rule out* the possibility that in some circumstances a particular sort of reaction may be a symptom of misunderstanding.)

A position of 'ethical neutrality' then, whatever exactly that might be, is not logically enjoined by the fact, if it is a fact, that different cultures have diverse moralities. And to this extent the anthropological critics of the relativistic conception of 'tolerance' preached by Franz Boas and his followers surely had some justice on their side when they argued that Boas himself, contrary to his own profession, was at least setting up tolerance as a positive cross-cultural value. On the other hand, it is by no means clear what the denial that there are any such general cross-cultural principles or values comes to. Though such a denial sometimes seems to be treated as though it were a straightforward registering of the facts of moral diversity, it is clearly not so. It leads even the usually clear-minded Hatch into confusion. Certain critics of relativism, he notes:

> may be right that we are not led directly to the concept of freedom by the supposed fact that there are no general cross-cultural principles. Yet the reverse does seem to hold. Given the value of freedom, or the moral belief that people ought to be free to conduct their affairs as they choose, it follows that we ought to be tolerant of other ways of life.[4]

But to call the second claim the 'reverse' of the first does seem to be to treat the claim that we ought to be tolerant of other ways of life as though it were equivalent to the claim that there are no cross-cultural ethical principles; and this obviously cannot be so. The phrase 'absence of cross-cultural principles' may mean several different things. It may mean absence of any principles on which the members of all cultures would agree. In that case it entails nothing either way about any duty to be tolerant. Or it may mean the absence of any principles which it is meaningful for members of one culture to apply to the institutions or practices of another culture. If so, it entails, so it seems, that there can *a fortiori* be no principle enjoining either tolerance or intolerance on our part towards the institutions and practices of another culture. Or again, it may mean

4 *Culture and Morality*, p. 98.

that if participants in one culture are bound by a certain principle it does not follow that participants in another country are similarly bound. If so, that entails only that *if* indeed *we* have a duty to be tolerant towards other cultures, it does not follow that participants in those cultures also have a duty to be tolerant towards us or towards each other. None of these conclusions seems to make any connection between tolerance and the facts of moral diversity. It seems to me that the very genuine problems with which in part ethical relativism is an attempt to engage have to be stated in different terms.

In fact these problems, though they affect our ability to evaluate morally alien institutions, traditions and practices, are not primarily problems which concern such evaluation *directly* at all. Rather, they concern our ability to understand the nature of those institutions, etc., to understand *what* precisely people in those cultures are actually doing in various contexts. If in a particular case we cannot do that, then of course we are in no position to make a responsible moral judgement about whatever it is. The matter is complicated by the fact that the nature of people's actions is itself affected, not to say permeated, by the context of moral evaluation surrounding the performance of actions of that sort. For example, what someone who borrows money is doing could hardly be grasped by someone unfamiliar with the obligations, moral and legal, generated by such an act, to say nothing of the complex network of legal, moral and social commitments involved in the concept of money. If there were occasion to make a moral judgement concerning the behaviour of someone who had made a loan, we would, I imagine, attach little weight to such a judgement made by someone whose understanding of what making a loan actually consists in were seriously deficient.

In thinking about the cultural relativity of ethics we are in danger of being dominated by a crude picture. On the one hand, we may think, are people's actions; on the other hand are the standards, ideals, principles, etc. that are applied to them. The former are open to public view and can be seen by anyone who looks carefully enough, irrespective of his cultural background. Cultural background becomes relevant only when it comes to passing moral judgement. Of course, the picture has only to be described in these explicit terms for us to see that it is a gross distortion. I think that something like this is all the same at work in many discussions of ethical relativism.

To understand all need not be to forgive all: it may lead to an increase in indignation. But if we do not understand, we are in no position to know what we are getting indignant about or, as the case may be, what forgiving. And there are indeed special problems of understanding involved when the parties involved in such transactions have to cross cultural boundaries.

14

Language, Belief and Relativism

It is one thing for a man to think that something is so and quite another thing for what he thinks to be so. This simple truism is fundamental to what we understand thought to be; for a thought is a thought about something – it has an object – and the kind of relation it has to its object involves the possibility of assessing the truth or adequacy of the content of the thought by confronting it with its object. All this would disappear, apparently, if there were no distinction between truth and falsity of a kind which presupposed a distinction between what is the case and what is merely thought to be the case.

However, it is considerably easier to recognize this as a truism than it is to understand exactly how it is to be applied in different areas of human thinking. The attempt to win clarity about such issues is philosophy. And the controversy surrounding different forms of 'relativism' is one large complex of aspects of this attempt.

The interesting difficulties appear when we ask under what conditions two people can be said to believe the same thing. It seems to me a failure to appreciate the nature and extent of these difficulties which has led some critics of earlier publications of mine[1] to suppose that I was denying the simple truth which I have tried to state in my opening paragraph. They have taken a situation like that comprising the Zande 'belief in witchcraft' and the twentieth-century European 'rejection' of such a 'belief' as a case of two sets of people, who respectively assert that p and that not-p. And they have misinterpreted my argument against such an assumption

1 Especially 'Understanding a Primitive Society' in Peter Winch, *Ethics and Action*.

as an espousal of a relativism which, if perhaps a little more sophisticated than that laid out above, is essentially open to the same kind of objection.

In 'Understanding a Primitive Society' I was discussing the conditions under which a European anthropologist can render the sense of what a Zande tribesman says when he talks of what the anthropologist translates as 'witchcraft', 'oracle', etc. We may speak of 'Zande witchcraft beliefs' in such a discussion. But what is being referred to is not the sum of particular beliefs held by individual Azande that this or that tribesman has exerted witchcraft; we are discussing rather the language in which such beliefs are expressed and which makes them possible.

The issues raised by such a discussion differ from those raise by the sort of relativism concerning truth which I have so far considered. Roger Trigg's *Reason and Commitment* provides an instructive example of the confusions which result from failing to observe the distinction. Trigg thinks that the following remark in 'Understanding a Primitive Society' is evidence of objectionable relativist leanings: 'Reality is not what gives language sense. What is real and what is unreal shows itself in the sense that language has.'[2] Trigg comments that while a language certainly 'expresses a community's beliefs about reality', reality nevertheless exists 'apart from people's beliefs', which may be mistaken. 'An essential function of language . . . is to concern itself with what is actually the case. Its business is to attempt to communicate *truth*.' It follows from my quoted remark that 'different languages cannot be thought of as different attempts to describe the same reality. "Reality" is made relative to a language, and if different languages portray the "world" differently, then there must be different worlds.'[3]

Unlike Trigg, I did *not* speak of a language as expressing a community's *beliefs* about reality. On the contrary, my main objection to Evans-Pritchard's treatment[4] of Zande thought was precisely that he did so treat their language. The confusions involved are highlighted by Trigg's talk of *language* as concerned 'to attempt to communicate truth', to 'describe reality'. It may indeed be argued – I have done so myself[5] – that there could be no

2 *Ethics and Action*, pp. 12–13.
3 Roger Trigg, *Reason and Commitment*, p. 15.
4 E. E. Evans-Pritchard, *Witchcraft, Oracles and Magic Among the Azande*.
5 Cf. 'Nature and Convention', *Ethics and Action*, pp. 50–72.

language whose speakers were not normally concerned to say what is true rather than what is false. But it is *speakers* of a language who attempt to say what is true, to describe how things are. They do so *in* the language they speak; and this language attempts no such thing, either successfully or unsuccessfully. Trigg is right to say that, on my view, 'different languages cannot be thought of as different attempts to describe the same reality', but wrong to suppose that the alternative which I must accept is that different languages attempt to describe different realities: they do not attempt to describe anything at all. If we do want to speak of a 'relation between language and reality', this is not a relation between a set of descriptions and what is described; although, no doubt, an account of this latter relation would have to form part of any account of the relation between language and reality.

The point may be brought out by the following consideration. If Tom believes that Harry is in pain and Dick that he is not, then, in the ordinary sense of the word 'belief', Tom and Dick have different beliefs. But according to Trigg's way of speaking, Tom and Dick, because they both speak the same language and mean the same thing by the word 'pain', share a common belief: even though their descriptions of Harry are mutually contradictory – indeed, precisely because they are – they in a sense share a common belief about reality: perhaps that it contains such a thing as pain. But if it is possible to affirm that there is such a thing as pain, it ought to be possible to deny it too. The language in which the denial is couched must be meaningful; and it must mean the same as the language in which what is denied might be affirmed, else the denial would not contradict the affirmation. So to deny that there is such a thing as pain, I must mean by 'pain' just what someone who affirms that there is such a thing means by 'pain'. Hence we are still both speaking the same language and still, according to Trigg's way of thinking, offering the same 'description of reality'. This incoherence illustrates how important it is to recognize that the grammar of a language is not a theory about the nature of reality, even though new factual discoveries and theoretical developments may lead to grammatical changes. What is difficult in particular cases, like that of Zande notions of witchcraft, is to understand clearly what belongs to grammar and what belongs to theory or 'belief'. I will return to this point later.

But first I should like to comment on another way in which we may be confused when we speak in this context about the relation of one 'language' to another.[6] On the one hand we speak of 'the English (French, German) language'; and on the other hand philosophers frequently use such expressions as 'the language of science (of religion, of morals, etc.)'. These two different ways of distinguishing between 'languages' raise different issues; but the two kinds of distinction overlap in certain cases, as they do for instance, very confusingly, when we compare the English language with the language of the Azande.

An Englishman who wants to learn French will have to master a new vocabulary having varying degrees of equivalence with the vocabulary of English, new grammatical rules of sentence-construction, declension, conjugation of verbs, and the like. All this takes place within the broad context of a shared culture. French and English life differ at various points, of course, and at such points there may indeed be difficulties concerning the translatability of sentences from one language into the other. How relevant such considerations are will depend on the kind of material to be translated and the purpose of the translation. A report of scientific experiments, for instance, will not bring to light the same kind of problem as a serious work of literature. But by and large such differences are marginal: there is so much common ground in respect of, for example, political ideas and practices, economic institutions, religious tradition, etc., etc., that learning French does not consist for the most part in learning to express radically new ideas, but in learning to express in a different medium of vocabulary and syntax the kind of thing which an Englishman is already perfectly well able to express in his own language.

Learning the language of mathematics on the other hand can hardly be distinguished from learning mathematics. To learn how to express commands in French is not to learn how to command or what it is to command. But if I learn how to formulate a mathematical proof (as distinct from how to operate with a particular notation), I am not acquiring a new way of expressing something I already grasp (namely mathematical proof). I am learning how to prove something – even *what it is* to 'prove' something mathematically. Correspondingly, while one would speak of a translation from English into French, one would hardly speak of a translation from mathematics into ... well, what? There is no such thing as a translation into non-mathematical terms of the phrase 'solution of a

6   See for instance Martin Hollis, 'Reason and Ritual', especially p. 236.

differential equation'. The concept of a differential equation belongs to mathematics and has to be expressed in 'the language of mathematics'.

When we are considering the 'translatability' of Zande into English these ways of distinguishing 'different languages' overlap. There would be little difficulty, over a wide area, in agreeing that certain expressions in the one language 'mean the same' (roughly) as certain expressions in the other. But in other areas, to demand a translation from the Zande into English would be like asking for a translation of something mathematical into something non-mathematical. Someone from a tribe with no knowledge of mathematics who wants to learn English will be able to find equivalents in his own language to much of what he learns. But if he happens upon an English textbook of mathematics he will not be able to proceed in the same way. If he does want to learn what is written there he will have to learn mathematics. In so doing he will not merely be learning new ways of expressing himself; he will also be learning new things to express. The English anthropologist is in a somewhat similar position when he tries to understand Zande talk of the poison oracle, of witches and of magic medicines. He has to learn not merely how the Azande express what they are doing when they consult the oracle, but what they are doing, *what it is* to consult the poison oracle. There is no more reason to suppose that the English language which he speaks will, without extension, provide expressions into which what the Azande say about this subject may be translated than there is for supposing that the language of a tribe with no mathematics will provide a means of translating expressions for differential equations.

However, an Englishman who wishes to understand the poison oracle will face additional difficulties. Even if I know little mathematics I have grown up with and live in a community which cultivates mathematics and I am familiar with the position it occupies in our cultural landscape. The poison oracle on the other hand is a feature of a cultural landscape which is itself alien to me. Our own culture provides a well-established and well-understood route by which a non-mathematician can learn mathematics. When learned, mathematics has a multitude of well-established applications in the lives people lead in this culture. But there is no place for any 'application' of Zande magical beliefs and practices in the life which it is open to anyone to lead in contemporary England. And the interest of an English anthropologist in learning about and trying to understand such beliefs and practices will not be directed towards any such practical application. Correspondingly, to raise the question whether we have properly 'understood' Zande ways of thinking will be to apply different criteria of understanding from those appropriate to the question whether we have properly 'understood' a certain branch of mathematics. The point is not that a 'greater or lesser degree' of understanding is possible in the one case as compared with the other. It is rather that 'understanding' takes different forms in the two cases (though there will be many points of connection). Moreover, though there is no room for a direct application in our own lives of what we may learn when we study Zande magical practices, this does not mean that we shall find no points of contact at all with elements familiar to us in our own cultural tradition. In 'Understanding a Primitive Society' I wanted to indicate that we are in danger of missing the useful points of contact if we concentrate too exclusively on the relation of Zande magical thought to our own scientific theories. This particular comparison is one which forces itself on our attention not merely because of the dominant position occupied by science in our culture, but also because of certain general ideas about the relation between thought and reality which we may find philosophically attractive and of which we may think (mistakenly) science provides a clear paradigm.

This brings me back to a point I raised earlier in discussing Trigg: that the grammar of a language does not constitute a theory about the nature of reality. Questions about the relation between language, thought and reality, as they are raised in philosophy, are characteristically connected with sceptical worries: worries about whether the world can be known to be such as our forms of thought seem to presuppose. But sceptical worries may have diverse sources and, according to the diversity of the sources, scepticism itself will take different forms which it is not always easy to distinguish. The scepticism which belongs to the stock-in-trade of Western philosophy is usually directed at ways of thinking which are fundamental to the way we live: for instance, our ways of thinking about time, about causality, about physical things in relation to our perception of them. Augustine fails to see how we can distinguish between a shorter and a longer period of time; Hume how we can say that one event is necessarily connected with another which we call its effect; Berkeley how we can speak of a physical object as existing when it is not being perceived. Much of the difficulty in all these cases springs from the fact that the forms in which we speak and think seem, on a certain sort of examination, to suggest a kind of application to the world which is not the application they in fact have. When we do, in the course of our lives, apply them in the appropriate way, the sceptical worries strike us, in Hume's phrase, as 'strain'd and ridiculous', but the worries are not laid to rest until we have succeeded in the surprisingly difficult tasks of attaining a clear view of the *actual* application of our ways of thinking and of the nature of the obstacles which stood in the way of our taking proper stock of these.

Such sceptical difficulties do not concern doubts about whether someone is right on a particular occasion in the claim he makes about how much time has passed, what caused such an event, what kind of object he is perceiving. They concern rather the possibility of making *any* such claims; they tend to undermine confidence in there being any genuine distinction between truth and falsity in such judgements; they attack, that is, the possibility of making any sense of them at all.

The scepticism to which we are likely to feel inclined when we contemplate the forms of thought of alien cultures is in many ways similar in form. We find a Zande tribesman asking whether such and such a man is a witch, or consulting an oracle to determine whether a proposed marriage would be propitious. We want to ask not whether he is right in the particular answers he arrives at, but whether he is asking questions to which there could be a right and a wrong answer, or whether the methods he customarily uses to answer his questions could conceivably serve to distinguish right from wrong answers. But, in contrast with the former cases, our scepticism here does not conflict with our settled thought habits. Like Augustine, we feel that we know what time is as long as we are not asked; but this is not what we feel about witches and oracles. Whereas, like Hume, we find sceptical arguments 'strain'd and ridiculous' as long as we are actually investigating the cause of something or establishing by observation the characteristics of some physical thing, we are never in the position of inquiring whether someone is a witch or of asking the advice of an oracle. Our scepticism does not evaporate over a game of backgammon. The arguments which will appear 'strain'd and ridiculous' are not those of the sceptic, but those of a philosopher who suggests that perhaps questions about witches, or inquiries of oracles, could be interpreted as logically perfectly in order.

Not only do we have no use, in the lives we lead, for notions like witchcraft and oracles but, more strongly, those lives seem to exclude the possibility of any such use. If I came across an Englishman in Richmond Park administering poison to a chicken while asking questions, I should not think he was consulting the poison oracle as a Zande tribesman might do; I should be at a loss as to what was going on – I might think him deranged, or perhaps perpetrating some bizarre 'happening'. Culture sets limits to what an individual can intelligibly be said to be doing. This is not to say that there cannot be new cultural developments ('happenings' constituted a new cultural development); but what can count as a new development is also limited by the cultural framework.

I have already said that the mere fact that we can find no application in our lives for a way of thinking which has an application in other cultural contexts is no good reason for arguing that it is 'in principle impossible to understand' it. That would be to employ criteria of 'understanding' inappropriate to the case in hand. It would be equally wrong to suppose that we are necessarily faced with the question who is 'right', we or the Azande. There is certainly *conflict* between European and Zande modes of thinking and even a sort of mutual exclusion; but this is not so far to say that they logically 'contradict' each other. It could be that people who interest themselves in cricket find it impossible to take baseball seriously, and *vice versa*: there would be conflict here too, but no contradiction. It would make little sense to ask, in the abstract, which game it was 'right' to support (though of course in particular circumstances a man might have reasons for supporting the one rather than the other).

Philosophical scepticism about such notions as time, cause and physical objects often represents these notions as 'incoherent'. I have suggested (and space precludes more than the suggestion) that the appearance of incoherence springs from our substituting for the actual application of such concepts another application, suggested by misleading grammatical analogies, which will not permit them to retain their original sense. When we are dealing with such notions as witchcraft and oracles among the Azande, we do not even have a first-hand unreflective mastery of their application and are the more easily misled into seeking analogies with concepts more familiar to us. Seeking such an application, we may well run into incoherences; but this is so far no argument for the conclusion that their proper application in their native setting has anything incoherent about it.

I shall try to develop this by considering some points in H. O.

Mounce's interesting paper 'Understanding a Primitive Society'. Mounce agrees with me that the notion of reality which Evans-Pritchard appeals to in his criticism of Zande thought cannot be given a sense independently of the practices of science and that, therefore, it can serve as a standard for criticizing magic only if magic is first shown to be a sort of science. He differs from me about how we are to determine whether Zande magical thought does 'make sense', that is, whether it involves an appeal to an independently intelligible notion of reality.

The philosophically important point here is not the correctness or otherwise of any particular suggested interpretation of Zande thought so much as the kind of reasoning needed to support an interpretation. Mounce's main criticism of me is that I argue from the established acceptance of a set of practices to the impossibility of questioning their sense, when the only premiss which would support such a conclusion is one concerning the established use of a set of *concepts*. He goes on to argue that Zande beliefs about witchcraft and oracles are not fully intelligible in themselves, but can only be understood as a confused application of concepts having their proper home in other contexts, generated by a sort of conceptual bemusement similar to that found in certain kinds of metaphysics. I shall not here examine Mounce's interpretation of my original argument, but try to identify a confusion about the relation between beliefs and concepts which Mounce's own discussion betrays.

In identifying superstitions, Mounce argues, we must distinguish between men's spontaneous reactions to certain situations and the beliefs which they may come to hold associated with those reactions. For instance, a married couple may be upset over the loss of a wedding ring; and there is nothing absurd or irrational in this. 'It is just the way many people, at least, happen to feel.'[7] But if they come to feel that the loss is a sign that their marriage will founder, this 'is just as absurd as anything held by the Azande'. Again, a man is distressed when induced to stick a pin into the eyes in a picture of his mother. This once more is just a natural reaction, 'neither rational nor irrational', But if, on his mother's eyes subsequently becoming diseased, he finds himself believing that this is somehow due to his action, then this *is* absurd.

Mounce rightly claims that such beliefs cannot be interpreted as simply 'mistaken'; rather, 'there is a certain craziness about this

7   Mounce, p. 353.

whole way of thinking'.[8] It is like the thinking characteristic of some forms of metaphysics, where we try to apply certain forms of expression in ways which the sense which we want them to retain will not admit. He suggests that Zande beliefs about witchcraft and oracles can be similarly diagnosed: they too apply notions like 'causal influence' and 'prediction' in situations where the conditions needed for making the sort of sense desired for them are lacking.

Mounce does not suggest any determinate aetiology for beliefs in witchcraft and oracles comparable to those he offers for his examples of superstitions. Neither does he consider whether any difference is made by the central position occupied in Zande life and thought by their magical notions, for which there is no analogy in his examples. Yet he does think that the reason why, in our society, a superstitious belief can be met with the rejoinder, 'Come now. Don't be stupid', is that 'such a belief will not fit into the network of beliefs about the physical world which has been developed by western science and which has been taught to us since childhood; or, rather, it does not even qualify as something which could possibly fit into such a network of beliefs'.[9] Such a resource is not obviously available within the context of Zande life.

A man who is distressed at having treated his mother's picture in the way described, and even more distressed when her eyes subsequently have become afflicted, may express his distress in the words 'I have injured her'. That he does so *may* be a symptom of superstitious confusions, but need not be. This will depend not on the fact that he uses that particular expression, but on *how* he uses it; it depends on the *kind* of 'connection' he sees between his action and his mother's affliction. He is not confused, but perfectly right, in thinking that there is *some* connection. He stuck pins into a picture of his mother, not any old sheet of paper; and he aimed for the eyes. If his mother had seen him do that she might well have been distressed and that would have been an injury to her. She did not as a matter of fact see him do it, but still, he is aware that if she had. . . . And he may also, not at all absurdly, feel that his action was anyway a betrayal of the respect and affection he owes her. Why should he not see that as an injury to her? And why should not his sense of that injury be heightened by her subsequent physical affliction?

8   Mounce, p. 354.
9   Mounce, p. 354.

We might speak here of the primitive reaction, which Mounce describes, as the basis for a new *concept* of 'injury', a concept the particular articulation of which may depend on the fact that the word 'injury' also has that other ('causal') use; but this latter use is not simply being taken over and applied in a situation where it does not belong. Its use is *modified* in the new circumstances and it thereby comes to bear a different sense. The point I want to make here is that though the thought 'I have injured her' *may* be a confused one, the mere fact that it is expressed in that way is not enough to show that it is. We need to see what other thoughts it is connected with, and how; we need to understand what role it is playing.[10]

Something similar may happen to the notion of 'prediction' when it is applied in the context of oracles. Mounce insists rather emphatically that the attitude of the Azande to the poison oracle shows them to regard it as a source of 'true statements about the future'; he thereby misses the variety of forms 'statements about the future' may take – even with us. (Compare, for instance, 'I will meet you at four o'clock; 'the government will be defeated at the election', 'Harold Wilson will go down in history as a successful prime minister'.) To understand precisely what sort of relation to the future these statements have (and hence what truth and falsity comes to in the various cases), we have to attend to, amongst other things, the kind of reaction which is appropriate to various eventualities; and this of course may be a complicated and unperspicuous matter.

The same goes for the poison oracle. Mounce himself claims that we must attend to the details of the Zande attitudes to the oracle. But when he comes to attempt this, he constantly appeals to analogies from other contexts. Thus he says that the Zande practice of asking the same question twice in the oracle's presence, interpreting the fowl's death as a 'yes' and a 'no' respectively on the two occasions, is analogous to the procedure of checking on the reliability of a witness. But we have to remember that though the oracle is consulted by administering poison to chickens, it is not the chickens that are being consulted, it is the oracle. So the grammar of the consultation is not that one *chicken*'s answer is being

10 There is a more extended discussion of analogous ways in which a concept may receive new applications and thereby develop a modified sense in my 'Ethical Reward and Punishment', *Ethics and Action*, pp. 210–28.

checked against another's. It is of one and the same oracle that the same question is asked twice; and what sort of 'check on its reliability' is that? What we must say is that two posings of the same question while *benge* is administered to two fowls constitute *one* complete consultation of the oracle. And there is an obvious rationale for this procedure quite different from the (confused) one suggested by Mounce. Given the importance of the *benge*'s being neither too weak nor too strong a poison – since this would predetermine the outcome and make the consultation nugatory – a good way of *checking on the goodness* of the benge is to do precisely what the Azande do do. This illustrates the importance of what I have wanted to emphasize: that we should view any particular utterance or procedure in the context of the other utterances and procedures to which it belongs.

The grammar of oracular pronouncements is determined by various factors: by, for instance, the procedure of consultation, the kind of question it is generally regarded as proper to ask, the kind of reaction considered appropriate to various kinds of outcome in relation to what the oracle has said. All this, and much else besides, constitutes a language in which certain kinds of thing can be said, certain kinds of question raised. A person *using* such a language may of course fall into confusion and into superstitiously expecting results which reflection would show it to be irrational to expect. But this would not show that there is anything confused, irrational or superstitious in the language itself.

There are consequences here for the methodology of ethnographic fieldwork. If the investigator interrogates native informants about the use of the poison oracle, he must be alive to the possibility that some of the answers he gets will betray such confusions. He must also be wary of reading such confusions back into the grammar of the mode of thinking he is trying to understand, for it is only against the background of that grammar that what is confused can be distinguished from what is not. Evans-Pritchard cites a consultation of the oracle to determine who was responsible for performing some specific act (placing magic medicines in the roof of a hut). Mounce comments, plausibly, that in this case what the consultants 'hope will be revealed is exactly what might have been revealed by adopting other, and to us, more normal procedures, if these procedures had been available.'[11] and, he clearly wishes us to conclude, this can only

11 Mounce, p. 352.

be regarded as an absurd superstition. Such behaviour may indeed be a case of superstition. This is a question that could be settled only in the light of much more information than Evans-Pritchard supplied: about the surrounding circumstances of the consultation, about what, if anything, is taken as 'independent evidence' concerning the same allegation, about the kind of use to which the oracle's answer is put – and much else besides. But even if, in the light of such information, we do conclude that there is a confusion of thought here, this is certainly not enough to show that 'the Zande belief in oracles' is confused.

As I read Evans-Pritchard's account, oracles are mainly consulted to determine whether it is propitious to undertake some important and potentially hazardous enterprise. Now though to say that circumstances are 'propitious' is in a way to make a kind of prediction, the relation of what is said to the future is very complex and indeterminate. For instance, that it is propitious to act in a certain way is no guarantee that so doing will be successful or turn out well: there are endless opportunities for explaining failure which do not conflict with the act's propitiousness. Again, there is ample room for debate as to what is to count as an action's 'turning out well'. The literature of oracular consultation in other cultures, the Greek for example, is full of cases in which an agent misreads the oracle's pronouncements because his ideas of what is and is not advantageous are distorted or blinkered; indeed it seems clear that one important role of oracles has been precisely to raise probing questions on this sort of issue. Such a literature is essential to our understanding of what the oracle was for the Greeks, for example, and to our understanding of what sort of pronouncements the oracle issued. Any analogue to this literature in Zande folklore would be an essential feature of the grammar of the Zande poison oracle; essential, therefore, too to the possibility of distinguishing between what is and what is not superstitious in the thinking of individual Azande.

I have wanted, in the foregoing discussion, to distinguish between the beliefs people hold and the language in which those beliefs are expressed and which makes them possible. And I have tried to undermine the seductive idea that the grammar of our language is itself the expression of a set of beliefs or theories about how the world is, which might in principle be justified or refuted by an examination of how the world *actually* is. This temptation is hard enough to resist in the case of our own language; so much the harder when we are dealing with a language the forms of which are alien, and even perhaps repugnant, to us. A large part of the difficulty springs from the fact that the distinction is not a clear-cut or stable one (as is brought out, probably more forcefully than anywhere else, in Wittgenstein's *On Certainty*). Furthermore, the grammar of a language has its concrete realization *in* the expression of particular beliefs (though not only there). The grammar of the word 'pain' finds expression in what we say about the pains (or absence of pains) of particular people. The grammar of the Zande word we translate as 'oracle' finds expression in what individual Azande say and do in connection with particular oracular consultations. But what we mean by 'pain' is not the sum of our particular beliefs about the pains (or absence of pains) of particular people; and what the Azande mean by their word for 'oracle' is not the sum of their particular beliefs about oracles. Indeed, the whole notion of a 'sum of beliefs' in this connection is highly suspect.

Of course, the influence of modern industrial civilization may (and does) tend to squeeze out the practices and judgements in which talk of oracles and witches finds its expression. But this is not to say that 'belief in oracles and witches' has been *refuted* – perhaps by showing that the world does not contain such things. This is no more so, than the decline in religious faith in industrial society is the result of its having been demonstrated that reality does not contain such a thing as a God. None of this is to say that belief in oracles and witches (or in God) cannot be criticized – there are more kinds of criticism than one. Though when we engage in such criticism we might do well to remember the parable of the mote and the beam. 'For with what judgment ye judge, ye shall be judged: and with what measure ye mete, it shall be measured to you again.'[12]

12   Matthew, 7: 3.

Bibliography

Anscombe, G. E. M., 'Times, Beginnings and Causes', *Collected Philosophical Papers*, Vol. II (Blackwell 1981)
——'Modern Moral Philosophy', 'Rules, Rights and Promises', 'On the Source of the Authority of the State' *Collected Philophical Papers*, Vol. III (Blackwell 1981)

Block, Irving, *Perspectives on the Philosophy of Wittgenstein* (Blackwell 1981)
Bowen, Elizabeth, *The Death of the Heart* (Penguin Books 1966)

Cavell, Stanley, *The Claim of Reason* (Oxford University Press 1979)

Descartes, René, *Philosophical Works*, trans. Haldane and Ross (Cambridge University Press 1979)
Donagan, Alan, *The Theory of Morality* (University of Chicago Press 1977)
Drury, M. O'C., 'Some Notes of Conversations with Wittgenstein' in R. Rhees (ed.) *Ludwig Wittgenstein, Personal Recollections* (Blackwell 1981)
Dummett, Michael, *Frege, Philosophy of Language* (Duckworth 1973)
Durrant, Michael, *The Logical Status of 'God'* (Routledge and Kegan Paul 1974)

Evans-Pritchard, E. E., *Witchcraft, Oracles and Magic Among the Azande* (Oxford University Press 1937)

Hatch, Elvin, *Culture and Morality* (Columbia University Press 1982)
Henry-Hermann, Grete, 'Die Überwindung des Zufalls', Minna Specht and Willi Eisler (eds) *Leonard Nelson zum Gedächtnis* Verlag Öffentliches Leben 1953)
Holland, R. F., 'The Miraculous' in *Against Empiricism* (Blackwell 1980)
Hollis, Martin, 'Reason and Ritual', B. R. Wilson (ed.) *Rationality* (Blackwell 1970)

Hume, David, *A Treatise of Human Nature*, 1739, 1740.

Ishiguro, Hidé, 'Use and Reference of Names', P. Winch (ed.) *Studies in the Philosophy of Wittgenstein* (Routledge and Kegan Paul 1969)

Kant, Immanuel, *A Critique of Pure Reason*, 1781
Kripke, Saul A., *Wittgenstein on Rules and Private Language* (Blackwell 1982)

MacIntyre, Alasdair, *After Virtue* (Duckworth 1982)
Malcolm, Norman, *Memory and Mind* (Cornell University Press 1977)
——*Nothing is Hidden* (Blackwell 1986)
Moore, G. E., 'Proof of an External World', *Philosophical Papers* (Allen and Unwin 1963)
Mounce, Howard, 'Understanding a Primitive Society' *Philosophy*, Vol. 48, No. 186, October 1973

Niel, Fernand, *Albigeois et Cathares* (Que sais-je?, No. 689, Paris 1974)

Orwell, George, 'Reflections on Gandhi', *Collected Essays, Journalism and Letters* (Penguin Books 1970)

Rhees, Rush, 'Questions on Logical Inference', G. Vesey (ed.), *Understanding Wittgenstein* (Macmillan 1974)
Russell, Bertrand, 'The Limits of Empiricism', *Proceedings of the Aristotelian Society*, 1935–1936

Singer, Isaac Bashevis, 'Stories from Behind the Stove', *A Friend of Kafka* (Penguin Books 1970)
Strawson, P. F., *Individuals* (Methuen 1964)

Tolstoy, Leo, *The Kreutzer Sonata and Other Tales* (Oxford University Press 1961)
Trigg, Roger, *Reason and Commitment* (Cambridge University Press 1973)

Weil, Simone, *First and Last Notebooks*, trans. Richard Rees (Oxford University Press 1970)
——*Lectures on Philosophy* (from the notes of Anne Reynaud), trans. Hugh Price (Cambridge University Press 1978)
——*A Simone Weil Anthology*, ed. Sîan Miles (Virago 1986)
Wiggins, David, *Sameness and Substance* (Blackwell 1980)
Williams, Bernard, 'Wittgenstein and Idealism', G. Vesey (ed.) *Understanding Wittgenstein* (Macmillan 1974)
Winch, Peter, *Ethics and Action* (Routledge and Kegan Paul 1972)
——'Apel's Transcendental Pragmatics', S. C. Brown (ed.) *Philosophical Disputes in the Social Sciences* (Harvester Press 1979)

Wittgenstein, Ludwig, *Tractatus Logico-Philosophicus*, trans. C. K. Ogden, (Routledge and Kegan Paul 1922)

——trans. D. F. Pears and B. McGuiness (Blackwell 1961)

——*Philosophical Investigations*, eds G. E. M. Anscombe, G. H. von Wright and Rush Rhees, trans. G. E. M. Anscombe (Blackwell 1958).

——*Notebooks, 1914–1916*, eds G. E. M. Anscombe and G. H. von Wright, trans. G. E. M. Anscombe (Blackwell 1961)

——'A Lecture on Ethics', ed. Rush Rhees, *The Philosophical Review* Vol. LXXIV, No. 1, January 1965

——*Lectures and Conversations on Aesthetics, Psychology and Religious Belief*, ed. Cyril Barrett (Blackwell 1966)

——*Zettel*, eds G. E. M. Anscombe and G. H. von Wright, trans. G. E. M. Anscombe (Blackwell 1967)

——*On Certainty*, ed G. E. M. Anscombe and G. H. von Wright, trans. Dennis Paul and G. E. M. Anscombe (Blackwell 1969)

——*Philosophical Remarks*, ed. Rush Rhees, trans. Raymond Hargreaves and Roger White (Blackwell 1973)

——*Remarks on the Foundations of Mathematics*, eds G. H. von Wright, Rush Rhees and G. E. M. Anscombe, trans. G. E. M. Anscombe (Blackwell 1974)

——*Philosophical Grammar*, ed. Rush Rhees, trans. Anthony Kenny (Blackwell 1974)

——*Lectures on the Foundations of Mathematics, Cambridge 1939*, ed. Cora Diamond (Harvester Press 1976)

——'Cause and Effect: Intuitive Awareness', ed. Rush Rhees, trans. Peter Winch, *Philosophia*, Vol. 6, Nos. 3 and 4, September–December 1976

——*Remarks on Frazer's "The Golden Bough"* ed. and trans. Rush Rhees (Brynmill Press 1979)

——*Culture and Value*, eds G. H. von Wright and Heikki Nyman, trans. Peter Winch (Blackwell 1980)

Index